MW00824176

THE GERMAN INFANTRY HANDBOOK • 1939-1945

Also by Alex Buchner

OSTFRONT 1944

Alex Buchner

THE
GERMAN INFANTRY
HANDBOOK
1939-1945

• ORGANIZATION • UNIFORMS •
• WEAPONS • EQUIPMENT • OPERATIONS •

Schiffer Military History
Atglen, PA

Translated from the German by
Dr. Edward Force, Central Connecticut State University.

On the Cover:
Background: Wehrmacht Officers Cap, c. 1941
Insignia: from Wehrmacht Officers Staff Car Pennant
Courtesy of the Military History Shop,
Kennett Sq., Pennsylvania.

Copyright © 1991 by Schiffer Publishing.
Library of Congress Catalog Number: 90-62983

All rights reserved. No part of this work may be reproduced or used in
any forms or by any means – graphic, electronic or mechanical, including photocopying or information storage and retrieval systems – without
written permission from the copyright holder.

Printed in the United States of America.
ISBN: 0-88740-284-4

This book originally published under the title,
Das Handbuch der Deutschen Infanterie, 1939-1945
by Podzun-Pallas Verlag, GmbH, Markt 9, 6360 Friedberg 3.
© 1987. ISBN: 3-7909-0301-9.

We are interested in hearing from authors with
book ideas on related topics.

Published by Schiffer Publishing Ltd.
77 Lower Valley Road
Atglen, PA 19310
Please write for a free catalog.
This book may be purchased from the publisher.
Please include $2.95 postage.
Try your bookstore first.

Contents

Equivalent Wartime Ranks of the
Waffen-SS, the Wehrmacht and the U.S. Army

Waffen-SS	Wehrmacht	U.S. Army
General Officers		
- No equivalent -	Generalfeldmarschall	General of the Army
Oberstgruppenführer	Generaloberst	General
Obergruppenführer	General	Lieutenant General
Gruppenführer	Generalleutnant	Major General
Brigadeführer	Generalmajor	Brigadier General
Staff Officers		
Oberführer	- No Equivalent -	- No Equivalent -
(Wore the shoulder strap of a Colonel)		
Standartenführer	Oberst	Colonel
Obersturmführer	Oberstleutnant	Lieutenant Colonel
Sturmbannführer	Major	Major
Company Officers		
Hauptsturmführer	Hauptmann	Captain
Obersturmführer	Oberleutnant	1st Lieutenant
Untersturmführer	Leutnant	2nd Lieutenant
Officer Candidates *(Basically equal to Oberfeldwebel & Feldwebel)*		
Oberjunker	Oberfähnrich	- No Equivalent -
Junker	Fähnrich	- No Equivalent -
Non-commissioned Officers		
Sturmscharführer	Stabsfeldwebel	Sergeant Major
Hauptscharführer	Oberfeldwebel	Master Sergeant
Oberscharführer	Feldwebel	Technical Sergeant
Scharführer	Unterfeldwebel	Staff Sergeant
Unterscharführer	Unteroffizier	Sergeant
Enlisted Men		
- No Equivalent -	Stabagefreiter	Admin. Corporal
Rottenführer	Obergefreiter	Corporal
Sturmmann	Gefreiter	Corporal
SS-Obersoldat*	Obersoldat*	Private 1st Class
SS-Soldat*	Soldat*	Private

---

*Note: Soldat is a general term. Other words here are Schütz, Grenadier, Füsilier, depending upon the combat arm to which the soldier belonged.

Source of U.S. World War II army equivalents: War Department Technical Manual TM-E 30-451, *Handbook on German Military Forces*, 15 March 1945.

Foreword

This book portrays the mass of the German field army in terms of an infantry division, as it fought and saw service in World War II, with its organization, uniforms, equipment, weaponry and individual units. For the basic portrayal, an active division already existing before the war began was chosen; infantry divisions established later show a few non-essential differences.

What with the extent of the subject on the one hand, and the available space on the other, it was impossible to include every detail. For that reason, for example, the weapons were limited to the most important ones; variations, special developments, captured weapons etc., which in any case reached the troops scarcely at all or in limited numbers, are not mentioned. It is to be noted as concerns the technical data for weapons and equipment that these often vary in the specialized literature that deals with them, so that in such cases the average was chosen, in order to attain accurate values even in large-scale statistics.

To avoid repetition as much as possible, such subjects as supplies are described precisely in only one chapter; they were similar in other units. For the same reason, corresponding references are added.

Despite painstaking research into still-available files and documents and checking by specialists, this book does not claim to be complete, nor can errors be ruled out. Additions and corrections will be accepted gratefully.

This book is dedicated to all the hundred thousands of German infantrymen, artillerymen, antitank troops, engineers, mounted troops, intelligence and communications men, medical and supply men, drivers and staff soldiers and all their officers who did their duty quietly, namelessly to the last day of one of the most terrible wars in the history of the world.

My special thanks for their cooperation go to my dear wife Margot and my energetic son Volker.

The Author

Introduction

The German soldier's oath, valid as of August 2, 1934:

"I swear by God this sacred oath, that I will give unlimited obedience to the Leader of the German Reich and People, Adolf Hitler, and as a brave soldier will be ready to stake my life for this oath at any time."

For this oath, approximately 2,960,000 German soldiers gave their lives in World War II. In addition, 1,400,000 soldiers were missing or died in captivity.

And after the lost war, it was written:

By a general:
"Not hate of others, not desire for war, nor understanding of the necessity of practicality provided the impetus for the workers, farmers, employees in field-gray uniforms to storm and fight, but only the obedience to an oath that gave no reasons."

By a major:
"Such hardships and demands will probably never again be made on a troop."

By a chaplain:
"The soldier and the war victim have never expected recognition, for every performance of duty speaks for itself. But a sense of justice rises up against every misunderstanding or negative judgment . . . It is to be hoped that the men will be better understood who, in the valuable years of their lives, were only objects of a terrible human tragedy and irresponsible highest command."

By a corporal:
"Fear, secretly – probably everybody had it. And everybody had to put himself to the test, anew again and again, before every action."

CHAPTER 1

The German Infantry Divisions 1939-1945

The mass of the German army, and above all the field army, consisted in World War II, along with panzer divisions, motorized infantry divisions, antitank divisions (Jägerdivision), mountain divisions (Gebirgsdivision) and such, of infantry divisions.

After Adolf Hitler came to power in 1933 and the Reichswehr was turned into the Wehrmacht, there were 21 active infantry divisions at the end of 1934. In 1935, the year of increased armaments and universal military service, came the further enlargement and expansion of the army, in which the last peacetime division was the 46th Infantry Division. Divisions with the numbers 13, 37, 40, 42 and 43 did not exist then or later.

During the war there were, in all, 35 so-called "waves of establishment" of divisions. The last high "house number" was the 719th Infantry Division, but this is deceiving, as there were only 294 definitive infantry divisions during the whole war, a number of which were disbanded or turned into motorized or pursuit divisions. All other divisions were field training divisions (Feldausbildungdivisionen), guard divisions (Sicherungsdivisionen), permanent sector divisions (Bodenständige Divisionen), coast-guard divisions (Küstenverteidigungsdivisionen), replacement and training divisions (Ersatz- and Ausbildungsdivisionen), so-called "shadow divisions" and ad hoc units established in the last months of the war, which were scarcely or not at all representative of a normal infantry division.

Operations of the Infantry Divisions

1939 – 37.5 divisions took part in the Polish campaign, 38 divisions were stationed on the western front.

1940 – 5 divisions took part in the Norwegian campaign.

1940 – During the western campaign the whole army consisted of 141 infantry divisions, of which 123 were in the west, 5 occupied Poland, 5 were in Norway and Denmark and 8 at home. After the western campaign, 23 divisions were disbanded or restructured.

1941 – 4 divisions served in the Balkan campaign.

1941 – At the beginning of the eastern campaign, the army included 152 infantry divisions in all, of which 99 were in Eastern Europe, 38 in Western Europe, 8 in Norway, 8 in the Balkans and one each in Denmark and Finland. Shortly after the eastern campaign began, the number there increased to 119 infantry divisions.

1944 – At the beginning of the Allied landing in the west in the summer of 1944, 17 infantry divisions were present there.

The Infantry Divisions as Organized for War[1]
(Example: 9th Infantry Division as of April 15, 1940)

Division Staff with:
  Motorcycle courier platoon
  Map office or printing platoon (2 IMG)

Battle Troops:
3 Infantry regiments, each with:
  Regimental staff
  Intelligence platoon
  Mounted platoon
  Engineer platoon
  Regimental band
Infantry gun company (horsedrawn) with:
  – 6 light 75mm and 2 heavy
  – 150mm infantry guns.
Panzerjäger company (motorized) with:
  – 12 36mm antitank guns, 4 light machine guns
  – 3 infantry battalions, each with:
  – Battalion staff and intelligence platoon
  – 3 rifle companies, each with 12 light machine guns,

---

[1]War organization or war strength instructions stated the numbers of soldiers, weapons, horses and vehicles determined by the General Staff of the Army/Organizational Section, and thus corresponded to the prescribed "should-be strength." The "is strength" was the strength actually present.

    The troops calculated according to total strength (that is, all soldiers, weapons, etc., belonging to the units involved, also including furloughed men, detailed men, weapons under repair, etc.), ration strength (that is, all soldiers present in the company, including members of supply trains, detailed VB troops of the artillery, sick men in the area, etc.), battle strength (which also included the field supply trains), as well as fighting or trench strength (that is, all soldiers and weapons that were actively in operations).

– 3 light grenade launchers, 3 A.T. rifles
– 1 machine-gun company with 12 heavy MG, 6 heavy grenade launchers.
1 Light Infantry Column.
　All the units in the regiment, except staff vehicles and antitank companies, were horse drawn.
1 Reconnaissance Unit with:
　Staff and intelligence platoon (motorized) with 9 light machine guns
Cycle squadron with:
　9 light MG, 2 heavy MG, 3 light grenade launchers.
Heavy squadron (motorized) with:
　– 2 light 75mm infantry guns, 3 37mm antitank guns, 3 light armored scout cars (Panzerspähwagen)
1 Panzerjäger Unit (motorized) with:
　– Staff and intelligence platoon
3 Panzerjäger companies, each with:
　– 12 37mm antitank guns, 6 light machine guns.
1 Artillery Regiment with:
　– Staff and intelligence platoon
3 light units, each with:
　– Staff, intelligence platoon and survey platoon
　-- 3 batteries, each with 4 light 105mm light field howitzers and 2 light machine guns
　– 1 artillery column
1 Heavy Battalion with:
　– Staff, Intelligence Staff and Surveying & Mapping Unit
　– 3 Batterys, each with 4 Heavy Field Howitzers
　– 2 Light Machine Guns
　– 1 Artillery Cannon
All the units in the regiment, except staff vehicles, were horsedrawn; later the heavy unit was also motorized.
1 Engineer (Pionier) *Battalion* with:
　– Staff and battalion band
　– 3 engineer companies (2 horsedrawn, 1 motorized), each with 9 IMG, 3 A. T. rifles, 3 flamethrowers
　– 1 bridge column B (motorized)
　– 1 light engineer column (motorized)
1 Intelligence Unit with:
　– Staff
　– 1 telephone company (partly motorized)
　– 1 radio company (motorized)
　– 1 light intelligence company (motorized)

Back-Line Services:
Administrative Services with
  1 victualling unit
  1 bakery company
  1 slaughtering platoon
  (all units motorized)
Supply Services with
  6 supply columns (3 horsedrawn, 3 motorized)
  1 fuel column
  1 repair-shop company
  1 supply company
  (all units motorized)
Medical Services with
  2 medical companies
  (1 horsedrawn, 1 motorized)
  1 field hospital (motorized)
  2 ambulance platoons (motorized)
Veterinary Services with
  1 veterinary company (horsedrawn)
Military Police Services with
  1 field police platoon (motorized)
Mail Services with
  1 field post office (motorized)

Most divisions also had one field replacement battalion with staff and 3 to 5 companies.

(The individual units were designated with Arabic and Roman numerals, for example, 1. = 1st company, I. = 1st battalion, Inf.Rgt.1, etc., thus 1./Inf.Rgt. 1 = 1st company of Infantry Regiment 1, or II./Art.Rgt.8 = 2nd unit of Artillery Regiment 8.

Even though the organization of the divisions in those established later were not completely uniform (for example, in the Panzerjäger units, etc.), there were generally few large-scale differences in the basic organization.

The strength of a division, according to war strength instructions (KStN), without a field replacement battalion, was:

518 officers, 102 administrators[2], 2573 non-commissioned officers,

---

[2]According to a directive of the OKH of May 23, 1939, all army personnel, including administrators, were "combatants" in the sense of the 1929 Geneva Convention, but did not belong to the fighting troops. For self-defense, they were armed with pistols. The weapon color for administrators was dark green. Wehrmacht administrators without officers' rank had light gray braid, administrators of officers' rank had aluminum-colored braid. In an infantry division there were the following administrators:

Futtermeister	Oberfeldwebel
Sekretär	Leutnant
Feldpotheker	Leutnant
Zahlmeister	Leutnant
Intendanturinspektor	Oberleutnant
Oberzahlmeister	Oberleutnant
Intendanturrat	Hauptmann
Kriegsgerichtsrat	Hauptmann
Oberstabszahlmeister	Major

and 13,667 men. This made for a total strength of 16,860 men.

Female infantry personnel such as intelligence assistants, Red Cross nurses etc., were not included in infantry divisions.

The complete armament, according to war armament instructions (KAN), consisted of:

3681 pistols, 12,609 rifles, 312 machine pistols, 90 A.T. rifles, 425 light machine guns, 110 heavy machine guns, 84 50mm light grenade launchers, 54 heavy 81mm grenade launchers, 75 37mm antitank guns, 20 light 75mm infantry guns, 36 light 105mm field howitzers, 12 150mm field howitzers, 9 flamethrowers, 3 light armored scout cars.

The following horses and motor vehicles were on hand:

1743 saddle horses, 3632 draft horses, 895 horsedrawn vehicles, 31 of them with trailers, 500 bicycles, 530 motorcycles, 190 of them with sidecars, 394 motor cars, 536 trucks, 67 of them with trailers.[3]

Rank Insignia at the Beginning of World War II

1. Schütze, Reiter, Kanonier, Funker, Kraftfahrer, Fahrer, Pionier, Sanitätssoldat, etc.
2. Ober- (added to terms listed in #1).
3. Gefreiter
4. Gefreiter/Unteroffiziersanwärter
5. Obergefreiter
6. Stabsgefreiter (as of 1942)
7. Unteroffizier
8. Unterfeldwebel, Unterwachtmeister in the Artillery
9. Fähnrich
10. Feldwebel or Wachtmeister
11. Oberfeldwebel or Oberwachtmeister, also Oberfähnrich
12. Stabsfeldwebel or Stabswachtmeister
13. Leutnant
14. Oberleutnant
15. Hauptmann, Rittmeister in reconnaissance unit
16. Major
17. Oberstleutnant
18. Oberst
19. Generalmajor
20. Generalleutnant

---

[3]While motorized and horsedrawn vehicles as well as horses were frequently brought up to war strength from the civilian sector in the mobilization of 1939, and later losses mainly replaced from the occupied areas, all weapons and guns, with a few early exceptions, were fully standardized.

Insignia of Rank at the Beginning of World War II

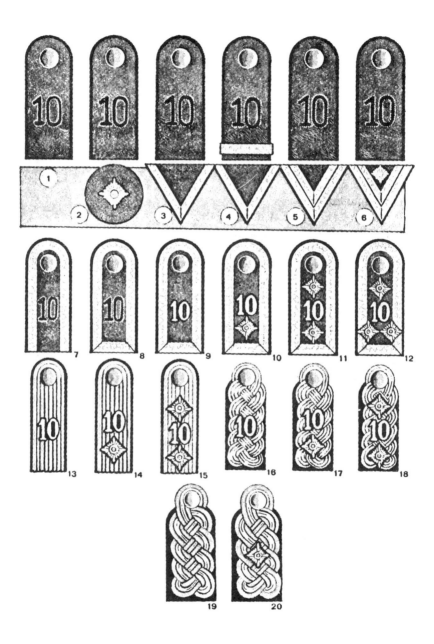

CHAPTER 2

The Soldier

The Uniform

For all soldiers in an infantry division there was the same field uniform. Ranks were distinguished only by their insignia. The only exceptions were riders and drivers (who will be dealt with briefly).

The field-gray uniform consisted of long gray cloth trousers, which were stuck into nail-studded jack-boots. The gray-green buttoned field jacket had two shoulder flaps, two breast and side pockets (over the right breast pocket the army eagle emblem was sewn on), and was equipped with two hooks in back to make the heavy belt more secure to wear. In the collar of the field jacket there was originally a built-in tie, later usually replaced by a neckcloth. On the upper left sleeve were the insignia of rank, on the lower right sleeve the insignia of activity. In the inner lining at the front of the field jacket was a large packet of bandages, with a small one in the right breast pocket. The field cap (or Schiffchen), with a small rosette in the Reich colors of black-white-red, served as a head covering. The underwear consisted of long white underpants, a collarless white shirt, and gray woolen socks with white rings to indicate their size. Foot wrappings were often used inside the boots as well.

Two other important things belonged to the uniform. In the left breast pocket of the field jacket was the service book. To a degree, it was the detailed personal document of the soldier. On the inside of the cover was his photograph with signature, on the first page were his army number, identification disc and list of promotions, on following pages a brief description, the address of his next of kin, clothing and equipment information, data on his weapons training, inoculations, wounds and hospital treatment, salary and special allowances, decorations, and furloughs of more than five days.

The other special item was the oval identification disc that hung on a string around his neck. It consisted of two separable aluminum halves, with his name and the number of his field post or replacement troop stamped on. When a soldier died, one half was broken off and turned over to the burial officer or division chaplain, who then passed it on.

In his trousers and jacket pockets the soldier kept the personal belongings that were important to him, such as letters, photos of family members, etc., plus various useful things such as writing and eating implements, handkerchief, matches, paper, candles, string, pocket knife, can opener, smoking articles, etc.

Winter clothing consisted at first of a field-gray cloth coat, a thin woolen vest, woolen gloves and body belt, a woven cap to pull on over his head, or earmuffs and a scarf.

This field uniform was retained to the end of the war. The only change made, as of June 1943, was the replacement of the "Schiffchen" cap with the uniform field cap with a peak, like the cap of the *Afrika Korps*.

An urgently needed change was made in the winter clothing, though too late, as of the winter of 1942/43. There was now a winter battle suit of thick, warm cloth, with jacket and trousers cut so that they would fit over the normal field uniform and could be worn with either side out (the one side white, the other in spotted camouflage colors), plus a fur cap and felt boots, plus pull-down padded trousers and fleece-lined jacket. For motor vehicle drivers, sentries and such, there were also sheepskin or fur coats.

Any additional clothing was carried in a knapsack and clothing pack on the transport truck: white fatigue jacket and trousers, laced shoes, spare underwear, washcloths, handkerchieves, sport and swimming clothes, running shoes and a woolen blanket, which were issued according to need and situation.

With this uniform and clothing, which were replaced at certain intervals according to use and condition, as well as availability, the soldier was in the field for nearly six years, in summer as in winter, in the west or east, north or south, on the very extended fronts.

As for special uniform pieces, riders and saddle drivers wore riding breeches with leather patches and riding boots with spurs. Motorcycle and other motor vehicle drivers had a long rubber raincoat that could be buttoned over the knees when driving.

The field dress of officers differed very little. They also wore riding breeches and boots, the usual field jacket with silver shoulder patches and lapels, a field cap creased at the front, with a black leather peak and rosette with insignia of rank. The shoulder belt that was still part of the uniform in the 1939 Polish campaign was eliminated by the 1940 western campaign, the wide brown belt was usually blackened and the shoulder flaps often covered, in order to make the officer as unrecognizable to the enemy as possible after already heavy losses.

Equipment

Among the standard equipment was a black leather belt, with a buckle that bore the eagle emblem and the motto "Gott mit uns" (God with us), as well as a sliding leather holster for side arms. On either side of the belt buckle were two black leather three-section bullet pouches (with further divisions internally), each of which could hold 30 bullets. On the right rear of the belt, the musette bag was fastened with two loops and a hook. It held the daily ration of cold food, a small round bakelite container for butter or fat, rifle-cleaning tools, spare ammunition, and at first also the "iron ration", consisting of a small bag with 500 grams of hard zwieback in small pieces and a 200-gram can of meat. It could be eaten only under orders in cases of the most extreme need, which soon proved to be unrealistic after the beginning of the eastern campaign. Fastened to the musette bag by a strap was the felt-covered three-quarter-liter field flask with a field cup carried over it.

At the left rear of the belt, in an open leather carrier, hung a short spade, to which the side arms were attached. The hand spade was also used as a weapon in hand-to-hand combat, and was used in trenching tasks such as digging shelter pits and foxholes, as well as digging cooking pits, knocking off branches and such (A folding spade that could also be used as a cutter by having a small roller on the handle did not prove practical).

On the left side too, the Model 30 gas mask was carried on a thin cloth belt over the right shoulder. In front, diagonally over the breast, there was until about the end of 1940 the gas shield, an oil-saturated, folded light cloth with which the soldier was to cover himself in a gas attack. For gas protection there was also a packet of *Losantine* tablets for use against the chemical warfare agent Lost. But the gas shield and Losantine were no longer used after 1940, since they had proved to be impractical and unnecessary.

The weight of the belt with all the pieces of equipment and contents that the soldier had to carry on the march and in battle is noteworthy. The weights were: belt 0.25 kg, two bullet pouches with 60 rounds 2.06 kg, musette bag (empty) 0.24 kg, bread 0.50 kg, small meat can 0.65 kg, one small fat can 0.15 kg, field flask (full) 1.07 kg, spade 1.11 kg, side arms 0.65 kg, gas mask 1.93 kg, in all over 8 kilograms.

Before battle, the field cap was exchanged for the dull gray steel helmet (Stahlhelm), which otherwise usually hung on the front of the belt over one of the two bullet pouches. The steel helmet was the standard Model 35 with two shield-shaped emblems, the colors of the Reich on the right and the service insignia on the left side. The steel helmet was made of smooth sheet steel, 1.1 to 1.2 mm thick, and was made in five sizes; it weighed 1.34 kg. Later in the war the application of the two symbols was eliminated; the use of camouflage covers made these emblems superfluous anyway.

But that did not complete the marching and fighting equipment.

There was also the assault kit.[1] This consisted of a leather harness that was attached to the belt at the front by two straps at the left and right and became a wider strap in the back that was likewise attached to the belt. To this harness there could be fastened, on the soldier's back: the two-part cooking utensil with lid and folding handle of aluminum (capacity 1.5 liters), with three eating utensils. If the cooking pot was not used to hold food, then it contained a cloth bundle of washing and shaving implements. Also fastened to the harness was the tent square, folded around the cooking utensils; along with the field flask and cooking utensils, this was one of the most indispensable pieces of equipment.

The tent square (Zeltbahn), with a weight of 1.27 kg, was of triangular form, measuring 202 x 202 cm on the sides and 240cm along the bottom, and was made of waterproof fabric. The front and back sides had camouflage coloration, with irregular brown and green angular spots and green lines running through them, one side somewhat lighter, the other darker. On each side there were twelve double buttons and just as many buttonholes, opposite each other, so that several tent squares could be buttoned together. Four tent squares, along with four tent poles and eight tent pegs (one pole and two pegs were also carried on the soldier's harness), made the customary tent for four men, but larger tents could also be made, using eight or more tent squares. The tent square also served to cover foxholes. In the middle of every tent square was a double attached, buttonable and unbuttonable cutout that provided ventilation for the tent in summer. But if one stuck his head through this opening, one could wear the tent square, buttoned around him in various ways, for good weather and rain protection. But the tent square did not offer just covering and protection from the weather; not the least of its uses was as an improvised stretcher for carrying injured men away from the front lines.

Field uniform, clothing and equipment remained essentially unchanged until the end of the war.

A few further remarks as to camouflage. At first the individual soldier had nothing for this purpose but his tent square, which could be used to provide camouflage. In the Polish and western campaigns steel helmets were camouflaged by stretching rubber bands or straps around the helmet and sticking small twigs, bunches of grass and the like in them. Helmet camouflage was later improved by pulling a camouflage net or cover of tent material over the helmet.

For the eastern campaign a white winter camouflage was urgently needed. Here the troops had to help themselves during the first Russian winter, covering their helmets with pieces of white cloth and their uniforms with white bedding. White snow jackets, snow coats and camou-

---

[1] If the harness was not available, the assault kit was fastened to the back of the belt.

flage covers were provided later. The reversible winter battle dress, white and spotted, that subsequently became standard provided full camouflage.

Armament

Every soldier was armed with a 98 k rifle, a bayonet and hand grenades (*see also* section on "Light Infantry Weapons" for greater detail).

The bayonet, as a belt weapon, belonged to dress as well as combat uniforms for all servicemen and non-commissioned officers up to the rank of sergeant and were also carried by mounted soldiers.

CHAPTER 3

Battle Troops

The Rifle Squad (Schützengruppe)

The rifle squad, the smallest unit of the infantry, with its white distinguishing color (waffenfarbe), consisted of the squad leader and nine riflemen, and thus had a strength of 1 officer and 9 men (the former division between light machine-gun troops and rifle troops no longer existed). During the course of the war, this strength naturally dropped, often to six or five men.

When the war broke out in 1939, the squad leader was still armed with a rifle, then as of 1941 with a machine pistol (MPi). Among his equipment were two pouches, each with 3 MPi magazines (32 rounds each), which were carried on either side of his belt, plus 6 x 30 binoculars, message bag, flashlight, marching compass and signal whistle. The squad leader, at first always a non-commissioned officer, in the later years of the war sometimes an experienced *Obergefreite* ("Backbone of the Army") or a tested *Gefreite*, was not only the leader of his men but also their defender, responsible for them day and night, handling all great and small needs and problems, a fixed point in all critical situations and a comrade among comrades. If he proved himself as a soldierly and human example on good and bad days alike, then the whole group was good; if he was not, then his men usually failed as well.

Gunner (Schütze) 1 of the group was its "sharpest-shooting" man. He carried and operated the light machine gun (lMG 34, later lMG 42) with its detachable parts and a 50-round belt. Also part of his armament and equipment were a Type 08 pistol (later a 38 pistol) with one 8-round magazine, the machine-gun tool kit, with spare parts and cleaning tools on his belt, and sunglasses. Gunner 1 fired offensively and defensively, with the gun supported on a bipod either in front or in the middle, and during an attack or penetration, with the bipod folded up, he fired the lMG from the hip.

Gunner 2 carried, on a carrying strap, the first ammunition supply of four 50-round ammunition drums (weighing 2.45 kg per drum) as well as an ammunition box with 300 rounds (weighing 11.53 kg), plus a sheet-metal barrel protector with two spare barrels. For short-range defense he also carried a pistol. Gunner "zwo" (2) was Gunner 1's assistant with the lMG. He supported the machine-gunner by supplying ammunition, changing a barrel or breech, and by removing hindrances. If Gunner 1 fell, he took the firing position behind the gun himself.

Gunner 3 was the ammunition gunner for the lMG. He was armed with a rifle and had the job of carrying two full ammunition boxes of 300 rounds each on either side, hanging on a strap. Early in the war he also had to handle the machine-gun tripod, unloaded from the army truck, in case of danger from the air, but later this was not used. But as the strength of the squad decreased, the role of Gunner 3 was eliminated. The ammunition boxes were then divided among the squad and had to be carried by individual soldiers in turn.

The remaining six men of the squad, including the deputy squad leader (Gruppenführer), were all shooters, armed with rifles. In the two belt supported ammunition pouches they carried 45 rounds, in clips of five rounds each, and in battle 15 more rounds from the truck. In addition, each man carried two or three hand grenades. Stick grenades (so called "Potato Mashers") were carried on the front of the belt or stuck into the boot tops, while hand grenades were carried in the musette bag or the trouser pockets.

Thus the firepower of the squad added up to one light machine gun, one machine pistol, two pistols, seven rifles and a number of various grenades.

The rifle squad was the smallest combat unit. In an attack it "developed" into the "rifle row" and "rifle chain" formations, normally with a distance of ten paces from man to man, which could also be increased depending on enemy action. An experienced battle group went into an attack spread out, supported each other mutually with fire, especially with the light machine gun, and penetrated enemy positions tightly grouped while firing the machine pistols and machine gun, throwing hand grenades, and shouting. Their battle cry provided much moral support and in numerous cases caused the enemy to give up his defense early. The squad could also handle small tasks such as guarding, scouting, etc.

The squad was not just a battle unit, but also a unit sworn to accept its fate; every member knew every other member inside and out, shared his joys and sorrows, and developed a true camaraderie that – as with all other units – has maintained unbroken to this day.

The Rifle Platoon (Schützenzug)

The rifle platoon was the next higher unit, consisting of the platoon leader, platoon troop, four squads (later fewer), light grenade-launcher troop and drivers, with a strength of 1:6:43 men. The platoons were originally led by a *Leutnant* (as leader of the first platoon in the company, he was the company officer), and an *Oberfeldwebel* or *Feldwebel*.

The platoon leader's armament and equipment consisted of a machine pistol with two magazine pouches, 6 x 30 binoculars, message case, compass and flashlight.

The platoon troop that led the platoon consisted of the platoon troop leader (*Unteroffizier*), and three messengers (originally one was also a bugler), all armed with rifles. Later the third messenger was also given a telescopic sight that could be attached to his rifle for sharpshooting. One medic, armed with a pistol, also belonged to the platoon troop. His equipment consisted of a belt attached medical kit, plus a water bottle (similar to but larger than a field flask), and on his back a medical pack with supplies to treat minor wounds or injuries, marked with a large red cross. The red cross armband, worn on the left arm until 1941, was usually done away with after the eastern campaign began, since the Russians often disregarded the red cross sign, and the medics, with their noticeable armbands, suffered high losses as a result.

The platoon troop also carried amongst themselves, wire cutters, flare pistol, signal flags and a small flashing light for optical communication (Blinkgerät). The signal flags and flashing light were soon dropped, as they did not prove useful in combat. Especially important, and regarded as indispensable until the war's end, was the flare pistol. With its white and variously colored flare and signal bullets, it served to light up the terrain briefly at night, aided in communication and contact, helped to indicate recognized enemy targets, aided in directing fire, etc. The flare pistol was not a weapon in the usual sense, but it could also be used successfully in close combat for direct fire against enemy gun positions, bunkers, etc.

The rifle squads, four in number, have already been described. The light grenade launcher troop with its troop leader and gunners 1 and 2 carried the troop's high-angle fire weapon, the 5-caliber light grenade launcher 36. The troop leader carried a rifle, binoculars, message case, three leg brace for the launcher, and in combat an ammunition box with ten grenades. Gunner 1, armed with a pistol, had the bottom plate, Gunner 2, likewise armed with a pistol, had the barrel of the launcher – both were carried on their backs. The launcher gunners also each carried two ammunition cases by hand. The grenade launcher was set up on its three legs and either aimed at a target or "zeroed in" with a few shots. This happened approximately in the following manner: Gunner 1: "Feuerbereit" ("Ready to fire"), troop leader: "350 (meters) – one round – frei (fire!)"; gunner 1: "Abgefeuret" ("Fired") Troop leader: "40 to the right – 50 shorter – one round – fire!"; gunner 1: "Abgefeuret."

The firepower of the rifle platoon consisted of 5 machine pistols, 4 light machine guns, 11 pistols, 34 rifles and one light grenade launcher.

For these weapons, a primary ammunition supply of 1048 machine pistol and pistol rounds, 4600 machine gun rounds, 2040 rifle rounds, about 60 hand grenades and 50 launcher grenades had to be carried into battle.

To every platoon there belonged at the beginning of the war a two-horse wagon (HF 1) with a driver; on the march, the light machine guns, the grenade launcher, tripods, hand grenades, tools, long trenching tools, tripwire, gun-cleaning tools, means of camouflage, and especially the ammunition not carried by the men could be transported. When they went into battle, the command "Equipment off!" ("entfaltete!") was given and the machine guns and grenade launcher, including the ammunition to be carried with them, were unloaded and taken over by the appropriate gunners. A new four-horse wagon made of steel, with rubber tires, introduced along with HF 1, could be used well on smooth roads (for example, in the western campaign), but was much too heavy for the bad roads and lanes in the eastern campaign, and was omitted after 1941. In place of it, the troops usually made use of one or two of the wagons native to that area, which could get through almost everywhere in spite of mud and dirt. In place of the wagon, some platoons had a one-horse infantry cart, driven by a driver, with a second cart in tow. In the first cart were the machine guns with their ammunition and equipment, in the second cart the grenade launcher, ammunition, equipment and grenades. When combat operations were about to begin, the wagon or cart joined the company's supply train, which was commanded by the company's *Hauptfeldwebel*.

In combat the platoon "unfolded" into a wide wedge, with three squads in front and one following them, or to a pointed wedge with one squad in front and three in back. The platoon leader and platoon troop always followed in the middle, from where the platoon leader could give his signals to the groups by voice, whistle, hand signals or messengers. The platoon was capable of handling larger combat tasks such as shock-troop operations and the like.

The Rifle Company (Schützenkompanie)

The rifle company consisted of:

– Company Chief, mounted (usually a *Hauptmann* or *Oberleutnant* as regulation leader of the company, during the war also a *Leutnant* who, as company leader, was entrusted with the leadership of a company for a shorter or longer time on account of a shortage of company chiefs).

  – Company troop
  – 3 rifle platoons (schützenzuge)
  – 3 antitank rifle troops (panzerbüchsentrupps)
  – Supply train
  – Commissary unit I

– Commissary unit II
– Pack train

The full battle strength added up to 2:21:178 men, the fighting strength to 176 men. Their armament consisted of 16 machine pistols, 12 light machine guns, 44 pistols, 130 rifles, 3 antitank rifles, 3 light grenade launchers, one saddle horse, 12 to 18 draft horses depending on their vehicles (see below), 8 bicycles, 1 motorcycle, 1 motorcycle with sidecar and 3 trucks.

To the company troop there belonged: 1 company troop leader (*Feldwebel*) with a machine pistol, 4 messengers (one originally also a musician), 2 messengers with bicycles, 1 groom with a bicycle, all with rifles, 1 medical non-commissioned officer with a bicycle, 1 medical soldier, with pistols. Along with the usual equipment, the company troop also had ten small ground panels (red and white cloths, 1.5 meters long). Laid out to form symbols and letters, they were intended to make communication with their own aircraft possible (for example, marking the front line, etc.). These cloths could only be laid out after several aircraft had appeared. So that enemy aircraft could draw no conclusions from these signs, they were to be removed immediately after their own planes were gone. In addition they could be laid out only at places in the terrain where they could not be seen by enemy ground forces.

Panzerbüchse troop:
with one troop leader (non-commissioned officer) with bicycle and three Panzerbüchsen to be served by two men each, with pistols (the Gunner 1 operated the Panzerbüchse, the Gunner 2 was the ammunition gunner with ammunition pouches on his belt for two bullet holders of ten rounds each). Generally there was one Panzerbüchse crew for each platoon.

To the supply train there belonged:
1 *Hauptfeldwebel* with pistol and bicycle, one supply train leader (*Gefechtstrossführer*) with rifle and bicycle, one weapons and equipment non-commissioned officer with pistol, 3 two-horse wagons with wagon drivers or 3 one-horse infantry carts, each with a driver, and one four-horse combat wagon[1] with one wagon driver and one saddle driver, one large four-horse field kitchen (150-liter kettle) with one wagon driver and one saddle driver, plus two field cooks and two orderlies, all with rifles.

To the commissary unit I (V I train):

---

[1]Throughout the war, the trusty two-horse light army vehicle 1 (HF 1) and the four-horse heavy army vehicle 2 (HF 2) were used as supply or field wagons.

belonged one quartermaster sergeant (*Unteroffizier*) as leader with bicycle, one soldier, one two-horse mess wagon with wagon driver, all with rifles.

The commissary unit II (V II train) consisted of one commissary *Unteroffizier*, one motorcycle driver with solo cycle, one 3-ton truck with driver and assistant, all with rifles.

The pack train included: one pay clerk (*Unteroffizier*) as leader, one pay clerk's assistant, one tailor, one shoemaker, one saddler, one motorcycle driver with cycle and sidecar, 1 3-ton truck with driver and assistant for company papers, spare clothing and tools, one 3-ton truck with driver and assistant for the soldiers' packs (knapsack and laundry), all soldiers with rifles.[2]

In mobile warfare the supply train and V I unit were directed by the battalion staff, the V II and pack trains by the regiment. In stationary warfare and times of rest, the trains were usually 3 to 5 kilometers behind the company sector or in the company's billet area.

The company, especially when strengthened by the heavy weapons of the battalion (*see also* section "The Infantry Battalion"), was capable of fighting alone, what with its strength and weaponry. In an attack it "took shape", like the platoons, in a pointed and wide formation and was thus assigned "attack sectors" by the battalion, while in defense it was assigned "defense sectors." The company could be deployed, for example, as a "shock company" to penetrate enemy positions, combined with motorized units as a spearhead, assigned to handle obstacle sectors or defend support centers, etc.

Just a word about the soldiers in the trains, who were often described unjustly, even by members of their own companies, as "baggage handlers"; despite all later "combing-out actions", they were absolutely necessary.

First of all, there was the company *Hauptfeldwebel*, recognizable by the two "Kolbenringe" ("piston rings") on the sleeves of his jacket, in peace as in war the "mother of the company", concisely and fondly called the "Spiess" ("spear") by the men. He was "in charge" in the company's rear zone and relieved the company chief or company leader, busy with fighting, of all possible matters that were not directly concerned with battle. Thus he commanded not only all the company trains, but also supervised the activity and work of all supply-train personnel and was in charge of discipline and order in the rear zone; in particular, after a long stay he immediately set up the company writing room in a suitable building, to serve particularly for service communications with commanders and home. The *Hauptfeldwebel* made sure that, even in war, the services of the company handled all necessary concerns as smoothly as possible. Thus

---

[2]Since the composition and strength of the trains were similar in other units too, they will not be described in depth again, for the sake of saving space.

he oversaw all the paperwork, including regular reports, arriving orders, promotions, arrivals and departures, inventories, reports and such. All communications from home concerning members of the company, death reports, inquiries from civil authorities, penal orders, etc., went through him, and he also sent the sympathy letters written by the company chief to the families of fallen soldiers. The "spear" examined and distributed the mail, and not the least of his jobs was maintaining a strict rotation for fervently desired furlough passes. He made sure of a fair division of no less desirable marketed goods, kept an eye on the food supplies and looked for the men who were sent back to the trains from up front, easing their lot by making a sauna or bath available, or even a small company building with tables and benches, plus straw sacks to sleep on. And if it became necessary, the "spear" also went forward to the fighting company to take the place of a platoon leader who was out of commission.

The *Fourier* and *Verpflegunteroffizier* were responsible for the correct and complete obtaining of rations, fodder and such goods, and for their storage and distribution.

The tailors, shoemakers and saddlers always had more than enough work, mending torn and worn clothing, equipment, horse tack and the like, until new supplies could be distributed.

The pay clerk and his assistants were in charge of the whole process of paying the company. He paid the soldiers' salaries whenever and however he could, even in the front lines, received payments, and was also in charge of the other payments, such as from sale of goods, company purchases, etc.

The medical non-commissioned officers and soldiers went to the battalion's troop dressing station. In times of immobile war or quiet, they set up a dispensary or field hospital in a suitable building in the company zone, where minor wounds, illnesses or convalescence could be taken in and cared for, treated and cured under the guidance of the battalion surgeon.

A few words now about the drivers, who always took care of their horses, often making up for a shortage of fodder by dangerous "hunting trips" into the country; along with the battalion foddermaster and blacksmith, they kept the horses in good condition, and drove their carts and wagons, often under terrible conditions, enemy fire and air attacks, over rough terrain, muddy roads, through deep snow and, when necessary, across country to follow the fighting forces everywhere.

Most important, though, was the field kitchen with its two cooks and their staff, jokingly-crudely called "kitchen bulls" ("Küchenbullen") by the soldiers. There was truth in the familiar saying, "An army marches on its stomach." The physical condition as well as the mood of the whole troop depended on its daily bread. Good field cooks were often true masters of their art and trained accordingly. The dinners that they conjured up out of their kettles out of the raw materials brought by the V-I and V-II trains from the division distribution centers may not have been banquet dinners, but they were ample and nourishing food, as was recognized with thanks by all the soldiers. Usually casseroles, it might also, depending on the place, time and opportunity, consist of several dishes, such as soups, roasts with gravy, potatoes and salad, prepared in special containers.To these hot field-kitchen food, when available, such things as fruit, chocolate, and dessert were added. The field cooks, along with the quartermaster sergeant, also distributed cold food in the morning and evening as well as special rations. The food provided in the usual way was, when possible, enhanced with fresh products from the country, obtained by purchase or trade – another duty of the *Hauptfeldwebel*. Commandeering was always strictly forbidden (re rations, *see also* section "Administrative and Supply Services").

The rations intended to be the morning, midday or evening meal could, naturally, not always be delivered at the regular times on account of the fighting. For this reason the field cooks had to be movable and able to improvise. While in times of quiet, every soldier in the assembled company came forward with his own utensils and field flask to get his food, in times of action the food was brought close to the front. In darkness the field kitchen was driven to a known, designated place, as protected as possible, to which the company's food gatherers (three to four men per group) came to get the warm and cold food for the following day; one man per group took about six full cooking pots for his comrades, a second had the field flasks filled with coffee or tea and slung on himself, and a third carried the cold food in a tent square or sack. Such a distribution of food was not without danger. The clearly audible rattling of the utensils, the flashes of flashlights and such often drew enemy fire.

The role played by food and the field kitchen for the soldiers is seen in the fact that, in the extended retreats later in the war, entire units were often shattered and torn apart. What reception lines, officers and military police could not accomplish – various field kitchens became gathering places for more and more soldiers, who could then be formed into units again.

Naturally, there were times of hunger and deprivation often enough, when supply problems or critical situations brought rations to a stop. But no soldier starved as long as he was with the troops (with the exception of the Sixth Army's defeat in the Stalingrad basin). And it probably would have been almost impossible for half-starved German soldiers to have marched forward and back for thousands of kilometers through all of Europe in campaigns that went on for years.

And this too is certain – unlike almost all other armies (with the exception of the Red Army), there was only a single food supply in the whole German Army, for officers and men alike – they all ate from the same food from the same field kitchens.

When things got rough somewhere and the enemy had penetrated far into the lines, then the supply-train soldiers, insufficiently trained and experienced in warfare, had to take up arms too. Then it was said later in one or another battle report:

". . . With quickly assembled back-line units, supply-train soldiers and such, the enemy advance could be stopped . . ." Medals were seldom given for it.[3]

Light Infantry Weapons
Among the light infantry weapons were:
- Side Arms
- Stick Grenade 24 and Hand Grenade 39
- Pistol 08
- Flare Pistol 38
- Rifle 98 k
- Self-Loading Rifle 41
- Light Machine Gun (lMG) 34
- Light Grenade Launcher (lGr.W.) 36
- Antitank Weapons (Panzerbüchsen) 38/39 and 41.

Side Arms
The short side arms, carried in a leather scabbard on the belt, consisted of a 26-cm one-bladed bayonet in a sheet-steel sheath, weighing 650 grams. The bayonet, attached to the rifle in combat, had long since lost the importance it had in World War I as a hand-to-hand weapon. This results from the fact that the Wehrmacht no longer provided bayonet training. To be sure, the bayonet was carried as the soldier's "side arms" to the end of World War II, but more for other purposes than for use in battle. Storm attacks and hand-to-hand combat with fixed bayonets were exceptions.

Stick Grenade (Potato Masher) 24 and Hand Grenade 39
The stick grenade, likewise stemming from World War I and subsequently improved, was first available when the war began. It consisted of a hollow wooden staff with a pull-out string, fuse and detonator, and the canister of thin sheet steel with the powder charge. The stick grenade had to be activated before use by unscrewing the safety cap on the stick end and inserting one of the detonators brought along in small cases.

To increase the shrapnel effect, a ribbed steel reinforcing cover was

---

[3]Activities, work and achievements of the supply trains could only be outlined in brief – as is true of all other units too – for reasons of space.

put around the canister as of 1941.

Technical data:

Weight	500 grams
Length	36 cm
Diameter (canister)	5.98 cm
Charge	165 grams of black powder
Delay	4 seconds
Range	up to 25 meters, depending on launcher
Shrapnel effect	15- to 20-meter diameter

The stick grenade could not only be launched individually, but also as a concentric charge, for example, in bunker fighting, or as an extended charge to blow up wire obstacles and the like.

In the concentric charge, 5 or 6 hand-grenade canisters were lashed in place around a central grenade with a stick, and the latter's detonator set off the entire bundle. In the extended charge, several hand-grenade canisters were fastened to a board, strong branch, etc., at about 15-centimeter intervals, with a stick grenade at the end. Here a long cord was tied to the trigger button to detonate it.

As of the spring of 1940, the stick grenade was complemented by the hand grenade. Compared to the stick grenade, it had the advantages of an already primed trigger button, was almost 50% lighter, easier to throw, and not as big and awkward to carry, so that the soldier always could take a few hand grenades along in his musette bag, coat or trouser pocket, close at hand.

Technical data:

Weight	298 grams
Length	7.6 cm
Diameter	5.0 cm
Charge	225 grams of black powder
Delay	4.5 seconds
Range	similar to stick grenade
Shrapnel effect	similar to stick grenade

The hand grenades were close-combat weapons especially suited to targets in or behind cover. They worked mainly through their shrapnel effect, but also by air pressure in a 3- to 6-meter circle, as well as affecting morale by the loud noise of their detonation. In an attack they were thrown just before the last storming and penetration, and were used defensively against storm attacks. They were also especially suitable for fighting in buildings, towns and trenches. Both grenades were used until the end of the war.

Pistol 08

This pistol was introduced into the German prewar army in 1908, proved itself excellently during World War I, and became widely known under the name "Parabellum." It was a semi-automatic self-loading pistol with a knee-joint which worked as a recoil self-charger. Aiming was done by notched backsight and foresight; firing was single-shot. It was a robust, reliably functioning weapon with great durability, and would, for example, shoot cleanly through a steel helmet at a distance of up to ten meters.

The ammunition per man consisted of one magazine in the pistol and a spare magazine in the leather holster. The 08 pistol was not manufactured after 1942, and was to be replaced by the 38 pistol, which was not introduced everywhere.

Technical data:

Caliber	9 mm (pistol ammunition)
Weight (unloaded)	870 grams
Length	22.3 cm
Range	up to 500 meters
Best range	25 to 50 meters
Exit velocity (V_o)	320 meters per second
Rate of fire	10 to 20 shots per minute
Weight of bullet	12 grams
Bullet feed	magazines of 8 bullets

The 08 and later 38 pistols were the standard weapons carried for close combat and self-defense by heavy weapons crews, "functionaries", medical personnel, officials and the like. Officers generally had various types of 7.65 mm caliber pistol which they had purchased.

Flare Pistol 38 (Leuchtpistole)

The 38 flare pistol was a single-shot pistol with a smooth barrel, stiffly bolted and tipping forward, without a safety catch, sights or a magazine. It was carried on a strap, as was its leather ammunition container, and was nicknamed "Klavier" (piano) by the soldiers because of its stepped design to make the individual cartridges easier to grasp.

Technical data:

Caliber	27mm
Weight	745 grams
Length	42.5 cm
Weight of cartridge	70 to 150 grams (depending on type)
Cartridge feed	one cartridge per firing

The ammunition consisted of flare and signal cartridges which made different-colored lights. The light cartridges began to take effect only after covering 25 meters, their maximum height was 80 meters, and their light lasted from 6 to 15 seconds. In the daytime, in good weather, they could be seen up to 2.5 kilometers; at light details could be seen in a 100-meter diameter. When a parachute flare was used, the light lasted for up to a minute.

The most commonly used light and signal cartridges for day and night, and their meanings (when not otherwise ordered and agreed on) were:

Light cartridge, white, and parachute light cartridge – To illuminate the terrain at night.

Signal cartridge, white – "Here is our front line" or "here are our units"

Signal cartridge, red, single fired or double star toward the enemy – "Enemy is attacking" or, "enemy is there" or "barrage fire ordered"

Signal cartridge, green, single or double star – "Lift the fire"

Multi-star cartridge, white, red and green – Usually to signal cooperation with heavy weapons, artillery, for storm action, disengagement, etc.

Signal cartridge, violet, and smoke cartridges – "Tank warning" or "enemy tanks are attacking here"

Whistling cartridge – "Gas alarm"

Rifle 98 k
There was no soldier in an infantry division, indeed in the whole Wehrmacht, who had not held the 98 k Rifle in his hand, had not been trained to use it and fire it, even if only on the firing range. And, for hundreds of thousands of soldiers it was their main weapon during the entire war – the 98 k rifle, was also known in jest as "The Soldier's Bride", but was also referred to as a "shootin' iron" by the soldiers themselves.

The 98 k (kurz: short) rifle was developed as an infantry handgun from the 98 rifle or carbine of World War I. It was similar to the old 98 rifle and differed essentially in having a barrel that was 14 cm shorter, a bent bolt lever, and a ring for the carrying strap on the side of the butt and butt plate. Like its forerunner, the rifle was a repeater, made for clips that held five cartridges, which were pushed into the box magazine by hand and locked in by the bolt lever via a turning cylinder lock. The sight consisted of a foresight with a V notch and a sliding sight that could be set from 100 (fixed sight) to 2000 meters.

Technical data:

Caliber	7.92 mm
Weight	3.9 kg
Overall length (barrel length)	1.11 m (59.4 cm)
Maximum range	2700 m
Effective range	400 to 500 m
Initial velocity (V_o)	755 m/sec
Rate of fire	up to 10 rounds per minute
Cartridge weight	23.7 grams
Cartridge feed	Charger (frame), 5 cartridges

The rifle could also be used as a sharpshooter's rifle. For that purpose the Zf 41 telescopic sight with small (2.5-fold) or the Zf 42 with great (five-fold) magnification could be screwed onto the rifle.

The 98 k rifle was the uniform weapon for the great majority of soldiers, who could use it as the occasion demanded, in shooting at targets, from the hip, firing grenades or rapid fire. Of course the rifle was primarily a firearm, but with its heavy wooden shaft, it could also be used as a thrusting and, with a bayonet, a cutting weapon.

The rifle was an absolutely reliable weapon for any good rifleman, and was retained until the war ended without any modifications. Then even the development of this, the most famous of repeater rifles, came to an end. There was no successor type.

Self-Loading 41 Rifle
With this self-loading rifle, which came out in two versions that were scarcely different, the attempt was made to equip the troops at least partially with a rapid-fire rifle. In this case it was a gas-pressure self-loader with support-flap locking and hammer bolt, air-cooling, a shaft like the 98 k rifle with a somewhat shortened foreshaft, and a box magazine for ten rounds (single shots) inserted from the bottom.

Technical data:

Caliber	7.92 mm
Weight	4.3 kg
Overall length (barrel length)	1.14 m (55.8 cm)
Sight	100 to 1200 m
Effective range	to 550 m
Initial velocity (V_o)	776 meters per second
Rate of fire	10 rounds in 12 seconds

The two rifle types, which were supplied the troops from the spring of 1942 on, were not as successful as had been hoped. They were not effective enough, often jammed, and were too expensive to produce. Cleaning the gas-pressure system was also difficult for the individual soldier. Therefore only a limited number of rifles was produced, and were usually issued as special weapons, equipped with telescopic sights, for sharpshooters.

Machine Pistol 40

For a long time, the German authorities could not decide whether or not to continue to develop the 18 machine pistol, also known as the MPi Bergmann, which had appeared during World War I, and put it into general use. In the western campaign in 1940 there were only three of them per company, one for each platoon leader. Only in 1941 did the MPi 40, a slightly improved version of the already developed MPi 38, reach the troops. The two models are almost identical. This machine pistol was a firearm made – for the first time – of stamped sheet metal and, as a recoil loader with a heavy spring breech, could be used only for sustained fire. It was usually fired with its shoulderpiece swiveled out, but could also be used with it folded in. The sight consisted of a fixed sight for up to 100 meters and a flap sight for 200 meters. Ammunition feed took place from a staff magazine mounted at the bottom.

Though most of its characteristics were good, the machine pistol had one serious fault. It was very susceptible to dampness, dirt and coldness, which often caused it to jam. In addition, its safety catch was not reliable enough, and often led to accidents. Even if it was set down on the ground a bit too hard, a loaded weapon could fire. The troops remedied that by making the safety a little firmer by adding a small belt. Then too, the spring of the straight magazine, with a full load of cartridges, lost its strength rather quickly, which in turn led to many jammings at decisive moments. This could be cured only by putting fewer cartridges in the magazine.

Technical data:

Caliber	9 mm (pistol ammunition)
Weight	4.1 kg
Length, shoulderpiece in	63.5 cm
Length, shoulderpiece out	88.9 cm
Maximum range	300 m
Effective range	200 m
Initial velocity (V_o)	381 meters per second
Rate of fire	400 to 500 rounds per minute
Cartridge weight	Same as 08 pistol
Cartridge feed	Staff magazine with 32 cartridges

Despite these weaknesses, which were later corrected, the MPi 40, along with the rifle, remained a standard weapon of the infantry, with which platoon and squad leaders in particular were armed. It was a short-range weapon particularly suitable for close combat, town and forest fighting. This machine pistol was issued in great numbers. The extent of production can be seen in the fact that in March of 1945 there were 48,300 of them manufactured.

Light Machine Gun 34

The 34 light machine gun, introduced to replace the earlier 08/15 machine gun used in World War I, was a gas-pressure recoil charger with air cooling. The sight range extended from 200 to 2000 meters. the lMG was set up for single shots and sustained fire, the latter meaning that – to keep on target – only quick successive bursts of 3 to 6 rounds could be fired. The folding bipod could be used in forward position for far and medium ranges, and in central position for close ranges, with a wider traverse. Ammunition feed was provided by metal belts with 50 rounds each or from metal drums (belt drums), also of 50 rounds. With the belt drum attached to the feed of the MG, the gun was immediately ready to fire (the empty belt automatically rolled up in the drum). Since the same ammunition was used as in the 98 k rifle, it could be exchanged from one weapon to the other if need be. The cartridges were inserted into the belts by hand, and on command, special ammunition (such as tracer bullets) could be inserted at intervals.

Gunner 1 usually fired in a lying position in moving warfare. When the situation required, the gun could also be fired standing up or over the shoulder of Gunner 2, who then held the bipod firmly.

Set on a telescopic tripod (aerial tripod – weight 6.9 kg), the lMG – equipped with a panoramic sight – could also be used as an anti-aircraft gun. These unhandy AA tripods, brought along in a platoon's equipment vehicle, were used rarely and soon dispensed with altogether. It was quicker and simpler to fire the MG at low-flying enemy planes from the shoulder of Gunner 2.

This weapon too had its weaknesses. When firing, the barrel became hot very quickly and thus had to be changed. When changing the barrel, though, one had to be particularly careful not to burn one's hands. It was impractical that in doing this, the lid of the MG had to be opened, the breech uncovered and the hot barrel removed with asbestos gloves or metal hooks, which was naturally quite difficult at night. In addition, the MG was very sensitive to dust, sand, snow, etc., and very expensive to produce.

Technical data:

Caliber	7.92 mm
Weight	12.1 kg
Length (barrel length)	1.22 m (59.6 cm)

Sight	200 to 2000 meters
Maximum range	3000 meters
Effective range	to 1500 meters
Initial velocity (V_o)	755 meters per second
Rate of fire	800 to 900 rounds per minute

The light machine gun provided the primary firepower of the rifle companies. Their light weight and low structure allowed their use in the front lines, in all battle situations, by just one shooter.

Light Grenade Launcher 36 (Leichter Granatwerfer)
The light grenade launcher consisted of two parts and was a muzzle loader with a smooth bore, mounted on a small baseplate. Aiming was done in a simple manner, when Mortarman 1 – sighting along a white stripe on the barrel or using two aiming rods – moved the launcher crudely into firing position. A fine adjustment was made by using the elevation and traverse controls, while a clinometer handled angles. The distances were marked on the left side of the holder as gradations on a line. Firing was done by an equally simple trigger lever.

For the light grenade launcher, only one basic charge was available, already within the grenade. Only explosive grenades with percussion caps could be used as ammunition. These grenades scattered a great number of small bits of shrapnel in a circle of some 20 to 30 meters, which was sufficient to put enemy troops out of commission.

Technical data:

Caliber	5 cm
Total weight	14.5 kg (barrel 5.6 kg, base 8.9 kg)
Maximum range	550 meters
Minimum range	50 meters
Most effective range	300 meters
Elevation	42 to 85 degrees
Traverse	17 degrees to left and right
Initial velocity (V_o)	75 meters per second
Rate of (effective) fire	6 grenades in 9 to 10 seconds
Ready to fire	2 minutes
Weight of grenade	900 grams
Flight time of grenade	ca. 13 seconds at ca. 200 meters
Crew	2 men

The light grenade launcher was intended to be effective at ranges between those of hand grenades and heavy grenade launchers. It was comparatively easy to transport and use, but was not durable. Since its effect against well-covered and built-in targets was meager, it was used gradually less and less. The rifle grenade later took its place (*see also* section "New Infantry Weapons").

Antitank Rifle 39 (Panzerbüchse)
The 38/39 "Panzerbüchse" antitank rifle was a weapon similar to a rifle, with folding bipod, shoulderpiece and pistol-like grip with trigger, which could be used by one man and carried by hand or over the shoulder. It was a single-shot weapon with which armor-piercing shells were fired.

The first version had been introduced to the troops as Antitank Rifle 38. Within one year, though, it was replaced by a refined version, Antitank Rifle 39, which was similar but 3.18 kilograms lighter. The antitank rifle was not semi-automatic, thus its recoil was stronger and its loading process slower. Instead of a cylinder breech like the 98 k rifle, it had a vertical-block breech. The strong recoil pushed the barrel back when firing and opened the breech. The single shell could be inserted by the shooter now, whereupon the breech locked itself and was ready to fire again. The ammunition was kept in a ten-round shell container on the side, near the grip.

Technical data:

Caliber	7.92 mm (special shell)
Weight	12.7 kg
Overall length (barrel length)	1.27 m (1.09 m)
Sight distances	to 600 meters
Effective range	under 200 meters
Initial velocity (V_o)	1210 meters per second
Rate of fire	10 to 12 rounds per minute
Penetration	30 mm at 60-degree angle at 100 meters, 25 mm at 300 meters
Special ammunition	(*see also* section "Ammunition").

The antitank rifles, intended for use by rifle companies against tanks, had already proved to have too-meager penetration (except against light enemy tanks) when the war began. Since they could not accomplish anything against the Soviet tanks from the beginning of the eastern campaign, they quickly went out of use. Further types were not developed.

Heavy Antitank Rifle 41
On the other hand, the heavy 41 antitank rifle had nothing in common with the other antitank rifles, even in terms of appearance. It was a special development in the manner of a small cannon on a short, simple special mount, with (or without) a small shield, muzzle brake and two cast spoked wheels with rubber tires. The conical barrel, narrowing to-

ward the mouth, was especially striking. Traverse and elevation aiming gear was lacking; aiming was done by using a sight. Antitank shells (full shells with hard cores) were used as ammunition. The heavy antitank rifle could also be disassembled for transport in five loads.

Technical data:

Caliber	2.8 cm, tapering to 2 cm
Weight	227 kilograms
Barrel length	1.71 meters
Arc of traverse	90 degrees at 0-degree elevation, 30 degrees at 45-degree elevation
Initial velocity (V_o)	1043 meters per second
Shell weight	130 grams
Penetration	55 mm at 30 degrees at 400 meters
Crew	2 men

Since the development of other antitank (Pak) weapons went on, the heavy 41 antitank rifle was only a type of stopgap solution for the infantry, and only a small number of them, 183 in all, were made. The numbers of these medium-performance and fully insufficient antitank weapons supplied to the troops in the army added up to the following:

Weapon	9/1/1939	4/1/1940	6/1/1941
Panzerbüchsen 38 & 39	568	1118	25,298
Panzerbüchse 41	–	–	183

CHAPTER 4

The Infantry Battalion

The infantry battalion (Inf.Btl.) was the smallest tactical battle group. The battalion (Btl.) had a complement of one commander, 13 officers, 1 official and 846 non-commissioned officers and enlisted men, plus 131 horses.

The battalion included:
- Battalion staff and understaff
- Intelligence unit
- Infantry engineer platoon
- 3 rifle companies
- 1 machine gun company
- Combat supply troop
- Supply troop I
- Supply troop II
- Pack train

The staff consisted of:
The battalion commander, originally an *Oberstleutnant* or Major, later often a *Hauptmann*, an adjutant, an assistant adjutant, a battalion surgeon, a battalion veterinarian.

The battalion commander was the responsible leader of the entire battalion in all ways and areas. He had the duty of carrying out orders and directives received from his superior officers, and gave the appropriate commands to his battalion.

In combat and action the battalion staff was divided into:

• Command staff of battalion commander, assistant adjutant, two horseholders (all mounted) and two mounted messengers, one of them with a scissor telescope. The command staff was located in the field or at the battalion command post, depending on conditions.

• Battalion command post with adjutant, one combat clerk, 1 artist.

The adjutant was the assistant, advisor and also the representative of the commander. He chose the command-post location, made sure that the other sections of the battalion staff and understaff were located at some distance from it, received incoming reports, evaluated them and passed important information on to all portions of the front lines, established liaison with the units to the right and left, set up the intelligence unit and observation post, saw to the immediate transmission of orders via telephones or messengers, maintained the position chart with appropriate markings, worked out commands and battle plans on the basis of reports received, wrote brief notes to be developed later for combat reports and diaries, informed and conferred with the commander on all important matters. The adjutant also made the daily report to the regiment, normally due as of 7:00 P.M. These reports included enemy movements, activity of the battalion's troops, special occurrences of the day, losses, ammunition needs, requisitions and any other pertinent matters.

The combat clerk wrote out dictated orders and instructions, handled duplication and distribution, registered commands and reports and kept one copy each for combat reports or diaries.

The artist prepared sketch maps, position maps, terrain and landscape drawings, firing plans, etc.

• The assistant adjutant was – when not with the command staff – the adjutant's assistant or representative. He directed the understaff, established liaison with heavy weapons, served as a reporting officer for particularly important reports to nearby units or advance posts and was responsible for the movements of the combat supply troops, including those of the companies. When the command post was relocated, he remained at the old position until the new command post was operational.

• Battalion command post with the chief of the machine-gun company, 2 clerks, the battalion surgeon and veterinarian, artillery liaison officer or command (AVKo), units subordinated or detailed to the commander (such as assault guns, anti-aircraft guns, etc.)

The chief of the machine-gun company (MGK), after his heavy infantry weapons were deployed, directed the command post representing the commander or adjutant. He saw to billeting and work assignments of the individual staff members, gathered and evaluated all reports on losses of soldiers, horses or equipment, vehicle breakdowns, ammunition consumption and supply, made supply reports and requested replacements and was also responsible for the morale of the troops and for enemy propaganda.

A clerk was available to serve as his assistant.

The battalion surgeon was responsible in his area for the health of the troops and their medical care, to the best of his ability, and transfer or transport of sick and wounded men to main dressing stations and field hospitals. He established the battalion's dressing station during action and the collecting stations and sickbays during quiet times. He was assisted by two medical corpsmen and, if needed, up to eight orderlies from the companies as well as stretcher bearers.

The battalion veterinarian was responsible for the health and performance capability of the horses, treated sick animals, carried out inspections of horses in the units and cared for the sick or wounded horses if there were large numbers of them, or in serious cases arranged for transfer to horse collecting stations or veterinary hospitals. In cooperation with the battalion surgeon, he was also responsible for the health of the troops through meat inspection, etc.

A clerk served both of them as assistant and secretary.

The surgeon and veterinarian were mounted and each had a groom on foot.

The artillery liaison officer maintained liaison with his own and other artillery units subordinated or detailed to the battalion, made suggestions for artillery deployment, carried out appropriate wishes of the battalion commander, saw to effective and quick communication with his unit, cooperated in making firing plans, etc. This also applied to the leaders of other subordinated or detailed units.

• Battalion understaff with leader (usually a *Feldwebel*) with bicycle, 1 battalion bugler, messenger unit (6 bicyclists, 2 drivers with motorcycles and sidecars, 2 drivers with motorcycles) and one driver of the command vehicle. The undertsaff leader was responsible for the construction and dismantling of the battalion and other command posts, shielding, covered approach and retreat routes, area security, aerial observation, air raid alarms, identification of friendly aircraft (one set of four large marking cloths was available), and division and organization of messengers and drivers. – The understaff also carried the triangular battalion standards.

Horse Unit:
This included all saddle horses of the staff with horseholders and grooms. Subordinated meant that the unit in question was fully under the command of the battalion commander at a given time. Detailed or in cooperation meant that the unit in question was fully subordinated to the battalion at a given time but received commands from its commander.

Although the battalion command post, battalion support posts and understaff were somewhat separated from each other, they were within hailing distance and formed one unit.

This organization of a battalion staff, as it still existed in the earliest days of the eastern campaign, soon proved to be much too expensive in terms of manpower and horses, and had to be reduced as manpower became shorter and shorter.

Intelligence Unit:
  – Leader (*Feldwebel*)
  – 2 small telephone troops a, each troop consisting of one *Unteroffizier*

and 3 men, for two telephone connections, as well as two small signal lamps for code transmission.

  • 4 portable radio troops d, with 12 men and 4 radios for 2 radio contacts in line communication, 3 contacts in radial communication.
  • One two-horse intelligence equipment wagon with driver, loaded with 8 km of light field cable, 2 km of heavy field cable, 6 field telephones, 1 folding cabinet, radio devices, tools and supplies.

The assignment of the battalion intelligence unit was to set up contact with the companies, the detailed heavy weapons and the next battalion on the right. Further connections within the battalion were handled by bicycle and motorcycle messengers (to the combat supply troop by bicycle messenger, to the general and combat supply troops by motorcycle messenger). Signal lights, flags and staffs were dispensed with soon after the war began as being too troublesome and often misunderstood.

Infantry Engineer Platoon: (Pionier)
This unit was assembled only when needed to carry out technical assignments of a simple kind. The rifle companies provided soldiers specially trained in infantry engineering service. This platoon was frequently used later in the war as a last reserve by the battalion commander.

  3 Rifle Companies (as described).
  1 machine-gun company (described below).
  Combat supply troop with:
   1 *Unteroffizier* as leader
   1 Foddermaster, mounted
   1 Armorer with bicycle
   1 Armorer's assistant
   1 Blacksmith (formerly "Fahnenschmied")
   1 Blacksmith's assistant
   1 Anti-gas Unteroffizier
   1 Medical *Unteroffizier* with motorcycle
   2 Field cooks
   2 Assistants
   (non-mounted or riding soldiers carried on wagons).
   1 Armorer's wagon
   1 Wagon with field smith and equipment
   1 Entrenching tool wagon
   1 Medical supply wagon
   1 Small field kitchen
   1 Fodder wagon
   (all wagons with two horses and one driver).

Supply Train I with:
  1 *Hauptfeldwebel* with 1 battalion clerk and writing room
  1 *Feldwebel* as battalion quartermaster sergeant with bicycle
  2 Two-horse wagons.
Supply Train II with:
  1 Paymaster
  1 Supply *Unteroffizier*
  1 Driver with motorcycle
  2 3-ton trucks with driver and assistant.
Pack train with:
  1 *Unteroffizier* as driver with motorcycle
  1 3-ton truck with driver and craftsman.

To outline a few assignments and activities briefly:

The foddermaster was responsible for orderly reception and division of delivered fodder, which he and the drivers tried to add to from the countryside. He was also responsible for the animals' health and for keeping contact with the battalion veterinarian.

Armorers and their helpers sought, when possible, to repair broken-down and damaged light and heavy infantry weapons, which were always urgently needed, tested their new weapons, examined captured weapons do determine their usefulness, and were responsible for the proper shipping and storing of reserve weapons and ammunition.

The blacksmith and his assistants worked together with the battalion veterinarian for proper shoeing in summer and winter, and also helped the veterinarian in treating sick horses.

The anti-gas *Unteroffizier* was responsible for the care and maintenance of gas-protection equipment such as reserve gas masks, gas-protection covers, sensors, signs of recognition, etc., an assignment that, as it turned out during the war that there was never a single use of gas, proved to be fully superfluous.

The two medical corpsmen assisted the battalion surgeon in his work and, at his direction, assigned the orderlies and stretcher bearers to their work.

To conclude this chapter, an often-twisted stereotype should be set straight, namely that of the "Zahlmops" who "enjoyed an easy life back in the office." This refers to the battalion paymaster (and along with him, any other paymasters). Holding an officer's rank, he was, along with his assignment as leader of the motorized supply train, also the man responsible for the sufficient and punctual supplying of the whole battalion, and was often underway to the divisional supply depots day and night, in all kinds of weather and through partisan-infested regions, to obtain the needed goods. In addition, he also had to handle all financial affairs, maintain direct contact with the division leadership, handle special items and additional supplies from the country, and do his best in every way to maintain the troop's fighting strength.

All of them, the countless unnamed and unknown foddermasters, supply officers, armorers, shoemakers, tailors, cooks and drivers, or whatever function and activity they may have had and practiced in the supply trains, and who never received praise or medals, about whom scarcely a word of recognition was spoken – all of them did their duty quietly and dependably for years in the war in order to make possible through their support the achievements of their comrades on the front lines.

Armorers and their helpers sought, when possible, to repair broken-down and damaged light and heavy infantry weapons, which were always urgently needed, tested their new weapons, examined captured weapons do determine their usefulness, and were responsible for the proper shipping and storing of reserve weapons and ammunition.

The blacksmith and his assistants worked together with the battalion veterinarian for proper horseshoing in summer and winter, and also helped the veterinarian in treating sick horses.

The anti-gas *Unteroffizier* was responsible for the care and maintenance of gas-protection equipment such as reserve gas masks, gas-protection covers, sensors, signs of recognition, etc., an assignment that, as it turned out during the war that there was never a single use of gas, proved to be fully superfluous.

The two medical corpsmen assisted the battalion surgeon in his work and, at his direction, assigned the orderlies and stretcher bearers to their work.

To conclude this section, an often-twisted stereotype should be set straight, namely that of the "Zahlmops" who "enjoyed an easy life back in the office." This refers to the battalion paymaster (and along with him, any other paymasters). Holding an officer's rank, he was, along with his assignment as leader of the motorized supply train, also the man responsible for the sufficient and punctual supplying of the whole battalion, and was often underway to the divisional supply depots day and night, in all kinds of weather and through partisan-infested regions, to obtain the needed goods. In addition, he also had to handle all financial affairs, maintain direct contact with the division leadership, handle special items and additional supplies from the country, and do his best in every way to maintain the troop's fighting strength.

All of them, the countless unnamed and unknown foddermasters, supply officers, armorers, shoemakers, tailors, cooks and drivers, or whatever function and activity they may have had and practiced in the supply trains, and who never received praise or medals, about whom scarcely a word of recognition was spoken – all of them did their duty quietly and dependably for years in the war in order to make possible through their support the achievements of their comrades on the front lines.

The Machine Gun Company (MGK)

The name deceived – for the machine gun company was not a company equipped only with machine guns, but a unit with mixed weapons, in which the heavy machine guns (sMG) and heavy grenade launchers (sGr.W.) of a company were gathered as flat and high-angle weapons (*see also* section "Heavy Infantry Weapons"); the later designation of "heavy company" was more apt. The machine gun company came after the three rifle companies, always being the 4th company of a battalion, and thus the 4th, 8th and 12th companies of the three battalions of an infantry regiment. They were always at the battalion commander's disposal with their heavy infantry weapons.

A machine gun company with a normal complement of three officers and 174 non-commissioned officers and men, with 58 horses, was divided into:

- Company chief (a *Hauptmann*), mounted
- Company troop, consisting of:

One company troop leader, 1 observation non-commissioned officer, two direction non-commissioned officers, one range taker, two bicycle messengers, one mounted messenger (also bugler), one horseholder (mounted). Intelligence unit with 6 telephone men and one two-horse equipment wagon with driver, loaded with 6 field telephones, light field cable and signal lights for establishing three telephone connections and one signal connection (later another telephone connection) for the purpose of fire control within the company.

• 3 heavy machine gun platoons, led by a Leutnant, each with two squads. Strength per heavy machine gun squad 1/10 and 2 heavy machine guns, total of 12 heavy machine guns. Plus a two-horse field wagon with driver for machine gun mantelets, equipment, ammunition and baggage. The heavy machine gun group consisted of a leader and two crews, each with one "gun leader", gunners 1 through 4.

• One heavy grenade launcher squad, led by a *Leutnant*, with platoon headquarters (1 non-commissioned officer, 3 messengers) and 3 heavy grenade launcher squads, 6 heavy grenade launchers in all. Each heavy grenade launcher squad consisted of a squad leader, a rangetaker and 6 grenade launcher gunners. Each heavy grenade launcher squad also had one wagon driver with a one-horse small-arms ammunition cart and trailer, in which the dismantled launchers, ammunition and telephones were loaded when on the march. The squad also included a two-horse wagon, which carried additional ammunition and the crew's baggage. In all, there were 48 grenades per launcher on the cart and wagon, of which

15 were taken into action as the first supply.
• Supply trains (similar to those of the rifle companies, plus fodder-master and blacksmith).

The heavy machine guns used by the machine gun companies were – as noted – the flat-fire weapons of the battalion and simultaneously represented the heaviest infantry firepower. They were used in all kinds of combat and formed the "backbone" of the fighting at medium and long ranges. Their assignment was to fire on all targets (other than tanks) that were most dangerous to the infantry. The heavy machine guns supported the attacks of the rifle companies by firing on and holding back the enemy, and provided the main defensive firepower in fighting off enemy attacks. Their effects varied and depended on the target. After ranging with short bursts of fire, they generally used only sustained fire, either as pinpoint fire against small and well-established individual targets such as machine-gun nests, or against bunker crews and the like, or as broad fire, swinging the gun back and forth, against open surface targets such as advancing or retreating enemy infantry, troop concentrations, etc. As a rule, the heavy machine guns were deployed in platoons or squads (combat units) in companies, and often subordinated to them for long periods, as directed by the battalion commander. It was even possible for single heavy machine guns, on account of their great firepower, to dominate and block important points and sectors of terrain, such as overflight paths, narrows, passes and such.

After receiving orders, a heavy machine gun platoon was ready to fire in about twenty minutes.

Before the beginning of a battle, the "gun leader" took the machine gun's sight and a case of ammunition from the cart, the Gunner 1 took the machine gun, Gunner 2 the folded mantelet, Gunners 3 and 4 carried two ammunition cases each, making a first supply of 1500 rounds.

In the first years of the war, every heavy machine gun platoon still had a two- or four-horse rubber-tired limber with a trailer. On the trailer was a twin mantelet on which two machine guns with annular sights were kept for use against aircraft while on the march. These anti-aircraft limbers fell into disuse shortly after the eastern campaign began, as they proved to be too ponderous and not effective enough.

The heavy grenade launchers were the battalion's high-angle weapons. Unlike the heavy machine guns, they could be used less against open and moving targets than for getting behind almost any enemy cover, while firing from under cover themselves. The heavy launchers' assignment was to act quickly, in both attack and defense, against built-in enemy targets that could not be engaged at all, or not quickly enough, with observed fire from flat-fire weapons, infantry rifles or artillery, if available, or not productively enough. In defensive action the heavy grenade launchers, like the other heavy infantry weapons, were fired at chosen barrage-fire areas. A heavy grenade launcher squad (combat unit) was generally subordinated to a rifle company, as were the heavy machine guns, and received its combat assignments from the company commander.

The heavy grenade launchers consisted of three parts: barrel, bipod and baseplate, and could be dismantled. Before combat, these three parts, each weighing over 18 kilograms, had to be picked up by a gunner and carried, while the two ammunition men each had two cases of three grenades each to carry, with a total weight of 22 kg. The leader carried not only the gunsight, but also a case of ammunition. With these burdens, it was not surprising that the grenade launcher squads and troops often hung well back in combat. Often rifle troops also had to be deployed to help carry the ammunition.

With their firepower, the machine gun companies formed the strongest support for the rifle companies. During the course of the war, heavy machine guns and grenade launchers provided full support wherever they were applied, and were irreplaceable to the end of the war.

CHAPTER 5

The Infantry Regiment

The Infantry Regiment[1] included:
- Regimental staff with staff headquarters
- Regimental supply train
- Regimental units, including
    Engineer platoon
    Mounted platoon
    Intelligence platoon
    Musicians
- 3 infantry battalions (1st to 12th companies)
  (*see also* section "The Infantry Battalion")
- 1 infantry artillery company (13th company)
- 1 Panzerjäger company (14th company)
- 1 light infantry column.

The regiment included 75 officers, 7 administrators, 493 non-commissioned officers and 2474 enlisted men.

Their armament consisted of 288 pistols, 180 machine pistols, 115 light machine guns, 36 heavy machine guns, 27 antitank rifles, 27 light grenade launchers, 18 heavy grenade launchers, 6 light infantry guns, 2 heavy IG and 12 antitank guns.

The vehicles available were 73 motor vehicles, 47 motorcycles and 210 horse-drawn wagons, plus some 600 horses including saddle horses.

Regimental Staff and Units
The regimental staff, with a commander, adjutant, assistant adjutant, intelligence officer and staff captain, was similarly structured to, and had similar assignments to, though on a higher level than, a battalion staff.

[1]According to an OKH ruling of October 15, 1942, all infantry regiments were renamed grenadier regiments, effective immediately.

Yet the regimental staff, including its understaff, was numerically larger, having more non-commissioned officers and enlisted men such as clerks, orderlies, messengers, drivers, etc.

Regimental Supply Train
The supply trains of the regiment consisted of:
  – Combat supply troop with one medical officer (staff surgeon) on a motorcycle, 2 veterinarians (one a staff veterinarian, mounted), one regimental armorer, one blacksmith, armory personnel with one two-horse armory wagon, kitchen personnel with one large four-horse field kitchen.
  – V I supply train with one commissary officer on a motorcycle, one two-horse wagon.
  – V II supply train with one senior paymaster (with the regimental cashbox) on a motorcycle, two trucks, square standard.
  – Pack train with one officer on a motorcycle, two trucks.
  (Naturally, all vehicles had drivers.)

Regimental Engineer Platoon (Pionier)
The engineer platoon was formed of:
  – 1 platoon leader (usually a *Leutnant*), mounted
  – Headquarters troop with troop leader, 3 messengers, one horse-holder, 1 medical NCO on a bicycle
  – 6 squads with a complement of 1/9 (the 1st, 3rd and 6th squads with one light machine gun)
  – 3 two-horse equipment wagons with entrenching tools, one two-horse wagon with weapons.

This platoon consisted of so-called infantry engineers, who also wore the white service-arm color of the infantry (as opposed to the engineers of the engineer battalions with the black service-arm color). The infantry engineers were only capable of smaller technical assignments such as limited mine removal, roadbuilding, trench and position work, etc. When needed, they were also deployed to assist the "black" engineers.

Regimental Mounted Platoon
The mounted platoon was composed of:
  – 1 leader (generally an *Oberfeldwebel* or *Feldwebel*)
  – Headquarters troop with one NCO and three men
  – 3 squads, each of 1 NCO and 7 men, each squad divisible into 2 "Abmärsche" of four men each.
  – 1 two-horse combat vehicle with one driver and one blacksmith, one small field kitchen with one driver and two field cooks, one pay clerk on a bicycle.
  Its fighting strength numbered 29 mounted men, with one horse in reserve.

Its armaments consisted of pistols for the leader and group leaders, as well as rifles and side arms for all mounted men. The mounted platoon did not have a light machine gun. As of about the middle of 1943, the 98 k rifle was replaced by the 44 assault rifle. The leader and group leaders were issued machine pistols. This greatly increased the mounted platoon's firepower.

Equipment and baggage (*see also* section "The Intelligence Unit – Mounted Squadron"). Appropriate to their assignments, the mounted platoons of the regiments were applied particularly in short-range reconnaissance, securing and messenger service. Their great test came in the eastern campaign, where daily rides of 70 to 80 kilometers during the advance were by no means rare. Ahead of the advancing infantry, the scout troops of the mounted platoons, like a thin veil, reconnoitered, quickly brought back important observations and reports, protected resting troops and columns and, going against their basic duties, had to take on light combat assignments in the very first year of the campaign, in which they were usually strengthened by rifle squads with light machine guns.

Some mounted platoons were replaced during the war by motorcycle platoons.

Regimental Intelligence Platoon
The intelligence platoon included:
 – 1 platoon leader (usually a *Leutnant*), simultaneously intelligence officer of the regiment and leader of the understaff, mounted
 – Headquarters troop with one radiomaster, mounted, and two signalmen
 – 1 small telephone troop a, 2 medium telephone troops b
 – 4 two-way radio troops d
 – 2 four-horse telephone wagons, one small two-horse radio wagon, all three vehicles with equipment and tools.
 The platoon had the following intelligence equipment:
 – 10 field telephones (troop telephone 33), weighing 5.9 kg, with induction current
 – 2 folding switchboards for small transmissions of 10 and 20 cables
 – 8 kilometers of light one-wire field cable, on large cable drums, with lengths of 500 meters each, for connections near the front
 – 14 kilometers of heavy one-wire field cable, on large cable drums, with lengths from 750 to 1000 meters (generally used material)
 – Portable radio set d (Dora), 3-watt transmitter portable by two men, with a frequency range of 33.8 to 38 MHz, set up for telegraph and telephone use, weighing 11 kilograms per case. Range for (Morse) telegraphy ca. 15 kilometers, for telephone about one quarter thereof. The power source was rechargeable nickel-cadmium batteries.

In addition to the intelligence troops, which also included the intelligence units of the divisions (*see also* section "The Intelligence Unit"), smaller intelligence units were designated as troop intelligence units. These included the regimental intelligence platoons as well as battalion intelligence echelons, the intelligence squadrons of the machine gun companies and infantry gun companies, as well as the intelligence echelons of the artillery.

The regimental intelligence platoon had the job of establishing and maintaining communication with the battalions, the next regiment on the right, and the units directly subordinated to the regiment, and if necessary also assisting the artillery intelligence platoons in establishing communication with the regiment.

Even though personnel doing their work well were able to attain excellent and uninterrupted telephone connections over great distances, nevertheless telephone connections, whether set up for line or radial use, had their share of weaknesses. Establishing connections, meaning setting up cables on foot, took up a lot of time. Under good terrain conditions, it took up to twenty minutes to lay one kilometer of light, and up to thirty minutes for one kilometer of heavy, field cable. The cables were sometimes strung in the air, but usually laid on the surface. In moving warfare it was particularly difficult to set up telephone lines. Then too, any external influence on the cables, especially enemy fire, but also heavy vehicles and the like, could interrupt communication. Then trouble-shooters had to go about replacing the damaged connections, and it was often dangerous and time-consuming to find and eliminate the problem, particularly at night, in mud or deep snow, or under enemy fire. In the foremost battle lines, only double cables were used. In these it was only possible to listen with intermediate switching or when a piece of wire was bare.

The portable (short-wave) radio set, on the other hand, was quickly ready for use, with readiness to send and receive attained in some 5 to 8 minutes. It had the advantage of also being usable while underway.

A portable radio troop consisted of the troop leader, the antenna material, spare batteries and tubes, headsets, writing instruments, etc., in an equipment container. One radioman carried the receiver when in motion, a second carried the transmitter in a box. But the radio equipment also had great disadvantages. They had a rather heavy weight and were one-way devices, as they could only be used in one direction at a time on the same channel, whether vocally or by Morse code. Their ranges, and thus their potential for being understood in the field, were much more strongly affected by atmospheric conditions. With the radio equipment available, the distances involved in actual use could be bridged only by telegraphy. The practical range for vocal communication was too short in any case.

Because of the danger of telephone or even telegraph communication being overheard, changing lists of code names for units and camouflaged terms for certain situations, such as enemy attacks, had to be employed.

Regimental Music

The regimental musicians wore the same field-gray uniforms as all other soldiers, but on their shoulders they wore the so-called "swallow's-nest" epaulets with white background and silver braid trim. They also had different titles of rank:

> Musiker = Soldat to Obergefreiter, with appropriate insignia
> Musikleiter = Oberfeldwebel
> Musikmeister = Leutnant
> Obermusikmeister = Oberleutnant
> Stabsmusikmeister = Hauptmann.

Men at or above the rank of Musikmeister wore the usual officers' uniforms. Their shoulder pieces bore four red longitudinal stripes and a golden lyre, plus the stars that represented their ranks. Unlike many other European armies, the German Army divided its musicians and instruments very precisely. Thus an infantry regiment included one *Musikmeister* and 37 *Musiker*, as follows:

Two musicians with two large and two small flutes in C, 2 musicians with oboes (for marching music an oboist played the glockenspiel, one bassoonist played the cymbals), 2 musicians with bassoons, 1 musician with a clarinet in E flat, 8 musicians with clarinets in B, 4 musicians with French horns in F, 2 musicians with soprano cornets in B, 2 musicians with tenor horns in B, 1 musician with a baritone tuba in B, 2 musicians with base tubas in E flat, 2 musicians with bass tubas or helicons in B, 2 musicians with trumpets in E flat, 2 musicians with trumpets in B, 3 musicians with tenor trombones in B, 1 musician with a small drum and 1 musician with a large (bass) drum.

It is worth noting that, in addition to the regimental music corps, every engineer battalion, as an exception, had its own military band with a *Musikmeister* and 27 *Musiker*.

A special feature of German military music was that each regiment had twelve Spielleute (6 drummers and 6 fifers), who were provided by the troop (1 *Spielmann* per company).

In the war, the musicians, whose instruments were transported by the regiment's motorized supply train, were used as temporary medical orderlies to rescue and treat wounded men, and were sent to dressing stations as needed. In quiet times they did their own work as regimental musicians for solemn occasions (burial of fallen soldiers, field religious services, etc.), or entertained at soldiers' homes or hospitals, gave concerts in occupied areas for soldiers and inhabitants, etc. One can, for example, read in the history of the 61st Infantry Division (summer 1942): Above all, though, the music corps, after being in the thick of the action for months, could finally return to their own assignment.

As of the end of May 1944, the OKH ordered regimental bands abolished; from then on there was only a small music corps with each division.

The Infantry Gun Company

Among the "heavy weapons" of the infantry were not only the heavy machine guns and grenade launchers of the battalions, but also the light and heavy infantry guns (lIG and sIG). They belonged to a separate company, the 13th company of each infantry regiment. With these guns, the regimental commander had his own "artillery."

The infantry gun company numbered some 180 officers, non-commissioned officers and enlisted men, and was fully equipped with 133 horses. The individual leaders were mounted, the crews rode on the limbers of the guns and the ammunition vehicles.

The company consisted of:

– Company chief (usually a *Hauptmann*), mounted

– Company headquarters troop with one intelligence NCO, 3 telephonists, 3 messengers, 2 surveyors, 2 calculators, 1 rangetaker, 1 horseholder (mounted) and 1 four-horse B-wagon with two drivers from the saddle

– 3 heavy infantry gun platoons, each with: Platoon leader and headquarters troop with deputy platoon leader, simultaneously position NCO, 2 directing NCO (I and II), 1 rangetaker, 1 messenger, 1 groom, all mounted. Not mounted were 3 telephonists and 1 messenger, who were equipped to set up fire control connections with telephones and signal flags.

– 2 75mm light infantry guns, each with four-horse hitch, limber and 2 drivers from the saddle, 1 mounted leader and a 5-man crew (gunner, loader, 3 ammunition carriers) plus 1 ammunition echelon with two four-horse ammunition trailers behind limbers with two drivers each from the saddle and 2 ammunition helpers. The 3 telephonists, the messenger and the gun crews rode on the limbers while on the march.

– 1 heavy infantry gun platoon with: Platoon leader and headquarters troop, same as the lIG platoon, two 150mm heavy infantry guns, each gun with six-horse limber with 3 drivers from the saddle, 1 mounted gun leader, and a 6-man crew (gunners, loaders 1 and 2, and 3 ammunition carriers) riding on the limbers. In addition, this platoon had two ammunition trailers with limbers plus its own ammunition echelon with 2 four-horse ammunition wagons.

– Combat supply train with 1 large field kitchen, 1 field smithy wagon, 1 blacksmith, 1 foddermaster and other personnel.

– Supply train I as in other units
– Pack train as in other units.

The infantry guns had the particular assignment of providing pinpoint fire on small open targets, hard to see and recognize, or targets in or behind cover, such as machine-gun nests, gun positions, etc., which were either too far away for heavy grenade launchers to reach, could not be hit by flat fire from heavy machine guns, or did not seem worthwhile to the artillery. They were also used with great success against hostile strong points such as bunkers, strongly fortified and extended support points, etc., against which other weapons could not offer sufficient performance.

In general, the lIG platoons of the infantry battalions were subordinated by platoons (the platoon with two guns formed the battle group), but single guns were also utilized. They received their combat assignments from the battalion commanders. To form focal points, regimental commanders could combine several lIG platoons and the two sIG under the leadership of an infantry gun chief.

The listed complements of soldiers, horses, guns and vehicles could not be maintained during the course of the war, and several changes were made. As of about 1942 the lIG platoons were integrated into the infantry battalions and replaced by sIG in the infantry gun companies. In newly formed infantry divisions, the lIG, which were often lacking, were replaced by twice the number of 81mm grenade launchers. Even though the grenade launchers were not precision weapons like the infantry guns, the effect of their shells was much the same, but the launchers were considerably less demanding in terms of personnel and transportation. As of 1943 the sIG were replaced in many regiments by twice the number of 120mm grenade launchers. In many infantry regiments the entire infantry gun company existed, as of 1942, as a grenade launcher company with 81mm launchers. The crews marched on foot, the dismantled launchers were either loaded into carts or towed, which meant a considerable saving in soldiers, horses and vehicles here too.

The Panzerjäger Company
The Panzerjäger company of the infantry regiment was fully motorized and consisted of four platoons, each with three antitank guns and a total of 12 light machine guns (structure etc., *see also* section "The Panzerjäger Unit").

The Light Infantry Column
The light infantry column carried the ammunition belonging to the primary supply. It consisted of the column leader (mounted), two motorcycle messengers and three platoons, each with a platoon leader and eight two-horse wagons with drivers and attendants. The column (like

others) was directed by the quartermaster section of the division staff.

Heavy Infantry Weapons
The heavy infantry weapons included:
- Heavy Machine Gun (sMG) 34
- Heavy Grenade Launcher (sGr.W.) 34
- Light Infantry Gun (lIG) 18
- Heavy Infantry Gun (sIG) 33
- Antitank Guns (Pak).

Heavy Machine Gun 34
The German Infantry of World War II was the first and only military power of the time to have one uniform machine gun, the MG 34, which could be used as either a light or a heavy machine gun (*see also* section "Light Infantry Weapons").

To be able to be used effectively as a heavy machine gun, the light MG had to be set on a mantelet, such as were used for heavy machine guns, without a bipod. With this mantelet, on which the machine gun was mounted firmly but on springs and able to traverse, the lasting recoil of a lengthy sustained fire could be absorbed and the shot ranges could be extended considerably. In addition, sustained fire could also be used at great distances, whereas the light machine gun could only fire short bursts.

The mantelet consisted of a three-legged standard with an adjustable forward and two hind legs, to the front leg of which two carrying pads were attached, as well as a mounting surface and a triggering apparatus for the machine gun. Folded up and with the legs telescoped in, the mantelet was carried on the back of Gunner 2. The heavy machine gun also had a gunsight apparatus for targeting. The heavy machine gun could fire with direct or indirect aiming. Direct aiming meant that the machine gun was fired from an open firing position and was aimed directly at the target via backsight and foresight or with the telescopic sight of the heavy machine gun's gunsight apparatus. In indirect aiming, firing was done from cover, and the target was aimed at using the directing telescope of the heavy machine gun gunsight apparatus. In indirect aiming, the shot ranges could be increased and, what with the naturally high, climbing trajectories, one's own troops could be fired over, as during an attack, and the enemy could thus be held back. The trajectories at a range of 1200 meters reached a zenith of 8.5 meters, at 2000 meters a zenith of 42 meters. To be sure, relatively little indirect aiming was done in the western campaign of 1940, and after that it was hardly used at all. It was also possible to create gaps in the enemy line, but the machine-gun fire could not generally fall less than 200 to 300 meters ahead of one's own troops.

Another noteworthy feature was the so-called "searching fire automat", which independently raised and lowered the shot trajectories toward the target in waves (alternatingly at higher and lower targets) and thus contributed to increasing the dispersion. Ammunition feed took place from the customary machine-gun boxes of 300 rounds, for which the individual 50-cartridge metal belts used by the light machine gun were fastened together.

Technical data:

Caliber	7.92 mm
Weight of gun, mantelet, sight	12.1; 18.1; 3 kg = total 33.2 kg
Maximum range in direct firing	3000 meters
Maximum range in indirect firing	3500 meters
Optimal ranges	1200 to 2000 meters
Initial velocity (V_o)	920 meters per second
Rate of fire	900 to 1000 rounds per min.
Crew	3 men

Heavy Grenade Launcher 34

The heavy (later medium) grenade launcher consisted of three individual parts: barrel with breech piece, baseplate and bipod with attachment and slider with spindle screw, which could be assembled to form a complete launcher within a very short time. Thus the launcher could be ready to fire in three minutes. Firing was done very simply, by a bolt in the inner end of the barrel, into which the loader let the primed grenade slide from above. The heavy grenade launcher was thus a muzzle-loader like the light launcher. Before being fired effectively, the launcher had to be settled in the ground by firing one or two grenades, so that the baseplate became stable. This "firing fast" was followed by homing in by means of "bracketing", with the first shot too far, the second too short, and the third on target. The primary charge (1st loading) was fired, followed depending on the range by up to four partial charges (2nd to 5th loadings), which were always attached to the end of the grenades, which had stabilizing fins. The charges were calculated by means of shot tables, and aiming was done with the RA 35 aiming apparatus. Thanks to the simple firing mechanism, firing in and bracketing could be followed by a high rate of fire, depending on the crew. When one considers that a grenade was in the air some 26 seconds, it can be seen that, in effective firing, a well-trained crew could have some 6 or 7 grenades in the air at the same time and falling on the target within about half a minute, with every grenade detonating and spreading a great many small and smaller splinters in a circle of 30-meter diameter. The launcher crew heard only the reports of firing; there was no howling noise to give a warning to take cover. Seconds after firing, a hail of grenades fell, without any indication of their direction and thus of the launcher's position. The launcher fired both explosive and smoke grenades.

Technical data:

Caliber	81mm
Weight of barrel, base, bipod	18.5; 18.3; 18.9 kg = 55.7 kg
Total weight ready to fire	56,7 kilograms
Barrel length	1.14 meters
Elevation arc	40 to 85 degrees
Traverse arc	9 to 15 degrees (depending on elevation)
Shot ranges	60 to 2200 meters
Optimal ranges	400 to 1500 meters
Initial velocity (V_o)	75 m/sec (1st charge) to 174 m/sec (5th charge)
Rate of fire	to 14 rounds per minute
Readiness to fire	within 5 minutes
Grenade weight	3.5 kilograms
Crew	3 men

Light Infantry Gun 18

The light and heavy infantry guns were both special guns. They combined the characteristics of cannon, howitzer and mortar and could fire either flat or high-angle fire, enabling their use at lower and upper angles.

Both types of fire were very precise and exactly on target, and had only meager dispersion in length and breadth.

Grenades with impact fuses, made for special purposes such as heavy cover and timed for delayed ignition, were fired. It was possible to overshoot one's own troops by about 200 meters with them. Since the firing positions were generally concealed, indirect firing was used. The ammunition used consisted, like artillery shells, of separately loaded grenades with case cartridges.

Because of their arched trajectory and low impact speed, these projectiles were not suitable for use against tanks.

The light infantry gun had been introduced into the infantry as early as 1927. It was light and handy, had a strikingly low structure with a simple box mantelet and a very short barrel, bedded in boxlike form and barely projecting beyond the shield, which was very far to the front. The hydropneumatic recoil and counterrecoil system was located in the cradle under the barrel. The shield consisted of five individual parts and could be folded down. Wooden wheels with iron rims and wooden spokes were typical, rubber-tired wheels less so. Aiming was done with the Z.E. 34 panoramic telescope. Thanks to its strikingly low construction and little smoke when firing, the gun was very hard for the enemy to locate.

Technical data:

Caliber	75mm
Barrel length	0.8 meters
Weight ready to fire	400 kilograms
Weight ready to march	560 kilograms
Elevation arc	0 to 75 degrees
Traverse arc	11 degrees to left and right
Initial velocity (V_o)	92 to 210 meters per second (depending on charge)
Shot ranges	800 meters (1st charge) to 3475 meters (5th charge)
Effective ranges	1000 to 2500 meters
Rate of fire	6 to 10 rounds per minute
Readiness to fire	30 minutes along with platoon
Crew	6 men

Heavy Infantry Gun 33

This gun, developed since 1926 and introduced to the troops in 1933, was the infantry's heaviest weapon. Built in conventional form, it had a particularly strong box-frame mantelet with recoil and counterrecoil system in the cradle under the heavy barrel. The shield mounts were far back, like those of the might IG, so as to allow as high a barrel elevation as possible. Similarly, two spring equalizers were attached to the sides of the mantelet to equalize the muzzle's heaviness. The divided shield to the left and right of the barrel was typical. The wide cast-steel wheels had full rubber tires.

Technical data:

Caliber	150mm
Barrel length	1.7 meters
Weight ready to fire	1750 kilograms
Weight ready to march	2872 kilograms
Elevation arc	0 to 75 degrees
Traverse arc	11 degrees to left and right
Initial velocity (V_o)	122 to 240 meters per second, depending on charge
Shot ranges	1475 meters (1st charge) to 4650 meters (6th charge)
Effective ranges	1500 to 3000 meters
Readiness to fire	45 minutes along with platoon
Crew	7 men

The heavy infantry gun was a very effective, reliable and durable weapon, but generally too heavy and unhandy for the infantry. There was no further development, though there were efforts made to lighten the gun, which succeeded only to a degree (from 1750 to 1550 kilograms).

Antitank Guns (see also section "The Panzerjäger Unit")
All heavy infantry weapons (with the exception of the 37mm antitank gun), like the light infantry weapons, had proved themselves and remained in use unchanged throughout the entire war.

Close Antitank Combat
Even during peacetime training, the procedure of the infantry during enemy tank attacks had been completely ignored. Dealing with enemy tanks was supposed to be left to the antitank companies of the regiments, or the antitank units of the divisions (later called Panzerjäger), whose guns and motorized vehicles were thought to be sufficient. In order to be armed against suddenly appearing individual enemy tanks, every rifleman was supplied at the beginning of the war in 1939 with ten SmKH (pointed bullet with hard core) cartridges in addition to his usual rifle ammunition. The SmKH ammunition, which later ceased to be produced, had a velocity of 930 meters per second and a penetrating power of 13 mm at a range of 100 meters. It was to be fired mainly at the viewing slits and optics of light and medium tanks. This special ammunition was retained until about the middle of 1941, and each platoon was also supplied between 1940 and 1941 with one "Panzerbüchse" for antitank use (*see also* section "The Rifle Company").

That worked well in the first years of the war. In the Polish campaign of 1939 the few, usually light Polish tanks, generally appearing alone or in small groups, quickly fell victim to antitank guns, tanks or artillery. In the Norwegian campaign of 1940 there were no enemy tanks at all, and the situation in Holland and Belgium in 1940, as well as in the Yugoslavian and Greek campaigns in 1941 was much like that in Poland. And even in the French campaign, where for the first time the enemy had superior numbers of tanks, including heavy and heaviest types, the tank was not seen as a particular enemy of the infantry. Again it was single tanks, 8.8 anti-aircraft guns, artillery and dive bombers that decimated the French tank battalions, which were usually used to accompany their infantry and thus tactically and operatively wrongly deployed. Yet the handwriting was on the wall – in May of 1940 French and British tank units attacked the Abbèville bridgehead, held by the 57th Infantry Division, for several days. The 37mm antitank guns positioned there proved to be completely powerless against the heavily armored tanks. Although the crews stuck to their guns bravely, 12 guns were shot down or rolled over. The troop units, frightened by the tanks, fled backward and could only be brought forward again with difficulty. One of the few serious crises in this campaign resulted. Only because the French infantry did not follow up the success of their tanks was the enemy not able to crush the bridgehead in the end. The losses of the 57th Infantry Division were very high. Here in these battles, numerous tanks were defeated with close-combat weapons for the first time.

When the campaign against Russia then began, the weakness of German antitank weapons became only too clear. Every rifleman still had his ten SmKH cartridges, and the platoon had an absolutely insufficient Panzerbüchse as its only antitank weapon. In the very first days of the campaign it could be seen that both were completely ineffective against the many light, medium, heavy and heaviest Soviet tanks, and in a short time the ammunition and Panzerbüchse were dispensed with. The 37mm antitank gun also proved to be without any effect against the giant Soviet tanks, especially the new T 34 which later became so famous. Their shells bounced off the heavy armor plate and ascended into the skies as glaring white fireballs. This inferiority was not yet so noticeable during the months of the 1941 advance against the Soviet tank units, which were still badly led and organized then, and that suffered heavy losses in the great pocket battles in the late summer and autumn. But like the whole Red Army, the Soviet tank units were strengthened remarkably quickly and entered the Russian winter offensive of 1941-42 at great strength. From now on there was scarcely one enemy attack that was not accompanied by numerous tanks, and in the times that followed, entire Soviet tank brigades and tank corps, well led and applied, worked either independently or together with the infantry – and more and more numerous and modern tanks rolled out of Soviet factories and depots to the front.

Their increasing numbers and fighting strength were felt more and more strongly, especially by the infantry, which was forced more and more into defensive action, since their own antitank forces (Panzerjäger) were still too weak, despite the 50mm antitank gun that had meanwhile reached the front. German 88mm anti-aircraft guns, artillery, tanks and dive bombers were not available everywhere on the vast front, and often not even in place. The infantry had to help itself – a time of close antitank combat began, and it was to last until 1944, when new defense weapons for the infantry (the Panzerfaust and Panzerschreck) reached the troops.

Close antitank combat was originally born of necessity – where enemy tanks broke into their positions, valiant and desperate men attacked the monsters and tried to stop them with any available means in unequal single combat – man against tank. And though they suffered losses, they had some success – there one tank was left motionless, there another was burning out, or the crew was forced to abandon it and fought down with hand weapons.

This success on the one hand, and the powerlessness on the other to make appropriate defensive weapons available in sufficient quantities at first, forced the high command, up to the OKH, to declare close antitank combat a new form of battle and institute the necessary training and instructions. The official directive now said: Every man must be capable of attacking and defeating an enemy tank by all means – and this applied to the infantryman at the front as well as the baker in the rear. They were told: Be ready to take on tanks and defend yourself against them at any moment!

The training that had generally been ignored previously now had to be made up hastily, since the infantry was engaged more and more in defensive action – with most of the soldiers trained where they were, and chosen personnel given quick courses and brief training close behind the front.

A distinction was made between passive and active close antitank combat. The *passive* aspect included:

Early tank warning (alarm) by purple smoke cartridges (as before).

The building on deep, narrow one- and two-man tank traps or ditches and positions.

Conquering fear of tanks – not to jump up and run away, but to roll out of the path of advancing tanks or let them roll over you in the ditches (and to practice this with your own ditches and tanks.

Tactically correct behavior – intense attacking, restraining and dividing the enemy infantry from their tank escorts, and isolating the tanks and firing on them to bring them to a stop, if possible.

Precise knowledge of enemy tank types, their strengths and weaknesses, armament, armor plate, hatches and openings, dead angles and areas, etc.

The *active* aspect consisted of:

Making and using makeshift close-combat weapons.

Knowledge of and familiarity with the close-combat weapons supplied to the troops. Learning to jump onto and off tanks (with practice on their own tanks) and bringing close-combat weapons into play.

All of this was to be learned quickly – but what it really meant to attack and defeat the colossal Soviet tanks such as the KW 1 with its 43.5 tons, 7.62 mm gun and two or three machine guns, or the faster T 34 that weighed 26.3 tons and had the same armaments, and that usually attacked in packs – that still had to be experienced. And it proved that since the beginning of this campaign many tanks were defeated in close combat, with increasing success. There was nothing for the soldier to do but attack the enemy tank with determination, using whatever weapons he had made or been issued.

Various weapons could be used for close antitank combat, depending on their availability and purpose. They were:

Makeshift Weapons
They provided a basis for fighting on, and did slight damage to tanks.

To rob moving tanks and their crews of orientation and sight and bring the tanks to a stop:
– Creating heavy smoke and dust by pouring gasoline and other inflammable fluids on prepared heaps of damp hay and straw, green twigs, etc., and setting fire to them by shooting with flare pistols, incendiary or tracer ammunition.
– Throwing rags or similar easily ignited material, soaked in oil and gasoline, onto the bows of tanks and igniting them.
– Pouring and throwing thick fluid mud, paint, chalk, dirty oil, etc. from containers kept in readiness, onto ports and optics, and throwing paper bags of dust, flour, cement, etc.
– Firing at optics with handguns and flare pistols.

In the case of standing tanks:
– Covering the ports and optics with covers, coats, tents, etc., or smearing them with paint, grease and the like.
– Shattering optics and machine gun barrels with iron rods or   other heavy striking implements.
– Tools such as axes, crowbars, levers, etc. kept in readiness can be used to open closed hatches, visors and armored covers, so as to put the crew inside out of action with pistol shots or hand grenades.
– Stuffing pieces of wood, stone, clumps of earth, etc. into gun   barrels in order to make the barrels burst, or even strike at the crews inside by sticking hand grenades in (the author has done this himself three times to T 34 tanks).

Hindrances (Means of Stopping)
These should serve above all to make tanks lose speed, stop, or force their crews to abandon them, and provide opportunities to apply means of crippling or destruction.

They include:
– Smoke hand grenades (producing fog lasting 2.5 minutes), thrown in front of or to the side of the tank, depending on the wind direction, should make the close-combat fighter's work easier.
– Smoke pots (smoking for 5 minutes – tied or wired in pairs and thrown over gun or machine gun barrels to bring the tank to a stop (likewise pairs of smoke hand grenades)
– Flares – the 1 H and improved 2 H flares were the most effective means of bringing moving tanks to a stop and, with a strongly irritating effect, even of forcing the crew to leave the tank. The fist-size flare consisted of a pear-shaped glass flask with inner and outer glass containers

holding two liquids that, when the glass was broken, mixed as they flowed out. There formed a strong, heavy cloud of smoke that lasted for some 15 to 20 seconds, and its main effect resulted from the suction of the ventilators and the pressure of the air, bringing so much smoke through the louvers and openings into the interior of the tank that the crew was compelled to leave the tank and then could be   fought outside it. These flares were best thrown against the   bow and driver's visor of the tank. They were carried packed in cardboard boxes of four, but had to be handled with care. These flares were the most effective means of blinding a tank.

Means of Crippling

They decreased the mobility or firepower of a tank by damaging the running gear or the engine cover, or even setting fire to the motor, and destroying the guns on board. Among them were:

Explosives
– Concentric hand-grenade charges (made by hand).
  The unscrewed casings of seven stick grenades were tied around one central hand grenade, complete with stick and charge, with wire or cord; it was ignited and thrown before the tracks of approaching tanks.
– Explosive blocks (1-kilogram charge)

One or more explosive blocks were attached to the running gear of standing tanks (laid on the tracks) and tore the track links apart when ignited. They were also a suitable means of destroying a tank's weapons. One had to be tied to a counterweight or two tied together with cord and thrown over gun or machine gun barrels to break or bend them on detonation.

It was also important to destroy the covering grid (usually of wire) over a tank's engine coolers. Clustered hand grenade charges and explosive blocks could be used for this purpose too. When tanks had been brought to a stop by hindering, blinding or crippling means, incendiary devices could be set afire on the rear of the tank at the engine's cooling vents.

Incendiary Devices
– Incendiary bottles (so-called Molotov Cocktails)
  They were made of bottles of any size, filled two-thirds full of gasoline and one-third of oil or incendiary oil. The bottles were plugged with hemp or with rifle plugs, and two special storm matches were taped to the bottles. Before being thrown, the plugs had to be thoroughly soaked in the inflammable liquid. Then they were ignited by using the matches just before being thrown, and the bottles were thrown at the tank (engine

compartment), where they ignited or were set afire by shots from a flare pistol.

– Gasoline canisters

Half-filled gasoline cans were also prepared by hand, first being perforated and then the holes being plugged with wooden plugs. A stick or smoke hand grenade was also attached to the canister. Shortly before attaching the canister to the rear of a tank with its engine cover, the hand grenade was ignited. The detonation tore the canister apart or drove the wooden plugs out of the holes and ignited the gasoline.

Means of Damage and Destruction

With their explosive effect, they could damage a tank in important parts of its running gear or weaponry and wipe out its crew. Among them were:

– Concentric engineer charges up to 3 kilograms (corresponding to 3 explosive blocks)

The concentric 3-kilo charge's light weight made handling easier when attaching to a tank or throwing. It penetrated some 6 centimeters of armor plate. To blow up heavier steel plate, such as on the bow, two or three charges had to be combined. They were used as an explosive charge with detonating fuses.

– T-Mine 35, total weight about 9 kilograms, weight of the explosive charge 5 kg. According to their intended use, they were ignited by detonator fuses (ripcord igniters with seven-second delay) or time fuses (pull igniters) with ten-second delay. With their own T-mine igniters (pressure igniters) the mines, made live and with safety catches released, were detonated with a pressure of some 190 kg in the center and ca. 100 kg at the edges.

The mines were thrown at tanks from foxholes individually with ripcord igniters, or were equipped with pressure igniters and thrown under the tracks. Experienced close-combat soldiers were also able to throw mines at moving tanks. Another way consisted of pulling a single mine out of a foxhole into the path of an approaching tank with thin wire or cord. Four to six mines could also be attached to a board at short intervals and pulled before a tank as a movable barrage prepared in advance. With enough time after a tank alarm, the mines could quickly be laid as a barrage on an open area in the expected path of the tanks. Their explosive effect ripped tank tracks to a width of 70 cm, if two thirds of their width touched the mine. The effect on the running gear, tracks and lower hull was destructive and brought the tank to a stop, immobilizing it, in any case.

When tanks had been immobilized, the concentric engineer charges and T-mines were pushed particularly between the top of the hull and the bottom of the turret, which destroyed the turret's turning track or could even blow the whole turret off.

It was particularly effective to throw charges and mines onto the rear to destroy the motor. It was important, though, to equip these explosive devices beforehand with wire hooks or to wrap them in rags so they would either catch on angles of the   tank or lie on it and not slide off.

Charges over five kilograms and T-mines penetrated armor 8 to 10 cm thick, had a powerful effect inside a tank, and were a   safe and effective means of destroying a tank.

– Magnetic hollow antitank charge H 3, issued as of the autumn of 1942, weight 3 kilograms, with high explosive and shock-wave effect.

The magnetic hollow charge consisted of a cylindrical body in which the charge was placed, a handle and a magnetically attached tripod. Ignition was provided by an igniting fuse that   was torn off and a detonator that was located in the handle. The duration of burning varied from the old to the new type of magnetic hollow charge, being between 4.5 and 7 seconds. The magnetic hollow charges were attached to any chosen spots on a tank by their magnetic tripods, most advantageously on smooth, steep surfaces, and usually with two of the three magnetic poles upward, and one had to make sure that they could not be knocked off by the turning of the turret. Since the magnetic effect failed on tank plates with a heavy layer of dirt or painted-on adhesive, the charges had to be equipped with chains   or hooks to attach them to suitable places on the tank. After igniting them, one had to take cover quickly. The magnetic hollow charges penetrated armor up to 14 cm thick, making a hole 3 to 5 centimeters in diameter; their explosive and shock effects were destructive. It was thus the most effective close   combat device and proved itself hundreds of times.

That all these devices, whether manufactured or cobbled up, were not just passing fancies, nor used just once in a while or just by single units, is indicated by the official Army Service Instruction (HDv) 469/4 NfD, "Guidelines for Close Antitank Combat" of October 7, 1942, in which, along with precise instructions, all the devices listed above and their uses are described. Well before that, many divisions had issued their own instructions for close antitank combat. For example, the 24th Infantry Division's "Command Directive No. 20, part i" of March 20, 1942 stated:

"Active antitank action in deep foxholes prepared and arranged in formation. Equipment: smoke bombs, concentric charges, explosive blocks, especially incendiary bottles.

It is to be striven for that the available materials are to be located at least every 100 meters in the main battle line (HKL), including places where no tank attack is expected. These devices must also be kept ready in the depths of the main battlefield (company to battalion command posts) . . ."

And on April 5, 1942 in an "Introduction to Close Antitank Combat":

"Determination, boldness, nerve are important.
1. Blind tanks early with smoke, thus throw smoke bombs at the right time and take wind direction into consideration.
2. Move in under cover of smoke, the nearer, the safer.
3. Throw incendiary bottles at the tank, especially at the motor.
4. Place concentric charges under the tracks or on the armor plate (find flat surfaces).
5. Throw hand grenades in opened visors and turret hatches.
6. Do not under any circumstances flee before the tank."

There was also new useful information from "above", such as a series of close antitank combat brochures dated November 1, 1943, in which the most important enemy tank types in the east and west were portrayed in pictures and outline drawings, with their dimensions, armor thicknesses, armaments, weak points, dead areas, etc. Information for firing, particularly for the later rifle and antitank grenades fired from launching cups, also reached the troops.

Since sufficient numbers of heavy antitank guns still had not been delivered to the infantry, which was under pressure from enemy tanks everywhere, they were to continue to fight against superior tanks in close combat. On May 13, 1944 the OKH issued a small booklet, Pamphlet 77/3, "The Tank Knocker", which animated close antitank combat through small scenes and verses, not to mention gallows humor.

Only with the introduction of the "Panzerfaust" in mid-1943 was the individual fighting man given a useful one-man antitank weapon with which he could take on a tank from a certain distance (*see also* section "New Infantry Weapons"). But this weapon reached the front only slowly, and so the antitank weapons of a company in the summer of 1944 still added up to just two Panzerfaust shells, two 3-kilogram and two one-kilogram engineer charges, two smoke grenades, two smoke blocks and two T-mines, which were carried on the combat vehicle.

Back to close antitank combat, of which it was said that the individual man must move right at the enemy tank to use his weapons. What calmness, cold-bloodedness and self-control it took to attack a rolling or halted steel monster of some 30 tons singlehanded and defeat it is, like so much else from the past war, hard to imagine today. It soon became obvious that the individual fighter, despite all his courage, often did not achieve the hoped-for success or even lost his life. For that reason the general advice was given: Safe and sure success is achieved by sensible cooperation of several soldiers in close combat troops. The composition of the troop should be – and was – varied according to the situation, units, weapons, etc. A close-combat troop could, for example, consist of three men, namely the securer, the blinder and the destroyer. Under the fire support of the securer against the infantry accompanying the enemy tank, the blinder first moved forward in order to take away the tank's sight with his weapons, and then he too worked as a securer. Then the destroyer sprang forward, utilizing cover and dead areas, and approached the tank to apply his incendiary or explosive devices. After the cry of "Burning!", meaning that the charge was ignited, the securer and blinder took full cover while the destroyer took cover by throwing himself to the opposite side of the tank.

No definite structuring was ordered by high officialdom, but an appendix to HDv 469/4 was issued.

Appendix for Structuring and Equipping a Close Antitank Combat Troop
(Addition to HDv 469/4, sections 44-48)

1. On the basis of past experience, the minimum strength of a close antitank combat troop is 3 to 4 men; the following structure has proved itself:

> 1 Troop Leader
> 1 Tank Blinder (if needed)
> 1 Tank Destroyer
> 1 Securer (simultaneously Carrier)

The strength can – depending on the situation – be expanded to a whole squad, and strengthening with heavy weapons is often useful.

There is always a leader who commands how, with what weapons and in what order the attack shall be made. Otherwise one waits for another or brings another into danger.

2. The equipment of a close antitank combat troop with weapons varies. It depends on the tank to be attacked, the situation and the available weapons. A machine weapon in the troop is advisable.

3. An example of the equipment of a 4-man troop lying in ambush:

Troop leader: Pistol (MPi or automatic rifle), one magnetic charge, two hand grenades, two twin smoke grenades, one short spade.

Blinder: Pistol, smoke bombs, two hand grenades, two twin smoke grenades, one short spade.

Destroyer: Pistol, smoke bombs, one magnetic charge, one T-mine with anchor hooks (or one 3-kilogram concentric charge) with detonator and three detonators (in reserve), 7 cm long, in a container, two hand grenades, one short spade.

Securer: Rifle, one magnetic charge, one T-mine with anchor hook (or one 3-kilogram concentric charge) and three detonators, 7 cm long, in a container, two hand grenades, one short spade. Additional personnel are to be equipped similarly to the securer.

4. The equipment for defense is more extensive than for attack and can include additional smoke, incendiary and explosive devices kept ready in foxholes, especially smoke grenades, stick grenades, incendiary bottles, smoke bombs and concentric charges.

5. According to its combat assignment, the close-combat troop – strengthened under some conditions – fights alone or within the framework of the squad or, as the case may be, the platoon; the tank destroyer and securer are generally located in one foxhole during defensive fighting for the sake of better cooperation.

As a decoration for a destroyed enemy tank (by the destroyer), a "special decoration for the defeat of tanks by individual fighting men" was introduced on March 9, 1942. And in special cases, the reward was the much more desirable furlough back home.

With what bravery, but also what courage of desperation, the infantryman, engineer, artilleryman or any other soldier defied the masses of enemy tanks is shown by the score of victories. According to it, *Generaloberst* Guderian stated the number of tank-destroying decorations awarded as of May 1944 at 10,000. There were 14,000 in all – or in other words, given the strength of a Soviet tank corps as something above 250 tanks, about fifty enemy tank corps were destroyed by close-combat soldiers.

CHAPTER 6

The Reconnaissance Unit

The reconnaissance units (partly motorized) with the golden yellow service-arm color were a remarkably mixed group. They did not exist in peacetime and were formed only upon mobilization in 1939, out of the thirteen cavalry regiments that were subordinated to the army corps at that time. At the end of the war, every cavalry regiment provided some three to five divisional reconnaissance units and one cavalry replacement unit, which at first remained at their peacetime garrisons. The cavalry regiments had thus ceased to exist, though they were partially reformed later.

The reconnaissance unit, also known as the "eyes" of the division, was to reconnoiter in advance and protect the division from surprises. For this it was often necessary in moving warfare to win superiority over enemy reconnaissance and securing forces in the reconnaissance area first, or at times to give way before superior enemy forces and seek success in another place. The units were also capable of securing open flanks in particular situations. During fast advances, they were applied along with individual engineer companies, batteries and Panzerjäger units as so-called advance units, in order to gain quick control of important points and sectors such as bridges, traffic intersections, dominating heights, etc.

The reconnaissance units of the infantry divisions, having been formed of disbanded cavalry regiments (and thus retaining terminology like "Rittmeister" and "Squadron"), were sufficiently suited for these short-term tasks in the first years of the war, but such a manifold type of fighting demanded a high degree of decisiveness and responsibility from all officers and leaders. It was also not easy to lead the whole of such a mixed unit, partly motorized, mounted or on bicycles.

Infantry divisions that were organized later generally were given a reconnaissance unit without a mounted squadron, and received a separate mounted squadron. The armored scout troops were replaced by re-connaissance units using motorcycles and motor vehicles.

The reconnaissance units had a total complement of 19 officers, two administrators, 90 non-commissioned officers and 512 enlisted men, making a total of 623 men.

Their armaments consisted of: 25 light machine guns, 3 light grenade launchers, 2 heavy machine guns, 3 antitank guns and 3 armored scout cars. The available vehicles were: 7 horsedrawn HF wagons, 29 cars, 20 trucks, 50 motorcycles (28 of them with sidecars). Their horses, including those of the mounted squadron, numbered 260, but in fact well over 300 horses were on hand.

The unit had the following structure:

Unit staff with:
– Commander, adjutant, assistant adjutant, leader of the intelligence column, veterinarian, senior inspector (leader of   the repair unit), senior paymaster and staff personnel (some mounted, some motorized).

It is noteworthy that the commander's car carried a 100-watt radio transmitter with receiver, which could be removed and used to maintain contact with the squadrons.

– Messenger unit with 5 bicycle and 5 motorcycle messengers.
– Intelligence platoon with
– 1 telephone troop (motorized) (1 Special Vehicle 15)
– 1 radio troop a (motorized) (1 Special Vehicle 15, 1 large radio truck [Funkwagen])
– 3 two-way portable radio troops b (mounted)
– 1 telephone troop (mounted)
– 1 intelligence equipment wagon (horsedrawn).
Strength: 1 officer, 29 NCO's and men, 25 horses.

1. *Mounted squadron with leader and squadron troop*
– 3 mounted platoons, each with one headquarters troop and 3 squads (each of 2 riflemen and 1 light MG "march"), each squad with 1 NCO and 12 riders.

The armament of the individual rider consisted, as in the regimental mounted platoons, of a 98 k rifle, originally carried in a carrying boot on the right side of the saddle, later slung over the rider's back. The saber still carried in the Polish and western campaigns had to be dispensed with and returned to the armories at the end of 1940 and the beginning of 1941, as they were no longer used; this was not done uniformly at first (the lances had already been done away with in 1928). Their equipment consisted of a belt with one bullet pouch at the left, saddlebags on both sides of the horse, 15 spare cartridges iron rations, 2 spare horseshoes and cleaning materials in the right one, and 1 bundle of toilet articles, 1 spare handkerchief, 1 pair of underpants, 1 pair of socks and small personal effects in the left one. A forepack carried over the saddlebags contained a gas mask, hand spade, food bag, field flask and cooking utensils. The rear pack consisted of a tied tent square, coat, blanket and halter, and the steel helmet on the back of the saddle. The horse carried a feed-bag on its neck.

The 1st to 3rd squads of each platoon had a pack-horse leader with a pack horse, which carried one light machine gun, plus ammunition cases left and right. The complement of each platoon included one officer, 42 non-commissioned officers and enlisted men, and 46 horses. The combat strength of the entire squadron was reduced, though, as a horse holder had to take every two horses away from the firing line when the riders dismounted to fight.

– The supply train included one horsedrawn field kitchen, 3 horsedrawn HF 1 wagons, 4 horsedrawn HF 2 wagons (one of them a blacksmith's wagon with a field smithy), 35 horses, 1 solo motorcycle, 1 motorcycle with sidecar, and 28 non-commissioned officers and enlisted men.

2. *Bicycle squadron with company chief (1 car) and squadron troop*
(two motorcycles)
– 3 Bicycle platoons, each with one platoon leader, 3 messengers, and 3 squads (each with 12 men and one light machine gun), one light grenade launcher troop (2 motorcycles with sidecars).

1 truck with spare wheels and repair shop.

The bicyclists had the heavy Wehrmacht Bicycle 38; on the luggage carrier or on the handlebars was an assault pack plus other equipment, and machine gun boxes were attached to the bicycle frame. Rifles and light machine guns were carried on the back or over the shoulder.

– There was also one heavy platoon with headquarters troop (3 motorcycles with sidecars) and one heavy machine-gun unit, consisting of two heavy machine guns with crews and 8 motorcycles with sidecars.

Including the supply train with field kitchen, commissary train and pack train, the bicycle squadron had a total strength of 158 men.

3. *Heavy squadron with leader and squadron troop*
– 1 cavalry gun troop (2 light 75mm infantry guns), drawn by
  six horses
– 1 antitank platoon (three 37mm antitank guns), motorized
– 1 armored scout troop (3 light 4-wheeled armored scout cars [Panzerspähwagen], armed only with machine guns, including one radio car [Funkwagen])

These three light scout cars were the only armored vehicles in the whole division. They proceed to be completely insufficient in terms of both quantity and strength.

– Combat supply train with 1 field kitchen (motorized), 1 ammunition truck, 1 repair and spare-parts truck, 1 fuel tank truck, 1 motorcycle with sidecar for the weapons and equipment.

NCO and armorer's assistant, victualling train (1 truck) andpack train (1 truck), plus one solo motorcycle each for the *Hauptfeldwebel* and the pay clerk.

Corresponding to their main assignment, either reconnaissance or as an advance troop for their division, the reconnaissance unit was located some 25 to 30 kilometers ahead of the division in advance combat, or was placed in gaps or on open flanks to the side of the division. During combat in the east in 1941 three combat-ready scout troops of the mounted squadron, composed of three squads each with a mounted radio troop, were usually located to the right and left of the advance course to a width of some ten kilometers, with bicycle scout troops at short distances, and the armored scout troop often covered side roads or parallel roads several times a day. The mass of the bicycle squadron and the 3rd squadron with its heavy weapons were at first held back to break weak enemy resistance.

By 1942, when the reconnaissance units were usually needed to perform infantry assignments, they were all too often not strong enough in terms of personnel, and also too weakly armed. Despite that, they were often thrown in as "division firemen", wherever the situation was serious and men were needed. With the obvious change in the eastern campaign at the beginning of 1943, the fate of the reconnaissance units was sealed. All the mounted squadrons were gradually withdrawn from the reconnaissance units and formed into new cavalry regiments. Since reconnaissance assignments rarely needed to be carried out any more, the remaining parts of the reconnaissance units were formed into so-called fusilier battalions (a type of light infantry, *see also* section "New Infantry Divisions") and thus strengthened the constantly sinking combat strength of the infantry divisions.

CHAPTER 7

The Panzerjäger Unit

The main source of antitank defense in an infantry division during the entire war was the antitank unit with its rose service-arm color. As of May 16, 1940 its name was changed from "Panzerabwehrabteilung" to "Panzerjägerabteilung." A division had one Panzerjäger unit, and each of the three infantry regiments had its own Panzerjäger company.

The Panzerjäger unit, the only fully motorized unit in a division, consisted of:
- Staff with intelligence platoon (as usual)
- 3 companies
- Supply trains (as usual)

with a total strength of 550 officers, non-commissioned officers and enlisted men, armed with 36 37mm antitank guns, 18 light machine guns, and equipped with 114 motorized vehicles and 45 motorcycles.

A Panzerjäger company included:
- Company chief (*Oberleutnant*) with company troop (13 men) using cars and motorcycles
- 4 platoons (I. and II. platoons led by a *Leutnant*, III. platoon by a *Feldwebel*, IV. platoon by an *Unteroffizier*)
- Combat supply train with one car, one large field kitchen, 3 trucks.

The company was armed with 12 antitank guns, 4 light machine guns, 86 rifles, 4 machine pistols and 10 pistols. Every antitank platoon consisted of:
- Platoon leader with headquarters troop (7 men)
- 3 37mm antitank guns with 6 men each, and one light machine gun troop with 3 men.

A gun crew consisted of a leader, gunner, loader and two ammunition loaders, plus the driver of a two-axle medium-size personnel car or a three-axle off-road limber vehicle Kfz 69, which carried both crew and ammunition, and on which the antitank guns were hung. The primary supply of ammunition consisted of 36 antitank and 24 explosive shells.

The antitank guns (the German abbreviation "Pak" stands for "Panzerabwehrkanone") were rapid-fire cannon-type weapons which fired antitank shells in flat fire, directly aimed using telescopic sights, primarily at enemy tanks but also at strongly fortified places (such as concrete bunkers) and explosive shells at infantry targets. These shells were cartridge ammunition (see chapter "The Ammunition"). The shot ranges were not decisive but depended above all on the penetrating power of the antitank shells against armor plate.

The 37mm Pak 35/36

From the beginning of the war until about the end of 1941 this was the standard gun for antitank use. Developed since 1933 and first issued to the troops in 1936, this antitank gun, like other weapons, saw service in the Spanish Civil War from 1937 to 1939 and proved itself under heavy fire. The 37mm Pak had a special mantelet with two tubular struts and a small angular shield, 50mm thick, raked sharply backward. The hydropneumatic recoil and counter-recoil system was located in the cradle. The barrel had no muzzle brake. The two wheels had rubber tires and individual air chambers, so they could not be shot completely flat. A special advantage was the low weight, which meant that the gun could be moved easily and quickly, even in rough country, and could even be hauled by manpower for short stretches, particularly on roads, so as to be put into service quickly in case of surprise tank attacks and change its position equally quickly.

Technical data:

Caliber	37mm
Overall length (including struts)	3.40 meters
Barrel length	1.66 meters
Weight ready to fire	435 kilograms
Elevation arc	-5 to +25 degrees
Traverse arc	60 degrees
Initial velocity (V_o) of antitank shell	745 meters per second
Rate of fire	16 rounds per minute
Weight of antitank shell	0.68 kilograms
Weight of cartridge (case)	1.32 kilograms
Penetrating power of antitank shell with steel core	at 100 meters, 35 mm armor
	at 500 meters, 28 mm armor
Of shell with hard core	at 100 meters, 60 mm armor
	at 500 meters, 35 mm armor
Crew	5 men

On September 1, 1939, as the war began, the army had over 11,250 of these guns, whose numbers grew to 15,515 by June 22, 1941.

The 37mm Pak was a generally useful design and was regarded, after experience with it in Spain, as a fully capable gun for antitank use from the beginning of the war on. It also proved itself in the Polish campaign of 1939 against the Polish tanks, which were usually light and rarely appeared in great numbers. In the only large-scale Polish tank attack, which took place at Warsaw on September 12, 1939, one Pak was able to destroy six tanks. But the picture changed in the western campaign of 1940. Its caliber and penetrating power were too meager and quite unsatisfactory against the numerous medium and heavy enemy tanks. When large-scale French tank attacks took place, the Panzerjäger suffered heavy losses. For example, the 57th Infantry Division lost 12 Pak shot down or rolled over in barely seven days at the Abbèville bridgehead, without having sufficient effect on the enemy. Tanks were generally shot down only when direct hits could be scored in favorable places, such as tracks, motors, etc.

Thus the penetrating power was first improved by the introduction of the Antitank Shell 40 with a hard core (tungsten), which had a heightened Vo of 1020 meters per second and could penetrate 65 mm of armor at 100 meters.

In spite of that, the inferiority of the 37mm Pak in the eastern campaign was quite obvious. In the beginning it could still prevail over the older types of Soviet tanks, but even in the first months of the campaign it became fully ineffective at times.

Against the heavy and extra-heavy tanks that appeared in ever-greater numbers, especially the T 34, KW I and KW II types, the "three-point-seven" was hopelessly inferior and no longer had any chance. So it was that the soldiers, threatened by enemy tanks, soon gave it the bitingly satirical name of "tank door-knocker."

Attempts were made to eliminate this inferiority by quickly developed makeshift equipment, which worked more or less. The 37mm stick grenade 41 is especially noteworthy. This was an over-caliber shell with a hollow charge, which was produced as of 1941. The shell consisted of a cylinder-shaped container with an explosive charge, clustered around an empty space and equipped with a perforated tubular shaft equipped with stabilizing fins. It weighed 8.6 kilograms, was 73.9 cm long, had a maximum diameter of 15.8 cm and a charge of 2.42 kilograms. This shell was propelled by a separately loaded normal 37mm case cartridge. The velocity was 110 meters per second, the effective range was at most 300 meters, and its penetrating power at any distance was supposed to equal 80 millimeters of armor plate. Yet its target accuracy from 200 meters on was meager, as the shell began to spin. Another disadvantage was that the 41 stick grenade had to be inserted into the barrel from the front.

Every 37mm Pak was equipped with two to four stick grenades in 1941, and a large number of Panzerjäger units or companies kept them on hand and issued them when needed. Conclusive evidence is lacking as to how successful the 42 stick grenade was. It went out of use in 1942.

The 42mm Pak

In 1941 a 42mm Pak was also introduced as a special antitank gun, but it was not used by all Panzerjäger units. Typical of this gun was the conical barrel, which had a caliber diameter of 42mm at the beginning of the riflings, decreasing to 29mm at the muzzle. Thus a particularly high muzzle velocity was achieved. This gun was very similar externally to the 37mm Pak, but had a changed chassis and a double shield with a 40mm gap.

Technical data:

Caliber	42mm
Weight ready to fire	642 kilograms
Elevation range	-8 to +25 degrees
Traverse range	60 degrees
Vo of the antitank shell	1265 meters per second
Weight of the antitank shell	bullet 336 g, cartridge 1.52 kg
Penetrating power	at 1000 m and 90-degree angle, up to 60 mm, at 60-degree angle up to 53 mm

This gun proved to have outstanding penetrating performance along with low weight, but the high wear of the conical barrel was a disadvantage. The production of this antitank gun had to be stopped as early as the summer of 1942 because of a shortage of tungsten for the production of special ammunition.

The 50mm (medium) Pak 38

To provide the Panzerjäger with a better and more effective gun, production and distribution of the 50mm Pak 38 were expedited. Developed in 1938, this gun only reached a few platoons of the Panzerjäger companies at the end of 1940.

The 50mm Pak also had a spreading mantelet with two tubular struts, a muzzle brake and thin, fully rubber-tired disc wheels with three-part profiling. A typical feature was the pair of curved shields, 24mm thick, with straight outer edges and mounted 25mm apart, making a double shield. The towing tractor was originally an Opel truck, later a light 1-ton halftrack tractor, which also carried the crew and ammunition. On short stretches the 50mm Pak could even be moved by manpower. It was also capable of firing over-caliber shells.

Technical data:

Caliber	50mm
Overall length	4.80 meters
Barrel length	3.0 meters
Weight ready to fire	986 kilograms
Elevation arc	-8 to +27 degrees
Traverse arc	65 degrees
Initial velocity (V_o) of the antitank shell	835 meters per second
Rate of fire	14 rounds per minute
Weight of antitank shell	2.10 kilograms
Weight of cartridge (case)	4.13 kilograms
Penetrating power of antitank shell with steel core	at 250 meters, 67 mm armor plate
	at 500 meters, 61 mm armor plate
with hard core	at 250 meters, 109 mm armor plate
	at 500 meters, 86 mm armor plate
Crew	5 men

On April 1, 1940 there were just two of these guns with the troops; on June 1, 1941, just before the eastern campaign began, there were 1047 of them. The ordered replacement of the 37mm Pak took a long time because of insufficient production and could not be carried out fully, especially for Panzerjäger companies in infantry regiments. Thus these companies had platoons armed with a mixture of 37mm and 50mm Pak. By the end of the war, of course, a great number of 50mm Pak had been put into service, but their performance was in no way satisfactory against the increasingly faster, more heavily armored and well-armed Soviet and Allied tank types that appeared in ever-growing numbers and finally in great masses.

The 75mm (Heavy) Pak 40

In order to meet the troops' constant demands for an effective gun for antitank use at last, no new gun was developed, but the former 50mm Pak was somewhat "enlarged" and equipped with a new larger-caliber barrel. Thus the 75mm Pak came into existence in short- and long-barreled versions, which were produced and first delivered to the troops as of late November 1941. They were so similar to the 50mm Pak that it was hard to tell them apart from outside. It had the same mantelet with spreading tubular struts and disc wheels with full rubber tires. The wheels were those produced for the 145cm heavy field howitzer. The longer barrel had a muzzle brake. The recoil brake and recuperator were likewise located in the barrel cradle. Two low, sharply raked shields of 4mm thickness, with a 25mm gap and an auxiliary partial shield that folded forward, protected the crew.

It was noteworthy that this Pak no longer fired explosive shells, but only antitank shells. The towing tractor was an Ost (RSO) caterpillar tractor, which also transported the crew and ammunition.

Technical data:

Caliber	75mm
Overall length	6.18 meters
Barrel length	3.92 meters
Weight ready to fire	1425 kilograms
Elevation arc	-5 to +22 degrees
Traverse arc	65 degrees
Initial velocity (V_o) of the antitank shell	792 meters per second
Rate of fire	10-12 rounds per minute
Weight of antitank shell	6.8 kilograms
Weight of cartridge (case)	8.1 kilograms
Penetration performance of the antitank shell with steel core	at 100 meters, 120 mm armor
	at 500 meters, 104 mm armor
	at 1000 meters, 76 mm armor
antitank shell with hard core	at 100 meters, 135 mm armor
	at 500 meters, 115 mm armor
	at 1000 meters, 96 mm armor
Crew	5 men

(Note: The penetration performance of all three antitank guns is listed for an impact angle of 60 degrees.)

Only with this 75mm Pak did the Panzerjäger receive a fully capable and effective gun with outstanding penetrating power, and which stayed in use to the end of the war as the new standard antitank weapon against nearly all enemy tank types. But the 75mm Pak had one big disadvantage – it had such a heavy weight that moving it by manpower, even on short stretches, was no longer possible for its crew; in fact, even moving it by towing on the battlefield, putting it into firing position and changing its position when necessary was often very hard to do. Changing its position during the day was all but impossible, since the towing tractor (RSO) was too easy to see. Thus it was unavoidable that, on account of their immobility, a great many of the guns were lost, particularly during the withdrawal fighting in the eastern campaign in the winter or the mud season.

The number of available 75mm Pak was also limited. In 1942 only 1360 of the guns had reached the front; on October 1, 1944 the number was up to 4805 (temporarily sufficient for some 80 divisions).

Examples of the total Pak supply of individual divisions in the summer of 1944:

12th Infantry Division: 7 medium, 22 heavy Pak

95th Infantry Division: 8 medium, 21 heavy Pak

197th Infantry Division: 11 medium, 20 heavy Pak

206th Infantry Division: 17 medium, 21 heavy Pak

252nd Infantry Division: 14 medium, 21 heavy Pak

267th Infantry Division: 2 medium, 22 heavy Pak

292nd Infantry Division: 7 medium, 25 heavy Pak

296th Infantry Division: 4 medium, 22 heavy Pak

(plus 1 assault gun battery as partial substitute for missing Pak)

Whenever possible, they were there when the infantrymen's call rang out: "Enemy tanks are attacking!" They, the Panzerjäger, were in the initial attacking operations of all campaigns, at the very front with the advance units and at the head of the attacking forces, standing by their small, light 37mm Pak until they were shot down or rolled over, forming the backbone of antitank defense, preventing tank breakthroughs and covering the steady withdrawals in the latter part of the war until their own troops could move out as the rear guard. They fired on infantry targets as well as bunkers and emplacements, and when their antitank guns allowed, they lived up to their task: Fighting off enemy tanks. Numerous armored monsters from east and west fell victim to the Panzerjäger with their 37mm, 50mm and 75mm guns.

CHAPTER 8

The Artillery Regiment

The artillery regiment with its bright red service-arm color was the "heavy hammer" of the division. With their well-directed, handy and heavy fire, they supported the hard-fighting infantry in attacking and defensive combat. They fired on enemy batteries, provided preparatory and barrage fire, smashed enemy forces that were setting up, and always provided a tangible release of pressure in any situation. When one reads divisional and regimental histories, one sees again and again what valuable help and support the division artillery provided.

An artillery regiment consisted of:
– Regimental staff with staff battery
– Three light units, each with a staff battery and three batteries of four light 18 field howitzers (FH 18) each, 36 lFH 18 in all
– One heavy unit with a staff battery and three batteries, each with four heavy 18 field howitzers (sFH 18), 12 sFH 18 each
– Supply trains.

Each battery also had two light machine guns for anti-aircraft use and short-range securing. The total strength of an artillery regiment consisted of 114 officers, 10 administrators, 427 non-commissioned officers and 2321 enlisted men (total 2872), plus 2208 horses (776 saddle horses, 874 light and 558 heavy draft horses), 48 guns, 240 horse-drawn vehicles, 76 cars, 80 trucks and 57 motorcycles, including eight with sidecars. The armaments used by the artillery included pistols, rifles and 24 light machine guns.

The *regimental staff* consisted of:

Commander, adjutant, first and second assistant adjutant, 1 artillery liaison officer (AVO), intelligence officer, victualling officer, regimental surgeon, regimental veterinarian, 1a clerk, armorer, equipment officer, radio master and staff personnel.

The *Regimental Staff Battery* consisted of:
the artillery liaison command (AVKo), intelligence platoon (telephone and radio troops), artillery surveying troop, printing platoon and weather platoon.

Every *Light Unit* was made up of:
– Unit staff with commander, adjutant, assistant adjutant, intelligence platoon leader, artillery survey troop leader, unit surgeon, unit veterinarian, paymaster, 1a clerk and staff personnel.
– Staff battery with intelligence platoon, artillery liaison troop (AVT) and survey troop.
– Intelligence platoon with:
   1 medium telephone troop a (four-horse wagon)
   1 medium telephone troop b (two-horse wagon)
   1 large telephone troop a (six-horse wagon)
   2 portable radio troops b (on foot)
   2 portable radio troops b (mounted)
   plus one battery charger C (*see also* section "The Intelligence Unit").
– 3 batteries
– 1 light artillery column (motorized) with 36 t.
The total strength of each light unit: 20 officers, 2 administrators, 82 non-commissioned officers and 505 enlisted men, 609 men in all.
The heavy unit with its three batteries was structured similarly, but each battery had a light artillery column (motorized) with 28 t each.
The total strength of the heavy unit: 20 officers, 2 administrators, 85 non-commissioned officers and 571 men, 678 men in all.

Every *Light Battery* consisted of:
– Battery chief with command echelon: Battery troop leader, 1 or 2 VB troops (forward observer with two radiomen), messenger, clerk, horseholder, 1 observation wagon.
– Survey echelon: Observation officer, observation *Feldwebel*, directing *Unteroffizier* I, calculating troop leader, scissor telescope *Unteroffizier*.
– Intelligence staff: Intelligence *Feldwebel*, 2 field cable troops on foot, 2 mounted telephone troops (carrying cable drums on pack horses), 2 radio troops on foot, one light telephone wagon (limber with single-axle cable wagon), telephone and communication personnel.
These three echelons included the leadership, observation, survey and calculation manpower of the battery.
– 2 gun echelons (battery officer, directing NCO II, fire control *Feldwebel*, 2 guns each and their crews, 2 light machine guns (on mantelets in vehicles for air protection when on the march).
– 1st and 2nd ammunition echelons with 4 ammunition wagons each.

A gun consisted of a limber pulling a light field howitzer, pulled by six horses, 1 gun leader (mounted) and 5 cannoneers (3 seated at the front of the limber vehicle and two at the back, with storage space for baggage between them). The drivers sat on the left-side horses (drivers from the saddle, saddle horses). The horses on the right side were called hand horses. The teams were called (in order from front to back) front, middle and hitch horses.

All wagons were six-horse except the telephone and anti-aircraft wagons.

– Combat supply train I with field kitchen, commissary NCO, repair troop and storekeeper with personnel

– Commissary train II with pay clerk, writing room with *Hauptwacht-meister* (*Hauptfeldwebel*)

– Pack train with saddler, shoemaker, tailor, etc.

The entire complement of a light lFH 18 battery included 4 officers, 30 NCO and 137 enlisted men, with 153 horses.

The structure of a heavy battery resembled that of a light battery. It had one more radio troop, though, and instead of the mounted telephone troop, the heavy howitzer battery had a second light telephone truck with personnel for installing lines.

Command and Fire-control Entities:

The unit (Abteilung) was a firing entity. Its action was commanded by the regimental commander, who was generally with the division commander. The artillery communications officer (AVO) maintained communication with the division.

The Artillery Communications Command (AVKo) (1 officer with an intelligence troop) was responsible for communication between the unit command and the appropriate infantry unit (infantry regiment, etc.).

At the main observation post (Haupt-B-Stelle) were the battery chief, the observation officer, telescope and direction NCO's, and the intelligence echelon leader with telephones and radiomen to direct the battery's fire. In addition, other observation posts could be set up if necessary. Combat assignments would have to be carried out by these observation posts.

They were the "eyes" of the artillery; from them as much as possible of the enemy, the terrain and their own troops needed to be seen. From the main observation post the battery chief also gave his commands for combat to the advance observers (VB), from here combat reports and position reports were made, and there was constant communication with the unit's command post.

An advance observer (VB), a *Leutnant*, *Wachtmeister* or, later, also an experienced *Unteroffizier*, was assigned to a focal-point unit or to the foremost point of the infantry, along with either a radio troop (radio troop leader, 1 radioman) or a mounted telephone troop (1 troop leader, 2 telephonists, 1 horseholder, 1 horse carrying cable drums). The VB accompanied the infantry in an attack or stayed with it during withdrawal fighting. With its intelligence troop, it made contact with the battery (firing position), reported observations of enemy actions, targets and distances immediately, directed the firing-in and observed the effect of firing, according to instructions from the battery and the unit or artillery regiment.

An lFH 18 battery was ready to fire 45 minutes after receiving instructions.

The Guns

The lFH and sFH 18 were howitzers that combined lengthened and shortened trajectories of their shells in the lower angle range of up to 45 degrees, in order to be able to hit both open targets and those under cover. Thus they did not use steep fire.

The **Light Field Howitzer 18** was put into service in 1935 to replace the earlier Light Field Howitzer 16 (which continued to be used, though). It was the most frequently used light field howitzer and remained in use among the division artillery throughout the war as a reliable and stable standard gun that was also simple to operate.The howitzer had a spreading mantelet with folding ground stakes, a recoil and recuperating system in which the barrel recoil brake lay in the cradle and the hydropneumatic recuperator, filled with compressed air, was above the barrel. The wheels were made with cast steel spokes and steel hubs.

Technical Data:

Weight ready to fire	1985 kilograms
Barrel length	3.30 meters
Shot ranges	3570 m (1 charge), 10,670 m (6 charges)
Elevation arc	-5 to +42 degrees
Traverse arc	56 degrees to left and right
Initial velocity (V_o)	200 m/s to 465 m/s (by charge)
Rate of fire	6 to 8 rounds per minute
Charges	6
Weight of the shell	14.8 kilograms
Shrapnel effect	30- to 40-meter diameter, 50 to 60 in ricochet fire
Crew	1 leader, 5 men

As of 1941 the lFH 18 was also provided with a muzzle brake* and called lFH 18M. The firing performance improved by about 18%.

The lFH 18, since it could be aimed quickly, proved itself well in action against enemy tank targets too and could be used as an antitank gun with hollow-charge shells. For this purpose, all batteries were supplied during the war with a set of HL shells (so-called red-head ammunition).

The **Heavy Field Howitzer 18** was developed between 1926 and 1930 and introduced to troop use in 1933-34. The sFH 18 had a similar design to the lFH 18, with rubber-tired aluminum disc wheels and iron hubs, plus a remarkably long barrel for a howitzer. The gun was transported in two loads drawn by six horses each, drawing the mantelet and barrel wagons, each behind a limber. Before marching, the barrel was removed completely from its cradle and transported on a two-wheel wagon. The mantelet, with its struts folded, was also carried on a wagon. Despite these two loads, the gun was much too heavy for the bad weather and road conditions in the later course of the eastern campaign, and teams of up to ten horses were often needed to move it. Some of the guns, in fact, remained far behind. Setting them up was also a laborious process, in which the barrel wagon was placed in front of the unloaded mantelet and, after the barrel wagon was unloaded, the barrel had to be "pulled over." This "pulling over" of the barrel to prepare for firing was backbreaking work for the twelve-man crew. Loading the barrel back on the wagon when changing position also demanded extreme strength.

Technical data:

Weight ready to fire	5512 kilograms
Barrel length	4.44 meters
Shot ranges	4000 to 11,400 meters (by charge)
Elevation arc	-3 to +60 degrees
Traverse arc	64 degrees to right and left
Initial velocity (V_o)	210 to 520 meters per second
Rate of fire	4 to 5 rounds per minute
Charges	7
Weight of the shell	43.5 kilograms
Shrapnel effect	50- to 60-meter diameter
Crew	1 leader, 12 men

As of 1942 this gun, now called the sFH 36, also was fitted with a muzzle brake, and its weight was decreased. It now weighed only about half as much as before, so that it could now be transported as one load,

---

*The muzzle brake helped to absorb the power of the recoil, which meant that stronger charges could result in greater shot ranges.

sometimes in motorized form, towed by an 8-ton towing tractor.

Both howitzers were used against enemy artillery, heavy fortifications, permanent structures used for defense, dug-in infantry in field positions, etc., at long ranges.

Ammunition and Ammunition Supply:

Aside from special shells, the artillery fired shells with a pressed or cast steel case. The interior was filled with an explosive charge (*see* photo section, "The Ammunition").

The effect of the shell was dependent on the number and combination of charges as well as the size and the wall and base thickness of the shell case. The explosive charge tore the case into many fragments, most of which flew roughly perpendicularly to the axis of the shell. The breadth effect of the shell was greater than its depth effect. The number of fragments grew with the angle of impact. The penetrating power of the fragments depended on their velocity, size and shape.

The points of the shells had a hole leading to the interior of the shell, into the threads of which the fuse was screwed.

A distinction was made between:

– Impact fuse (Az.) regular. Because of greater penetration depth, part of its effect was absorbed by the earth.

– Impact fuse sensitive. Here the shell exploded as soon as it struck the ground, with greater shrapnel effect.

Both fuses had double settings: with delay (m.V.) and without delay (o.V.).

A shell with impact fuse and delay (Az.m.V.), the delay being 15 seconds, was called a "ricochet" shell. In this case the shell touched the ground but then bounced up some 15 meters and scattered its fragments to all sides from that height.

– Double fuse (DoppZ.) with clockwork and usual impact ignition

– Double fuse with powder-burning ignition and sensitive impact ignition. Double fuses could be used with any set time in impact or powder-burning ignition form.

One special type of shell was the smoke cartridge, in which part of the explosive was replace by fog.

In all shells the bullet and cartridge case were separate. The cartridges were given different charges for different ranges. The light and heavy field howitzers, as opposed to the heavy infantry weapons, fired ammunition that was loaded separately (likewise the infantry guns).

Every lFH 18 carried a primary ammunition supply of six shells, every ammunition echelon had 240 shells, so that a battery's supply added up to 504 rounds. A light artillery column carried 136 rounds. An artillery regiment carried a total of 4536 shells of lFH ammunition, weighing 104.3 tons.

The primary supply of a heavy unit numbered 60 shells available immediately, and the ammunition echelons carried 150 rounds.

An artillery regiment carried 720 shells in all (weighing 43.2 tons). A division carried an additional 5328 rounds for the lFH units and 1080 rounds for the sFH units, weighing 187.4 tons, in its supply columns.

Constant reconnaissance and observation of the enemy, quick readiness to fire, simplicity of the firing process, effective fire control, quick concentration of fire and close cooperation with the infantry were the great advantages of the division artillery that stood out all through the war.

CHAPTER 9

The Engineer Battalion
(Pionier)

They wore the black service-arm color, and to distinguish them from the infantry engineers they were usually called "black engineers." The men of the engineer battalions were practically "maids of all work" – road builders, path breakers, workers, technicians and soldiers. Engineers formed a troop that, because of their training, knowledge, equipment of tools, apparatus and weapons, were able to help other parts of the division and support them, when, where and however it was necessary. Among their main jobs were:

– **On the March**: Advancing the movements of their own troops, in fact often making them possible in the first place and thus quickly eliminating artificial and natural barriers such as obstacles placed by the enemy (roadblocks, mines, explosives), and making natural barriers (such as bad roads, swamps, muddy fields, etc.) passable on foot or by vehicle.

– **Crossing Rivers, Streams and Other Waterways**: Setting troop units across waterways with inflatable or assault boats and ferries, as well as building military or temporary bridges or repairing damaged bridges.

– **When Attacking**: When storming strongly fortified positions, bunkers and fortifications: blowing gaps in barbed wire or minefields, removing barricades, etc. Applied as shock troops: Bringing supplies of weapons and ammunition, blowing up support points, bunkers and fortifications or smoking them out with flamethrowers.

– **In Defense**: Building positions of all kinds, such as trenches, dugouts, covers, placing barricades like wire barriers, barbed-wire obstacles, minefields with antitank or anti-personnel mines, tripwires with charges, masking and camouflaging paths and terrain features, creating fields of fire, etc.

– **In Retreat**: Blocking and slowing enemy pursuit with mines and barricades on roads and paths, blowing up bridges, passages and structures, destroying or interrupting transport lines, etc.

– And not least, often seeing service as combat troops equal to infantry units in the last years of the war.

The engineer battalion (partly motorized) was made up of battalion staff, intelligence platoon (mot.), 1st and 2nd engineer companies (horsedrawn), 3rd engineer company (mot.), bridge column B (mot.) and light engineer column (horsedrawn). Its entire complement numbered 17 officers, 1 administrator, 60 non-commissioned officers, 442 engineers, 14 saddle horses, 38 draft horses, 19 horsedrawn vehicles, 9 cars, 24 motorcycles and 38 trucks (not counting the bridge and light engineer columns).

The structure consisted of:
– Battalion staff with battalion commander, officer z.b.V., adjutant, commissary officer, surgeon, assistant surgeon, veterinarian and staff personnel, 36 officers and men in all.
– Intelligence platoon with a complement of 1 officer, 4 non-commissioned officers and 27 men.
– Battalion band, with 1 music master and 27 musicians. (The engineer battalion was the only battalion in the division that had its own band. The musicians served as auxiliary medical personnel in the field.)
– 1st and 2nd engineer companies with a total complement of 4 officers and 187 men each, with 4 saddle horses, 16 draft horses, 8 horsedrawn vehicles, 1 car, 5 trucks and 5 motorcycles.

Per company:
– Company troop, complement of 1/7, with 2 saddle horses, 1 car and 2 motorcycles.
– 3 platoons, each with 52 engineers, divided into headquarters troop 1/5, 3 squads, each with 1/14 (arms: 9 light machine guns, 3 flamethrowers, 3 Panzerbüchsen), plus 1 two-horse field wagon.
– Ammunition and machine troop of 14 men with 3 medium trucks, two with trailers (air compressors).
– Combat supply trains I and II with 1 two-horse field wagon, 1 field kitchen, 2 bicycles.
– Supply trains I and II with 1 two-horse field wagon, 1 medium truck.
– Pack train with 1 medium truck – 15 men in all.
– 3rd engineer company (motorized) with 4 officers and 194 men, 6 cars, 16 squad trucks of Henschel type (which were both personnel and equipment transporters) and 7 motorcycles, plus the usual supply trains.

Equipment of the 3 Engineer Companies:

Tools:
- 9 large air compressors
- 20 power saws
- 6 cutting torches
10 hand flashlights

plus tools of all kinds such as axes, picks, saws, etc., long trenching tools such as spades, shovels, pickaxes, as well as mallets, pile-drivers, etc. There was also special clothing such as watertight chest-high overalls, leather gloves and much more.

Barricade Materials
- 306 K rolls
- 100 S rolls
- 73 rolls of barbed wire
- 21 rolls of plain wire

plus 1550 sandbags (empty) for use in constructing positions. The S rolls were prepared rolls of barbed wire, rolled up for quick use by unrolling to provide a barricade 6 to 8 meters wide.

The K rolls were similar, but consisted of plain wire.

The rolls of barbed wire were rolls that had to be cut to size before being used in making barricades, obstacles, etc.

The plain wire was used to make tripwires of thin wire, etc.

Explosive and Incendiary Devices
- 351 kilograms of engineers' explosives
- 23 glow igniters
- 2600 meters of explosive fuse
- 936 smoke grenades and smoke candles.

Explosive ammunition included explosive substances (usually TNT = trinitrotoluene) which was stable in storage, safe to transport and insensitive to dampness, and so could be taken along. These explosives could be drilled into, cut with a knife or tamped in with wood, as needed. Charges of various sizes could be made as required, such as concentric, stretched and row charges, borehole and quick charges, etc. In ordinary fire the explosive burned slowly and detonated only at 300 degrees.

The most frequently used prepared explosives were:
- Borehole charge 28, cylindrical form, size 10 x 3 meters,
  weight 100 grams of explosive
- Explosive charge 28, rectangular form, size 4 x 5 x 7 cm,
  weight 200 grams of explosive
- Explosive block 24, rectangular form, size 5.5 x 7.5 x 20 cm,
  weight 1 kilogram of explosive

– Concentric charge, rectangular form, size 7.6 x 16.4 x 19.5 cm,
  weight 3 kilograms of explosive (with carrying ring).

These explosives, made in varying forms and strengths for different uses, could be ignited, meaning made to detonate, by fuses. The fuses were devices that ignited small amounts of highly sensitive explosive by striking, pushing, spark, flame or glowing wire, and thus provided the heat to make the explosive detonate. There was a basic distinction among powder-train ignition, transmitted ignition and electric ignition. The fuse of powder-train ignition was a time fuse, a black cable filled with black powder. It burned at a rate of 1 centimeter per second (including under water). It was lit by a match, slow-match, time-fuse igniter or explosive fuse, a green cable filled with highly flammable explosive, which immediately burned (detonated) in its entire length when ignited at one end, and could be used as both a fuse and an explosive. Its burning time or detonation speed was 7000 meters per second. The explosive fuse had an additional igniting section of flammable explosive. It could be used to detonate several charges simultaneously and was ignited by time fuse linked to an ignition cap or a cap igniter. The ignition cap with cap igniter had to be handled carefully, since it was sensitive to being struck, bumped, rubbed and shaken. The cap igniter was a prepared combination of a piece of time fuse and a fuse igniter.

For power-train ignition there were various combinations of individual means of ignition that were prepared and used by the engineers themselves.

Electric ignition was used primarily to ignite charges at a definite time or at great distances. Glow igniters or devices like the glow ignition device were used for ignition, and could likewise be combined in various ways.

Mines
The battalion carried with it:
    – 1140 T mines
    – 1934 S mines.

These mines were standard mines made of metal and manufactured in great numbers, but not sufficient by far; they had to be changed somewhat and complemented by other types of mines during the course of the war. There were antitank mines for use against enemy tanks and antipersonnel mines for use against enemy infantry. They were ignited by mechanical means, more precisely by pressure (pressure detonator), pulling (ripcord detonator) or electric ignition. The best-known T-Mine 35 (T for Teller: plate) had a diameter of 32 cm, weighed 9 kilograms including 5 kg of explosive, and was equipped with a pressure detonator. It served excellently for antitank use (*see also* section "Close Antitank Combat"). Later the Tellermine 42 was made, with a weight of 8 kilograms including 4 kg of explosive.

The S-Mine 41 (S for Schütze: rifleman), 10.5 cm high with its detonator screwed in, in the shape of a pot with 200 grams of explosive, was used against enemy infantry. The anti-personnel mine could be detonated by either pressure or pulling. When buried, the mine could be detonated by stepping on it,whereupon it rose some 1.5 meters and spewed 350 flattened steel balls in that direction at that height, in a 50-meter circle. Its fuse, which could be used only for that mine, had a double safety catch and was supplied to the troops with its detonating cap already in place.

Mines were used singly, in rows, or in the form of minefields at intervals of 2 to 4 meters and at depths of 10 to 20 centimeters, regularly or irregularly, scattered or underground, or on the surface for quick use.

All kinds of mine barrages especially useful in carrying out parts of a defensive plan, in which artificial barricades, other obstacles and the effects of light and heavy weapons and artillery were combined or complemented each other. The mine plan – documentary evidence of the mine barrages in a certain defensive sector – gave information as to the type, exact location and extent of the placed mines. It allowed checking and completion of the barricades, was necessary if the mines were to be taken up, made mine lanes for scout and shock troops clear and was likewise of great importance when positions were turned over to relief units.

But the engineers not only laid mines but also had to find and remove enemy mines, and do it by hand. Side arms, heavy wire, pointed wooden sticks or mine-searching rods or detectors were used. When mines were discovered, they had to be dug out carefully, defused or exploded. There were also partially electromagnetic mine detectors, which emitted a high, shrill sound in the presence of metal at a depth of up to 30 centimeters, but did not work with, for example, Russian wood-case mines.

In order to indicate cleared mine paths for passage, including in their own minefields, white strips of tracing tape, or even weighted strips of paper, were used.

Bridging Materials
　　– 36 small float bags (rubber boats)
　　– 36 large float bags (rubber boats)

The small float bag with a wooden bottom had a length of 3 meters, a width of 1.15 meters and an air chamber diameter of 35 centimeters; when not inflated it weighed 50 kilograms, and it could carry 300 kilograms = 3 to 4 men. It took five minutes to inflate with a bellows.

The large float bag, likewise with a wooden bottom, had a length of 5.5 meters, a width of 1.85 meters, a diameter of 60 cm and a weight of 150 kg. It could carry 1.5 tons. Needed to move it were one steersman of "Schlagmann" (an engineer) and six oarsmen (usually infantrymen). The large float bag could be loaded with 12 men and one light machine gun (roughly one squad), or one 37mm Pak and its crew, etc.

The equipment needed to use the float bags, which were packed in carrying bags and carried by the engineer companies, included short oars with holding lines, and bellows.

Five small float bags could be used, when the current was not swift, to make pontoon bridges with a length of up to 24 meters, with a superstructure of planks and boards on which infantry could cross in a double line, or motorcycles or heavy weapons pulled by manpower. More lightly built bridges could only be crossed by infantry in single file, at intervals.

Numerous large float bags with a superstructure of planks and boards could also be used to make temporary ferries, which could carry larger vehicles, etc., and be propelled by storm boats or run as ferries.

Float bags were particularly useful bridging materials for a surprising, quick river crossing. But since inflating the large ones with two bellows was audible for some distance, they had to be brought to the water, ready for use, by eight men. In addition, the rubber skin of the boats was sensitive, and they could only be carried on the men's shoulders or by the mooring lines on the sides.

Flamethrowers

Along with the treacherous mines, a particularly fearful weapon of the engineers, against which there was no cover or protection, was the flamethrower, of which every company had three. These were the Light Flamethrower 35. It consisted of a carrier apparatus with two belts, the tank with its contents, and at its lower end a short, movable hose with nozzle. The device, which an engineer could carry on his back, had a rather heavy weight of 37 kilograms when filled. The tank was filled with easily flammable oil, which was pressed out by nitrogen; the flammable material and gas were under pressure in the container. An ignition jet at the mouth of the nozzle ignited the oil as it came out. With the flamethrower, bursts of flame some 25 to 30 meters could be given off, lasting 45 seconds per burst (one filling gave about 35 bursts of flame).

The Flamethrower 40 weighed only 22 kilograms and was somewhat similar to the Model 35, but had a shorter effective time (some ten to twelve bursts reaching 20 to 25 meters).

Before firing a flamethrower, the engineer pressed the nozzle trigger to a certain point. This released the nitrogen alone and ducted it past an open glow plug powered by a battery. This created a nitrogen flame, and now the moment had come to press the trigger the rest of the way and release the flammable oil from the tank under strong pressure. It was ignited by the nitrogen flame at the mouth of the nozzle and produced a jet of flame. This electric ignition made it possible to produce flames of varying lengths.

Careful maintenance of a flamethrower was necessary; improper handling and faulty maintenance often led to failure. The flamethrower was a weapon that was used particularly against bunkers, fortifications, strong enemy positions, large nests of opposition, and in street, building and forest fighting. Their effect was a combination of the jet of flame and a heavy cloud of smoke. The shock effect of a flamethrower attack on an enemy was also great.

Engineer flamethrower troops were used along with engineer or infantry shock troops. Successful action was usually possible only when the flamethrower troops could be held ready unseen just a short distance from the action. A combat principle was that one flamethrower operator was never deployed alone, but that two men were always used together, so they could support each other when advancing and fighting. Thus the strength of a flamethrower troop was to consist of one troop leader and one flamethrower operator with auxiliary men.

Other than the weapons named above, there were no heavy or special weapons in a normal engineer battalion of an infantry division.

The Light Engineer Column

The light engineer column, led by a column leader, consisted of three platoons, each with three two-horse wagons. They carried ammunition, close-combat and explosive devices, mines, trenching and other tools, and served as a supply train for engineering equipment and materials, and also made repairs.

The Bridge Column B

The erection of military bridges over larger rivers by engineers, especially in moving warfare (especially while advancing), would not have been possible without the fully motorized bridge columns with their mobile Military Bridge Device B (dating from 1934). The Bridge Column B of an infantry division was only an equipment unit in peacetime, and was brought up to full strength only when the war began. It had only a small complement of 2 officers, 13 non-commissioned officers and 87 men (including 39 drivers). Its personnel was not intended for bridgebuilding, but chiefly for transportation, maintenance and servicing of important equipment, and thus was not included among the combat troops. Military bridges could be built only by the engineer battalion of a division, which had the necessary work force.

The Bridge Column B consisted of:

– Leader Squad (1 officer, 5 NCO and men) with one car and 3 motorcycles.

– 1st pontoon platoon (1 officer, 35 NCO and men), with 1 car, 1 motorcycle, 4 medium (8-ton) halftrack towing tractors, each towing a two-axle pontoon wagon (carrying half a pontoon), 4 medium cross-country 3-axle trucks, each towing a two-axle pontoon wagon (carrying half a pontoon), 2 medium trucks with 2 trestle wagons in tow, 2 medium trucks with 2 shore transom wagons in tow, 1 medium truck with a single-axle trailer for a motorboat (M-blat).

– 2nd pontoon platoon (36 NCO and men) like the 1st pontoon platoon but with a two-axle trailer carrying 6 storm boats.

– Replacement platoon (8 men) with one motorcycle with sidecar, 2 medium trucks with 2 ramp wagons in tow, 1 medium truck with a single-axle ferry-line trailer.

The platoon's trucks carried tools, equipment, float bags, bridge components, etc.

– Supply and pack train (1 administrator, 15 NCO and men), with 1 motorized field kitchen, 2 motorcycles with sidecars, 1 light truck, one fuel truck.

The entire supply of heavy equipment consisted of:

– 16 half pontoons = 8 whole pontoons
– 8 trestles
– 2 ramps
– 8 shore transoms
– 8 16-ton crossing rails
– 6 storm boats
– 1 motorboat
– 20 small float bags
– 24 large float bags

Storm Boat: It was made of wood with very low draught (it floated unmanned in 10 centimeters of water) and had a 4-cylinder outboard motor and a speed of 30 kph. The crew consisted of a boat driver in the rear and an assistant in the bow. The passenger load was six men.

Motorboat: It was used to pull and push ferries and bridge components, especially in ferrying and bridgebuilding.

Half Pontoon: Every half pontoon had a length of 3.20 meters and a weight of 750 kilograms. It was unloaded by 20 men, carried to the shore and placed in the water. A Bridge Column B could build ferries or bridges with these devices.

– 8 ferries of 4 tons each, or

– 4 double ferries of 8 tons each, or

– 2 ferries of 16 tons each, or

– 1 ferry of 20 tons (capable of carrying, for example, a 150mm heavy field howitzer with towing tractor.)

The pontoon ferries were driven by two outboard motors, pushed or towed by storm boats or motorboats, or drawn by cable. An 8-ton ferry, for example, after casting off from the dock, was rowed into position and then – on a cable – was pushed across the river by the current. On the other side of the river, the cable was firmly anchored and ran over a drum.

The Bridge Equipment B could be used to build:

– a 4-ton military bridge about 130 meters long (on half-pontoons with a simple single-lane roadbed) for light horsedrawn wagons, anti-tank guns, light infantry guns, etc.

– an 8-ton military bridge about 80 meters long, (on half-pontoons with a simple single-lane roadbed) for all heavy horsedrawn wagons, light artillery and all of the division's motor vehicles.

– a 16-ton military bridge (maximum load raised to 20 tons in 1939) about 50 meters long (on full pontoons, double-strength single-lane road-bed) for the heaviest motor vehicles, heavy artillery with towing tractors, etc.

By using additional equipment, the lengths could be increased by some 2 to 5 meters. By changes in the construction, the Military Bridge Equipment B thus allowed a higher load limit, though at the cost of length, and vice versa.

These bridges generally consisted of a fixed and a floating part. On the fixed sections at both sides, the so-called "bucks" were set for support. The ramp or shore beams and transitional pieces linked the fixed with the floating section of the bridge. The ramp sections rested on the shore transoms at the shoreward end and on the first pontoons or first ferries at the other end. The floating part of the bridge consisted of complete or half pontoons, connected together to make ferries and moved into the line of the bridge, depending on the form of the individual bridge.

Erecting a bridge was usually done in the following manner:

First came a concerted examination of the area in search of approach routes, cover, riverbank and water conditions (estimated widths, current speeds), weather conditions, etc. The length, capacity and construction of the bridge for its expected loads had to be calculated and determined. In addition, the necessary work forces had to be gathered and readied. Finally, a bridgehead had to be established on the far shore, which was usually heavily defended by the enemy. After preparatory fire, and under cover of fire, engineers ferried infantry units across to the far shore in rubber boats and storm boats, usually in the morning twilight. As soon as the first opposition had been put down and a small bridgehead had been established there, the engineers built a temporary bridge of float bags on which additional forces could cross to strengthen and expand the bridgehead and take control of the riverbank. Then it was their job to ferry heavy weapons across in rubber boats or pontoon ferries and to build exit and entrance ramps of bucks and transoms. Finally they turned from ferrying men and equipment across to building a military bridge, in order to bring artillery, ammunition carriers and finally the entire division across the river.

After all pontoons were unloaded, additional ferries were built. All of these individual ferries were towed into the so-called bridge line from both sides by motorboats and storm boats and linked together.

The important and not always simple "closing" of the bridge took place approximately in the middle. Then the superstructure (a covering of planks) was put in place, and ropes were added on both sides. In about eight hours a finished bridge had been erected. Finally, entrance and exit routes had to be prepared. Engineers in the pontoons guarded the bridge and the traffic that crossed it.

The building of the bridge itself was not all there was to the job. Bridges were naturally a favorite target of the enemy, who tried to stop or delay bridge building as well as transportation, using artillery fire and air attacks. When a bridge was hit, damaged parts had to be replaced immediately and the bridge repaired as quickly as possible. Where it was necessary or advisable on account of the width of the river, several bridge columns, sometimes as many as 15, were combined from the division and the corps.

All of these military bridges were replaced as soon as possible with more permanent bridges made of materials found in the area, or damaged bridges were repaired or new permanent bridges built, so as to free the vital mobile bridge columns for new assignments, for the advances in all campaigns that continued up to 1942 constantly required new river crossings.

CHAPTER 10

The Intelligence Unit

The intelligence unit (partly motorized), with its lemon yellow service-arm color, had as its main task the preparation and maintenance of telephone and radio connections within the division, for communication between the division command and the various large troop units, thus providing for quick transmission of commands and reports. So it was necessary to set up and, if necessary, dismantle as complete a communications network as possible. When possible too (especially in defensive action), the communications connections were made double.

The intelligence unit had a total complement of 474 officers, non-commissioned officers and men, plus 103 motor vehicles, 32 motorcycles, 7 horsedrawn wagons and 52 horses. Its armament consisted of pistols and rifles plus 17 light machine guns.

As was the case with infantry weapons and artillery guns, most intelligence equipment had been put into service before 1939, so that by the beginning of the war its development was largely completed. Individual new devices or improvements were added later.

The unit (*see also* section "The Infantry Regiment – Regimental Intelligence Platoon") consisted of:
   – Unit staff
   – 1 telephone company (partly motorized)
   – 1 radio company (fully motorized)
   – 1 light intelligence column (fully motorized)

The unit staff was composed of:

Commander, adjutant, leader of intelligence operations (LdN), technical inspector, leader of the motor vehicle repair echelon, troop surgeon and paymaster (the latter also commissary officer).

The telephone company had a strength of 5/40/190. It was composed of: Company troop, 5 telephone platoons, combat, commissary and pack trains.

In the platoons were:
- 11 large telephone troops (motorized) of 1/6 each
- 6 large telephone troops (horsedrawn) of 1/8 each
- 3 medium telephone operations troops (motorized), of 2/6 each
- 2 small telephone troops (motorized) of 1/3 each

plus 22 sets of switches for field phone cable and two sets of underwater cable.

It was the telephone companies' assignment to provide the division with reliable telephone connections to its units. In the first years of the war, so-called "tree connections" ahead to the troop were built, with individual branch connections to various units, but in the often hectic forward movements of the troops, the intelligence soldiers often had no chance to do this. The situation was similar in offensives and large-scale attacks. For that reason, large-scale telephone connections were usually set up in defensive and stationary warfare.

Every member of a telephone company had to be fully trained in telephone service; he had to know how to set up telephone lines, eliminate malfunctions of all kinds and also work in the transmission shack. The company construction troops worked with single-line heavy field cable in lengths of up to 1000 meters, on cable drums. The small installing and operating troops also used single-line light field cable in 500-meter lengths, or two-line twisted heavy field cable in 300-meter lengths.

Placing heavy field cable was usually done on foot, the cable carried on the men's backs when being laid at ground level, or by means of cable forks when mounted above ground; it could also be laid from a vehicle. When single-line cable was used, the second connection was made through the ground by using ground plugs.

The installation troops also had cordless connectors by which it was possible to connect with a civilian postal network. Such lines, when available, saved valuable heavy field cable, and the installation troops also had climbing irons for telephone poles. The lines from the operating troops (the transmissions) to the participants were installed by the small telephone installation troops, the connection troops, by using double-line heavy field cable.

The operating troops had large FK 16 folding field telephone switchboard, which could be used for up to 60 participants.

At the beginning of the war, a telephone company still had two carrier frequency devices with which additional calls could be carried on an existing line. These devices were used when needed and constantly improved, so that several calls could be made on one line.

The radio company, with a complement of 5/41/197, was composed of: Company troop, 4 platoons, combat, commissary and pack trains. The platoons included:

- 3 medium radio troops b (motorized) with 100-watt transmitters, each with a complement of 2/6, on a Kfz. 61 vehicle
- 2 small radio troops c (motorized) with 30-watt transmitters, complement 1/2, on a Kfz. 17.
- 8 small radio troops a (motorized) with 5-watt transmitters, complement 1/6, on Kfz. 15 or 17
- 4 portable radio troops b (motorized) with 5-watt transmitter, complement 1/4, on Kfz. 2 or 15
- 4 portable radio troops d (motorized) with 3-watt transmitters, complement 1/2, on Kfz. 2 or 15
- 3 listening and 1 surveillance troops (intelligence reconnaissance platoon
- 1 code troop.

It was the radio company's duty to establish radio or radio/telephone connections as quickly as possible. As compared to telephone lines, radio connections had the advantages that they could be set up faster and that messages could be sent while in motion. But they had the disadvantage of being easy for the enemy to hear and jam. Radio communication was also very dependent on distance, location and atmospheric conditions. Radio telegraphy, the sending of Morse code by means of electric waves, and radiotelephones, with which one spoke into a microphone and was heard by a receiver, were also used.

Every soldier in a radio company had to know how to send and receive; he had to know the Morse alphabet, be able to send Morse code with a transmitter and receive it, and also to send code with a hand code device or the hand-operated "ENIGMA II" device. Error-free sending and receiving of Morse code up to a "speed of 100" was taken for granted by the radiomen as average performance with full concentration. Since radio transmissions could also be heard and understood by the enemy in certain areas, permanent radio positions had to be encoded before their transmission, and then decoded by the receiving troops. There were often times when the radiomen worked at encoding and decoding under highly unusual conditions. The general and technical knowledge of the troop leaders and communications personnel were above average. In the so-called operating books and radio records, all messages and times were documented, and these documents became part of the military archives.

The type of connections to be set up depended above all on the range of the transmitter that could be used for radio and radiotelephone transmission. Under normal conditions, these amounted to 200 and 70 kilometers for a 100-watt transmitter, 150 and 50 km for a 30-watt transmitter, 90 and 30 km for a 5-watt transmitter, 25 and 10 km for a b portable transmitter, and 17 and 4 km for a d portable transmitter. The portable transmitters could be set for long-, medium- and short-wave transmission.

Among these various transmitters, the portable b type served as a receiver. It was found just as often among the portable radio troops in the front lines of the infantry as in the medium and upper command staffs. With its comparatively large range of frequencies from 96.6 tp 7096 kilohertz (long, medium and short waves), this receiver could be used for long and short ranges alike. At radio positions with simultaneous connections to various other radio transmitters, several receivers of this type were often in use around the clock, in order to be able to pick up several neighboring positions at the same time (this was called radio alert). The 100-watt transmitters had a Small Machine Set C as a power source, plus a U 100 transformer powered by an Akku 12 B 105 battery. The 5-watt transmitter had the U 5 transformer with the same power source, and both transmitters could be used while underway. For this reason, Vehicles 17 and 61 each had a telescopic mast built into the vehicle, but should also be equipped with pole masts. The Kfz 17 trucks were later equipped with roof antennas. When stationary, the 5-watt transmitter was powered by a gasoline-driven emergency generator or a foot-cranked generator on a bicycle-like apparatus which a man had to operate. This device was also the power source for the small radio troop a. Both transmitters included a b receiver, which could pick up the frequencies most often used by the army, and was powered by a 90-volt anode battery and an NC 2 B 38 battery.

The portable radio devices had built-in power sources like those of the receiver b.

In the company supply train there was, interestingly enough, a battery truck with a single-axle trailer carrying Charging Set D. The truck had a workbench for minor repairs as well as cabinets for NC 2 B 38 batteries, which had to be kept charged constantly for use by the individual troops. In the trailer was Charging Set D, including six battery chargers with which batteries, including those of the motor vehicles, could be charged.

The deployment of the individual troops was limited by the ranges of their transmitters. As a rule, the medium radio troop b handled connections to the higher command posts at the rear, the small radio troop a worked forward to the regiments, independent units or neighboring units, and the portable radio troops were usually located where they were needed or where only short-time communications were required. On the basis of wave lengths, 100-watt (1500 – 250 meters) and 5-watt transmitters (316 – 96 meters) could work together, and in the borderline area of 100 to 96 meters the 5-watt transmitters could also work together with the portable radio set b (100 to 60 meters), though this was often difficult.

In practice, intelligence transmission was done exclusively by telegraph, since it had quickly been learned that the range of the available apparatus for spoken communications (telephones) did not live up to the actual requirements and conditions.

The light intelligence column consisted of:

1 car for the leader, 1 truck for telephone operating and radio equipment, 1 truck for telephone installation equipment and field cable, 1 truck as a workshop vehicle, 1 truck for other equipment and a trailer for Charging Set D (battery chargers), 1 truck with fuel.

The light intelligence column was a unit that had the job of serving not only for its own companies but also the troop intelligence units of the division. The main need was for heavy field cable on wooden drums, but light field cable and twisted heavy field cable were also needed. Just as important for the radiomen was a constant supply of charged batteries. One or two of the large devices, such as the big FK 16 folding switchboard, transmitters and receivers, and generators were supposed to be sufficient for replacement. In addition, various devices such as small folding switchboards, transmitters, transformers, hand generators, field phones, etc., had to be kept on hand. There were also the usual small supplies, from insulating tape to small tools, tubes, flashlights, etc. Necessary repairs had to be made in the workshop truck.

The soldiers of the intelligence units were only lightly armed for self-defense and did not normally fight with weapons in their hands. Their jobs included the fast and purposeful deployment of their means of intelligence, essential for efficient operation, close cooperation of all units, and transmission of commands and reports. The great success of the first war years depended in no small measure on the sure command of even the smaller troop units through telephone and radio communication. The intelligence reconnaissance platoons also performed important services by surveillance and decoding of enemy radio communications, and could often inform the division commander of the enemy's location and plans. Even in the later war years, as conditions grew tougher and tougher, the intelligence soldiers, under the most demanding conditions, in the worst weather and terrain conditions, and often enough under enemy fire, performed their duties which were important for the combat of the whole division.

CHAPTER 11

Back-Line Services

Administrative and Supply Services

An infantry division could not just march and fight; its soldiers also had to be supplied, and had to receive timely and sufficient supplies of everything they needed for their daily lives. And this was equally true of horses and motor vehicles. Among the so-called back-line services, the administrative and supply services (light blue service-arm color) carried out this work. They were subordinate to the quartermaster unit of the division under Ib. The leadership of these services included a commissariat officer, designated IVa in the division staff (see chapter "The Division Staff").

Administrative Services (Supply Services)

With a complete complement of 3 officers, 28 administrators and 195 NCO and men, they included:

    — Commissary unit with 7 administrators, 15 NCO and men, plus 1 car, 3 trucks and 1 solo motorcycle

    — Bakery company with 2 officers (including a company chief), 2 administrators, 138 NCO and men, plus 5 cars, 24 trucks (7 of them with trailers, and 5 of them with mobile field baking oven trailers), 4 solo and 2 sidecar motorcycles.

    — Butcher platoon with 1 officer, 1 administrator, 42 NCO and men, plus 1 car, 6 trucks, 1 solo and 1 sidecar motorcycle (as well as butcher companies of appropriate strength at times).

    — Field post office with 1 field postmaster, 17 administrators, plus 2 cars and 2 trucks.

All of these services were fully motorized and could fully supply a war-strength infantry division. For self-defense, the soldiers (like those of the supply services) were armed only with handguns (pistols and rifles), and each unit had one light machine gun (and later antitank weapons). To fulfill their duties, the administrative services had a variety of field equipment. As a rule, when circumstances permitted, the commissariat, bakery and butcher units worked in buildings in towns, available bakeries, slaughterhouses, etc., in order to preserve their valuable field equipment. Where such facilities could not be found, which was often the case in the vastness of Russia, the field facilities had to be set up under cover. This cost a great deal of time, and work was often done in heavy trucks with permanent box bodies. Electric power for the whole facility was produced by 15.0-kilowatt generators, which were transported on special trailers. Water tank trucks provided the great amount of water needed, almost 15,000 liters per working day. All facilities and vehicles were usually kept outside the effective range of enemy artillery. But since it could not be dug in because of its great extent, it had to be separated sufficiently and well camouflaged to avoid air attacks. To protect the soldiers, slit trenches were raised, and readiness to defend the area was maintained by constant sentries and observers, which also defended against robbery by civilians and sneak attacks by partisans.

This whole equipment and vehicle park had to be established and dismantled often, especially in mobile warfare, to be as close as possible to its own division, at a distance of 20 to 30 kilometers, which was especially difficult in the later retreating movements. Timely information as to roads, paths and bridges were thus just as important as the location of buildings or good locations for facilities.

The Commissariat

This unit was assigned by Ib to supply the units, according to their supply complements as reported daily, with the correctly calculated quantities and regular supplies from the army commissary depots and replacement commissary stores on the one hand, and the division's own bakery company and butcher platoon on the other. After the goods were picked up in cooperation with the supply company made available by the division supply leader and the appropriate columns, they were divided according to receiving certificates and distributed to the V II trains of the units at specially established commissary distribution centers, normally daily, but also for several days during moving warfare.

The soldier's normal daily ration, which was widely followed and – except in times and situations of crisis – actually distributed most of the time, included, for example:

Cold rations
– 750 grams bread
– 45 grams butter or fat
– 120 grams sausage (fresh or canned), fish (preserved), cheese
   (in tubes, etc.)

- 200 grams jam or artificial honey (delivered in pails or cans and divided)
- 7 cigarettes, 2 cigars, 1 roll of candy drops or the like.
  Warm rations
- ca. 750 grams potatoes, vegetables, baked goods, etc., with 120 grams fresh meat
- 45 grams vegetable or animal fat
- 15 grams sauces
- 8 grams bean coffee and 10 grams ersatz coffee (or tea).

The fresh meat, fat and sauces were worked into the warm food from the field kitchens, and the specified quantities of coffee and tea were also given out as field-kitchen beverages.

These commissary supplies, always calculated according to the reported strength of a unit, were provided from delivered Wehrmacht supplies and in part also from the country, depending on the season. The latter particularly included fresh and dried potatoes, baked goods, rice, shortening, barley, corn, fresh and dried vegetables, various fruits, fresh meat, soup greens, poultry, eggs, fish, fat, butter, jam, artificial honey, cheese, etc.

To provide a conception of troop consumption and thus of the achievements of the supply services, let us take the 12th Infantry as an example. The strengthened division had, for example, in the first six months of the eastern campaign (from June 22 to December 31, 1941), a strength of some 20,000 men and 5500 horses, and a total consumption of 8110 tons of food and fodder, making about 45 tons per day.

In addition to the normal cold and warm rations, the following items were also supplied during those six months:

– Drops	245,000 packages
– Dextro Energen	408,800 packages
– Chocolate	6,516 kilograms
– Dried fruits	1,735 kilograms
– Lemons	954,000 lemons
– Biscuits	444.5 kilograms
– Cigars	1,350,000 cigars
– Cigarettes	15,100,000 cigarettes
– Alcohol	98,000 liters

and much more.

Another example that might be cited is the 6th Infantry Division, whose full daily ration of food at normal strength added up to 30 tons.

Along with the daily warm and cold rations for the troops, the commissariat issued additional and special rations at irregular intervals (according to instructions and availability from oversupplied warehouses or supplied by the division itself), for example, for sickbays, hospitals, or special events or holidays, including desserts, cake and other baked goods, etc. – to say nothing of the canteen goods so popular with all the soldiers. The latter included, in addition to tobacco and alcohol (in which case three or four men had to share a bottle of cognac, wine or champagne), useful and necessary items such as toilet articles, writing implements, stationery, etc.

How mobile a commissariat had to be at all times and in all lands is shown by the example of the 6th Infantry Division: From June 22, 1941 to June 1, 1942 the trucks of Commissariat 6 covered 178,419 kilometers in the eastern campaign.

The Bakery Company

This company was specially equipped with heavy 4.5-ton trucks that towed five special trailers of Type 106, plus two water tank trucks. In these five twin-axle mobile field baking ovens, with their high smokestacks that could be folded down while on the march, a maximum of 12,000 loaves of bread per day could be baked. The baking temperature of 220 to 260 degrees was attained by a wood fire in a relatively small burning chamber at the front of each field oven, from which a system of tubes carried the warmth not only to the baking grilles but simultaneously into the ovens. These tubes were empty of air, in order to provide the special conditions for conducting heat. The sourdough system, in which a definite temperature had to be maintained while baking, was particularly important. The supplies of flour, salt and water had to be used very carefully, for 10.5 tons of flour were used every day, along with hundreds of pounds of salt and tons of water. Production could not fail if the daily portion of 750 grams of bread per man was to be provided constantly.

Along with the field baking ovens, the heavy equipment included dough dividing machines, dough kneaders, dough rolling machines, etc. The great need for water was provided for in the western countries mainly from large water sources, in the east usually from available bodies of water. In the process, doctors and veterinarians always tested its quality. The high temperatures of the baking process sterilized the water, and beyond that, the bodies of water in Russia were usually in a natural state and thus clean. The article usually baked was the well-known 1.5-kilogram gray bread generally known as "kommissbrot" (commissary bread). But the bakers were also able to produce other baked goods. When appropriate additional items were supplied, hospitals, soldiers' homes, and sometimes entire troop units were issued baked goods such as cake, Christmas cookies and the like for special occasions. When the supply of flour was delayed but grain was available, an electric mill mounted on a trailer was used to grind up to six tons of grain per day, for the mills in the country were often not in condition to provide flour or had been destroyed by the enemy. Wherever it was possible, they were repaired and put into service, and the civilian population was also supplied.

To give an example of the achievements of a bakery company, the 6th Infantry Division's Bakery Company 6 baked 2,380,000 loaves of bread from June 22, 1941 to June 1, 1942.

In the strengthened 12th Infantry Division, Bakery Company 12 baked 2,012,180 loaves of bread plus 20,000 Christmas cakes and other items in the first six months of the eastern campaign.

The Butcher Company

The butcher company was capable of slaughtering 15 cattle, 120 hogs or 240 sheep and making up to 3000 kilograms of sausage daily. As on a normal civilian farm, all animals were officially inspected by the veterinarians for trichinosis and other diseases. An auxiliary crane and a slaughtering apparatus, plus a bolt gun, guaranteed – at any location – a painless large-scale slaughtering operation. Along with the delivery of fresh meat to the field kitchens, a spice truck and a smoking truck with four smokehouse compartments were available for making sausage. Bacon slicers and sausage-stuffing machines were supplied with power from 10.0-kilowatt generators, a boiling-kettle truck allowed the preparation of boiled meats. Rotwurst, liverwurst and fleischwurst were generally produced in rotation. The animal skins were salted and sent to the rear; otherwise nothing was left but horns, hooves and eyes. Of course the natural casings acquired in slaughtering were not sufficient for sausage production; thus artificial casings were kept on hand. The production of imperishable foods was not done at all; these were provided from Wehrmacht supplies. The dampness of the air resulting from the water consumption when the butcher company was in full operation was considerable. There was always a telltale cloud of water vapor hanging over the active butcher company, which meant that the work often had to be done at night.

Two examples:

6th Infantry Division: Butcher Company 6, with 20 butcher soldiers, slaughtered 4488 full-grown cattle, 928 sheep and 2700 hogs from June 22, 1941 to June 1, 1942.

12th Infantry Division: Butcher Company 12 slaughtered 3340 cattle, 1568 hogs and 190 sheep from June 22 to December 31, 1941, and provided 333,038 kilograms of beef, 124,818 kilograms of pork and 2489 kilograms of mutton, as well as 33,854 kilograms of fresh sausage.

The production and delivery data cited here were high points that were no longer necessary as the strengths of the divisions steadily decreased. On the other hand, there was naturally a correlation between unit strength and supplies provided. The soldiers sent to the combat troops became steadily younger, and as of 1943 there were shortages of equipment and supplies that could not be made up. In the new 43rd Division, the administrative and supply services were correspondingly restructured.

In addition to the rations which the soldiers needed every day to survive, the second most important supplies were ammunition, replacement weapons and combat equipment of all kinds, in order to be able to fight. The following example shows something of the quantities that had to be delivered and issued to the troops:

5th Infantry Division – ammunition consumption in the eastern campaign, August 7-22, 1941:

Infantry ammunition	126.2 tons
Light artillery ammunition	437.4 tons = 17,496 rounds
Heavy artillery ammunition	335 tons = 5,103 rounds

The four-legged comrades also had to be supplied with fresh fodder. Each horse received a daily ration of 5 kilograms each of oats, hay and straw. With some 5400 horses in the division, this added up to 70 to 80 tons per day, a quantity that often could not be provided, what with the numbers of horses and lack of fodder.

Other than food, fodder and munitions, many other items necessary for living and fighting had to be provided in large quantities from major clothing depots, fuel depots, engineer and motor vehicle parks through Ib via the quartermaster department to the administrative and supply services.

For example, the 12th Infantry Division was supplied with the following new clothing in the first six months of the eastern campaign:

38,000 pairs of socks	7,500 pairs of trousers
12,700 shirts	5,500 combat jackets
14,700 pairs of undershorts	2,500 pairs of boots
13,000 handkerchiefs	

The winter clothing of a division in 1943-44 amounted to an average of 9000 winter combat uniforms, 1000 fur coats, 1000 fur jackets, 12,000 pairs of felt boots, 7000 sets of underwear, 8000 body belts, 10,000 pairs of mittens and much more.

And that was by no means enough – other items that had to be shipped up from major depots to the rear and distributed included pieces of equipment, medical and engineering supplies, plus material and equipment for housing and position construction, and everything from boards and planks, stoves and lamps, to the last nail.

The Field Post Office

The smallest but by no means the least important unit in the whole division was the field post office, which maintained constant contact between front and home, between the soldier and his loved ones.

The personnel in the field post offices were serving in their positions, as administrators, under a special oath. They wore the same uniform as other soldiers, but were marked by a black armband on their jackets and coats, with the silver lettering "Feldpost." They handled the daily incoming and outgoing mail and often worked under the worst of conditions, as did the government postal service in peacetime. The personnel staked their honor on moving the mail to the folks back home or delivering it to the troops as speedily as possible. Other than in times of crisis, normal mail movement between the front and home, or in the opposite direction, during the eastern campaign took about 14 days. Cards, letters and small packets of prescribed sizes, shapes and weights were moved (for example, in the summer of 1941 the weight limit for the eastern front was 1000 grams). In addition, the field post office delivered troop periodicals such as corps and army newspapers for distribution.

Many unfair negative comments about the field postal system were made in postwar years, including verbal and written allegations of censorship and snooping. Mail from the soldiers and from home was generally not censored unless there was particular reason for suspicion. According to instructions from the Field Postmaster, though, field postal personnel were required to take samples of the mail. Negative results and resulting punishment were few.

Under normal conditions the soldier could write at any time, with the exception of before or during particular events such as large-scale troop movements, concentrations on the front, offensive preparations, retreat movements, etc. At such times the postal facilities were closed for a specified time, and mail was not distributed either.

The soldier was required to write his name and rank on each piece of mail, but instead of his unit, only the applicable field post office number. To guard against espionage, no military matters could be mentioned in the mail, and small packets could contain no dangerous or perishable contents (for example, ammunition or war souvenirs – such a case once set fire to a whole wagon of field mail and destroyed it all). Mail from the front was postage-free (mail from home to the eastern front in 1941 was free up to 250 grams). This mail was stamped at the field post office with the word "Feldpost", plus date and national emblem. Although the amount of field mail grew steadily as the war went on, very little mail was lost – other than as a result of enemy action and other misfortunes – and the soldier in the primeval forests of Karelia received his mail just as reliably as the one in the Caucasus Mountains.

Very little became known of the achievements of the field postal personnel. The following can offer some indication:

In the 18th Army zone alone, during the last five months of 1942 a total of 371,100 bags of mail, holding about 3.5 million pieces of mail, were processed.

Supply Services

All of the great amounts of provisions, munitions, fodder, clothing, war materials of all kinds and other goods naturally had to be transported, moved and taken along constantly until they reached the distribution depots set up to issue them to the troops. This was the job of the division supply troops, under the command of the division supply leader (Dinafü), holding the rank of major. His staff (half of it, the other half being located at Division Staff Ib) consisted of an adjutant, z.b.V. officer, senior paymaster, column surgeon and veterinarian, 24 non-commissioned officers and enlisted men, with 24 cars, 3 trucks, 3 solo motorcycles plus 1 with a sidecar. Subordinate to the Dinafü were

– 1st to 3rd small truck columns with 3 officers (column leaders) and 90 NCO and men, with 3 cars, 33 (3-ton) trucks, 3 solo and 8 sidecar motorcycles. Each column could move a total of about 30 tons.

– 4th to 6th horsedrawn columns with 3 officers (column leaders) and 90 NCO and men, with 36 two-horse military wagons (700-kg load limit), 3 cars, 3 solo and 3 sidecar motorcycles.

– 7th fuel column with one officer (column leader) and 34 NCO and men, with one car, 11 trucks (capacity 25 cubic meters of gasoline), 1 solo and 2 sidecar motorcycles.

– Supply company with 5 officers and 240 NCO and men, with one car, 14 trucks, 1 solo and 6 sidecar motorcycles.

– Repair shop company with one officer (company leader), seven administrators or engineers, and 94 NCO and men, with 6 cars, 19 trucks (4 with trailers), 1 solo and 5 sidecar motorcycles. The company was composed of a repair-shop platoon, armorer's platoon and motor vehicle repair platoon.

– Supply trains.

The job of the columns, along with the administrative services, has already been outlined in brief; the division supply leader had the job of coordinating and regulating the work of the columns.

The supply company provided the personnel for setting up the various distribution centers, usually in the form of a distribution depot to which the supply trucks of the units were driven.

The assignments of the repair-shop company can be illustrated by an example: Repair-shop Company 6 of the 6th Infantry Division returned to operation in the first year of the eastern campaign: by the repair-shop platoon, 442 horsedrawn wagons, 54 field kitchens and 181 bicycles; the armorer's platoon repaired 1191 handguns, 699 machine guns, 171 heavy infantry weapons and 70 guns; the motor vehicle repair platoon returned to service 999 cars, 430 trucks, 787 motorcycles and 342 special vehicles.

These few examples with their statistics, similar to those of all the infantry divisions, show that the administrative and supply services could not lead a lazy "holiday camp" life, all the more so on account of the wretched climate, weather and road conditions they had to face, not to mention their need to defend themselves with their few handguns against partisan attacks or enemy troop breakthroughs in the back-line division area.

Apart from the great events, far from combat and slaughter, they naturally did their work in the hinterlands, unknown and unpraised, gaining neither medals nor renown, but without them, the soldiers at the front would not have been able to go on living and fighting. Day by day, week after week, month upon month, year after year they had to supply the front-line troops, whether advancing, holding positions or retreating, in selfless service, as best they could, with everything they needed; that was their quiet but great job, which they often had to carry out under the worst of conditions.

Medical Services

In peacetime the medical corpsmen of all ranks – the "Sanis" – were often satirized as pill-rollers and apostles of castor oil, and the song of *Sanitäatsgefreiten* (Medical Corporal) Neumann and his wondrous healing salve was only too well known. Jokes about the senior and staff surgeons were also numerous. But when things got serious, and when the men had to go to war and the fights, battles and slaughters, especially in the eastern campaign, got worse and worse, countless soldiers cried out for the "Sani", gasping and pleading, in greatest need and with greatest pain. And "Sani" soon became an honorable name for all ranks of medical corpsmen, orderlies as well as surgeons, not a few of them sacrificed their blood and their lives to save and help the sick and wounded.

The service-arm color of the soldiers in the medical corps was dark blue, and their identifying mark was a red cross armband on their left sleeve. Medical officers (surgeons) wore the same shoulder patches as other officers, plus the staff of Aesculapius.

The levels of rank, though, were different, and were as follows:
– Feldunterarzt = Oberfähnrich Oberstabsarzt = Major
– Assistenzarzt = Leutnant Oberfeldarzt = Oberstleutnant
– Oberarzt = Oberleutnant Oberstarzt = Oberst
– Stabsarzt = Hauptmann

Since the number of surgeons active in the army in peacetime was not sufficient during the war, numerous doctors were inducted from civilian life when the war began, from private practices, clinics and universities, including experts from all areas of medicine. Young doctors, newly trained in medical schools, followed them into service.

The insignia of rank for non-commissioned officers and enlisted men were like those of the other troops, but the ranks were prefixed with "Sanitäts", for example, *Sanitätssoldat, Sanitätsgefreiter,* etc. In addition, medical troops wore the staff of Aesculapius on their right sleeve. They spent half of their basic training with the troops, followed by training and testing at a medical-corps school. The medical corpsmen received their training in first aid with the troops, from the troop surgeons. Many pastors, priests, monks, etc. served with the medical corps in the war. There were no Red Cross nurses in the medical services of a division.

According to an OKH directive of May 23, 1939, according to which all Wehrmacht personnel were combatants, the officers and men of the medical services were armed, but only with pistols. According to the Geneva Convention of 1929, they had the right, and indeed the duty, to defend themselves and any persons in their care (wounded and sick) with this weapon, in case of, and for the duration of, urgent danger. All members of the sanitary services were protected by the terms of this same convention and were not allowed to be attacked, fired on or involved in combat on the ground, in the air or on the sea. Therefore they were to wear their red cross armbands clearly visible on their uniforms. The red cross also had to be displayed, visible for some distance, as a protective sign on buildings, tents, vehicles, etc. used for medical purposes, or the latter were to be marked with flags. This symbol could be used only for the care, housing and transport of wounded and sick.

The medical units were divided into the troop and division medical services.
Troop Medical Services:
Every rifle platoon (or similar unit) with a trained medical soldier.
In the company, the company headquarters troop had a medical NCO and a medical soldier, who generally worked with the battalion surgeon in combat. These medical soldiers, plus auxiliary stretcher bearers when needed, served to rescue wounded men on the battlefield. They set up nests of wounded men in the country, gave first aid and provided for further transport to the troop dressing stations of the battalions, using stretchers and other available means.

Every battalion or unit had a surgeon (Assistenz- or Oberarzt = Truppenarzt) with two medical corpsmen. This medical group set up a troop dressing station (TVP) in a suitable place during combat, using the troop's medical equipment. Here the battalion surgeon provided the first professional care such as correct bandaging, splinting and bone-setting, applying tourniquets or otherwise stopping heavy bleeding, injecting anti-tetanus serum, dosing with pain-killing or circulation medicines, providing thirst-quenchers or tonics, preparing patients for transport and filling out patient charts with information on the wound and treatment given. There was no possibility of surgery at the troop dressing stations. When on the march, the battalion surgeon carried necessary medication with him in a large medical bag. Injections and needles were kept in a small container filled with alcohol, for they could naturally not always be boiled and sterilized. This was done to prevent infection.

Among the duties of the battalion and unit surgeons in quiet times were advising the troop leader on all medical matters, taking preventive measures against the spread of disease through distribution of appropriate medicines (such as atabrine and quinine, well known to every former soldier), and supervising the hygienic measures in dwelling areas (including kitchens, toilets, etc.), as well as instruction and health warnings when necessary.

Among the troop surgeons there was also the regimental surgeon, usually an *Oberstabsarzt* or *Oberfeldarzt*. He supervised the battalion surgeons, the medical facilities in the companies, battalions and regiment, arranged for transport of wounded and sick men, as well as for supplies of medical materials, and maintained direct contact with the division surgeon. In times of combat, for example, the regimental surgeon could also utilize the regimental musicians as auxiliary stretcher bearers and medical care personnel.

Division Medical Services:
At this point the medical services of the division began their activities, their main task being thoroughgoing care and, when necessary, further transport of wounded or sick soldiers in the entire division area. It is noteworthy that these services were not included in a single unit and thus had no commander or staff. The individual units were always led by medical officers. The direct and highest officer of all medical services was the division surgeon (*see also* section "The Division Staff"), who also regulated the movements and actions of the medical services.

The medical services of the division consisted of a full complement of some 16 medical officers (surgeons) and 600 men:
– 1st medical company (horsedrawn), with 5 medical officers, 2 administrators, 160 NCO and men (as medical ranks and soldiers, stretcher bearers, care givers, drivers, etc.), with 17 horsedrawn vehicles, 45 horses, 1 car, 1 truck, 1 solo and 1 sidecar motorcycle, 1 bicycle echelon
– 2nd medical company (motorized), with 184 medical officers, ranks and soldiers, with 4 cars, 21 trucks, 2 solo and 4 sidecar motorcycles.

Every medical company was commanded by a *Stabsarzt* or *Oberstabsarzt* as company chief and consisted of the leader's group (chief surgeon and surgeons) and three platoons. Later in the course of the war, a 4th platoon (delousing platoon) was added. In addition, in the Polish and western campaigns of 1939 and 1940 there was also a dog echelon, with dogs trained for medical work at the Military Medical Dog School in Berlin.

The 1st platoon of every medical company, led by a specialist, was the stretcher-bearer platoon. It helped the medical orderlies and auxiliary stretcher bearers of the troop in searching the battlefield for wounded men. In action, the platoon also set up wagon stops (occupied by a medical rank) to take charge of wounded or sick men from the troop dressing stations and other medical stations and transport them by horsedrawn or motor vehicles to a main dressing station (HV-Platz). In moving warfare this platoon also was in charge of collecting areas for wounded and sick and their transportation farther to the rear.

The 2nd platoon was the main dressing station platoon. It was led by a surgeon and had the duty of setting up a main dressing station some three kilometers behind the front (beyond the range of heavy infantry weapons). An HV-Platz could be set up in large tents (with operating, treatment and care tents), and in immobile warfare also in safely covered bunkers without dependence on permanent buildings, though the latter were also preferred if available. This 2nd platoon had a complete operating facility packed in portable containers, with full lighting and a light field X-ray machine as well as appropriate post-operative care facilities for soldiers. The platoon could form one or two operation squads; an OP squad consisted of: 1 surgeon, 1 or 2 doctors to assist him, 1 instrument handler, 2 anesthetists, 2 sterilizers, additional surgical assistants and a care group.

The 3rd platoon of every medical company, likewise commanded by a surgeon when possible, was the replacement platoon and carried reserve equipment and materials. The platoon provided necessary extra personnel for the other two platoons and helped to set up collecting stations for slightly wounded or sick men.

In every medical company there was also a field pharmacy with all necessary bandaging materials and medicines. The pharmacy was commanded by an army pharmacist (administrator) and an assistant pharmacist (medical rank). The so-called "Pharmacy Set B" was carried by a 3.5-ton truck.

In addition, every medical company had a dental station with a dentist and an assistant. Every company also had a paymaster, writing room and field kitchen with kitchen personnel. Of them, at least one cook had to be capable of preparing special rations for patients. Both medical companies had the personnel and equipment to set up two main dressing stations. At the main dressing stations the wounded men were examined, new dressings applied and minor treatment given immediately. But the surgeons on duty there were also capable of performing the most urgent and difficult operations successfully (for example, to treat abdominal wounds, head wounds, perforated lungs, or badly injured limbs), and to treat severely injured or sick men, who could then be housed, treated and prepared for further transport. But because of the great influx of wounded men, especially in times of heavy combat, the main dressing stations could only be transitional stations to the field hospitals.

Also part of the medical services was a field hospital (motorized) with an Oberstabsarzt as its chief, five surgeons, four administrators and 66 men as its medical personnel, plus 6 cars, 11 trucks and 2 motorcycles with sidecars.

Field hospitals were set up at least 25 to 30 kilometers behind the front, usually in connection with existing hospitals, schools or other suitable large buildings. In addition, there were individual operating, treatment and care tents as used at the main dressing stations. Here the emphasis was on specialized treatment of seriously wounded or sick men, particularly by surgeons or physicians specializing in internal medicine, and on keeping them there for a limited time. A field hospital was intended to provide treatment and lodging for some 200 to 300 patients, who could be placed in beds or on straw sacks, for some time, with ongoing treatment and ample care. Field hospital personnel were also active in providing drinking water, the hospital having its own drinking-water preparation facility, and in combating vermin and epidemics (delousing station). Special temporary isolation stations were set up for infectious diseases such as dysentery and typhus.

The field hospitals, though, were too insufficiently staffed, and in the course of moving warfare their purpose, in comparison to that of the main dressing stations, disappeared more and more. Then too, since the field hospitals often had to be transferred, patients who were actually in no condition to be transported had to be sent farther back (*see also* section "The New Infantry Division 43").

Finally, the medical services of a division also included two ambulance columns, commanded by an *Oberleutnant* or *Leutnant* and divided into three platoons each, each platoon with 40 men and 12 ambulances popularly known as "Sankas", plus two cars and 8 sidecar motorcycles.

The ambulance platoons were also independent units directly subordinate to the division surgeon, who regulated their use. The platoons had the duty of transporting wounded or sick men from troop or main dressing stations and similar areas to field hospitals or other back-line hospitals, to hospital platoons, medical aircraft or hospital ships. As needed, they were they were deployed to focal points from so-called ambulance parks, or temporarily detailed to the battalion and regimental surgeons to transport wounded or sick men.

When these vehicles were not sufficient or were hindered by weather or terrain conditions, a great number of other means of transporting patients were used, of which only a few can be named here. In the eastern campaign the light Panje wagons were often used, filled with straw and covered with a tarpaulin, providing a fairly comfortable ride even for longer trips. In the winter, similarly equipped sleds became indispensable means of transportation. Akjas also provided good service.

Reports on the construction and readiness for service of main dressing stations and field hospitals were sent to the division surgeons, who passed them on.

A short example of the significance of the medical services and their facilities within a division: Aside from the less serious cases handled among the troops, in 1942-43 some 47.7% of the sick and wounded men sent to the field hospitals returned to the troops, ready for active service again.

They were always there, the men of the medical services, always ready for action and with a strong desire to help under any conditions. The medical orderlies and stretcher bearers often rescued the wounded in the midst of enemy fire and gave first aid during combat. The ambulance drivers were underway day and night, usually on the worst roads, to bring back, as quickly as possible, the wounded and sick entrusted to them. Like them, the doctors and assisting personnel worked ceaselessly at the troop and main dressing stations and field hospitals, doing their duty under the worst conditions and on the verge of collapse, until the last wounded man was treated. Hundreds of thousands of German soldiers owe their health and life to the doctors and medical corpsmen.

Veterinary Services

The task of the veterinary services was to assure the mobility of the various units that used saddle horses and horsedrawn wagons, and thus to keep the horses healthy, treat wounded and sick animals, and provide care of all kinds for the whole complement of horses in the division, numbering more than 5000 saddle and draft horses.

The regimental and battalion veterinarians of the infantry regiments, the unit veterinarians of the artillery regiments, the engineer battalions, the reconnaissance and intelligence units and the back-line services, as well as the veterinary companies, were directly subordinate (through their commanders) to IVc of the division staff (*see also* section "The Division Staff").

The regimental, battalion and unit veterinarians, so to speak, formed the backbone of the veterinary service, for they were located right with the troops and thus on the spot where the horses were. Among their tasks were checking and relief during exhausting marches, providing fodder, keeping horseshoes in good condition, finding places to keep the horses, and building stables in static warfare, recognizing diseases and epizootics in their early stages, separating wounded and sick horses and sending them away, etc. Horse inspection in the units served as a regular check of the health and care of the animals. In the same way, the veterinary officer regularly supervised the drivers and other unit personnel who worked with the horses. The blacksmiths under the master smith helped him in his work.

There were about thirty "apprentices, journeymen and masters" active in a division as veterinary officers, wearing the carmine red service-arm color and the vertically entwined snakes without the staff of Aesculapius. The veterinarians in the war were, like the officer corps of the troops, mainly reserves who had been called up, in other words, practicing veterinarians from rural areas, a fact that was of much benefit to the great numbers of animals and the soldiers who worked with them. Inevitably, some of the approximately 30 veterinary officers were in hospital, on furlough or detailed elsewhere from time to time, so that it was often not very simple to accomplish all of their varied tasks. For that reason, field under-veterinarians who had not yet been approved were sometimes used. The levels of rank ranged from *Oberfähnrich* to Major (*Feldveterinär* = Leutnant, *Feldoberveterinär* = Oberleutnant, *Stabsveterinär* = Hauptmann, *Oberstabsveterinär* = Major).

A *Veterinary Company* consisted of:
1 company chief (*Stabsveterinär*), 6 veterinary officers (including three echelon leaders), 1 administrator, 24 non-commissioned officers, 203 enlisted men, 88 horses, 21 horsedrawn wagons, 1 car, 9 trucks, 1 solo and 2 sidecar motorcycles.

The company was made up of:
– Collecting echelon with several veterinary officers, transport vehicles and veterinary equipment for setting up horse collection centers where wounded and sick animals usually received their first adequate treatment. Every animal sent to a veterinary hospital took with him a patient chart that was attached to its mane or tail and included information on the reason for sending it and the treatment to date.
– Hospital echelon (commanded by the company chief) with one veterinarian and one under-veterinarian. This echelon looked for a safe place to set up a veterinary hospital when possible, including facilities for unavoidable operations and further treatment – and when possible, transfer to army veterinary hospitals. In addition, horses suspected of having contagious diseases were isolated and given special treatment here.
– Supply echelon with one *Oberveterinär* to handle cured horses and those that were transferred from army remount stations or army veterinary hospitals. These animals were sent on to the troops. In addition, this echelon was responsible for supplying veterinary medicines, bandages,

blacksmithing equipment, etc.

Normally every company, battery or unit had a blacksmith or black-smith NCO. In the battalions and similar units, and in the veterinary companies there were master blacksmiths (*Beschlagmeister*), and in the regiments, *Oberbeschlagmeister*. The significance of this blacksmithing personnel was made clear by their own activity emblem in the form of a horseshoe. The blacksmiths proved to be thoroughly dependable, indispensable helpers in the veterinary service, and often pitched in as veterinary assistants. They often undertook the first aid and care of sick and wounded animals.

It is not generally known today that the German Army of 1939 – and the situation did not change significantly through 1945 – was, particularly in the infantry divisions, up to 90% horsedrawn rather than motorized. The watchword when the Wehrmacht was being expanded was not "horse" or "motor", but "horse and motor." Thus it happened that the German field army of 1939, aside from some modernizations and motorized or armored divisions, went into the Second World War just as it had gone into the first, overwhelmingly mounted and horsedrawn. And this was not a disadvantage, especially in the course of the eastern campaign with the climate, weather and terrain that prevailed there.

This gave the veterinary service its importance, for without a sufficient, healthy and capable complement of horses, by far the greatest part of the infantry divisions would have been unable to march out of the unloading stations after being transported by rail; the infantrymen themselves could have marched, but without field kitchens, supply trains, ammunition vehicles, artillery, commissary columns and the like.

When even the motorized vehicles failed in the eastern campaign, the horsedrawn wagons became the only means of transportation.

The War Horse

The scene that looked so old-fashioned at the beginning of World War II, more reminiscent of the old army of World War I than a new, modern German army, was that of soldiers marching on foot and the long columns of horsedrawn guns and wagons of the infantry divisions, and in the eastern campaign at the latest, it proved to be an advantage not striven for, to be sure, but of incalculable value.

For during the summer months the engines of motor vehicles were eaten by sand and dust, in the spring and fall, whole columns of motor vehicles were stuck in the mud, and in the snowy winters motor traffic often came to a complete stop; the horse always came through.

In no war in world history were more horses put to use than in World War II. According to budgeting statistics, when the war began in 1939 the number of horses and mules (for the mountain troops) in the German Army was 573,000. By 1940 there were already 771,000 animals.

In the summer of 1941, shortly after the eastern campaign began, the number of horsedrawn infantry divisions rose to 119, the number of animals included some 88% of all active divisions and already numbered almost a million war horses in action.

They suffered great losses in the terrible Russian winter of 1941-42. From December 1, 1941 to March 15, 1942, 179,600 horses were lost, usually to cold and hunger, while only 20,000 horses could be replaced in the same period. Further replacements of 129,000 horses reached the army in the east by May 1, 1942 to make up for the heavy losses, including some 60,000 that had to be led over distances up to 1000 kilometers during winter marches. But as the failure of numerous motor vehicles made the needs of horsedrawn units increase even more, a further 118,000 horses had to be provided in the occupied eastern territories. Beyond that, the troops themselves commandeered many captured horses, including native Panje horses. Thus the numbers of horses and pack animals, despite further high losses, could be increased to 1,380,000 by 1943.

In all, there were about three million horses and mules that saw service from 1939 to 1945. 1.7 million of them were lost, and only a very few of the rest saw their homeland again, as they were seized by the victors.

These are the official figures, as far as is known. The unofficial figures cannot be determined but were surely much higher.

As for the "non-budgetary" animals, particularly the Russian Panje horses, more and more of these light horses had to be put into service, though it was not planned,when the need for army horses could by no means be met during the course of the eastern campaign. They were very tractable, rugged, insensitive to heat and cold, and very placid. But since they naturally had less physical strength, they could draw only light burdens and could not be used as draft horses for the artillery, heavy weapons and wagons.

Horses – they were always there, these four-legged army buddies, in the oppressive heat of summer and the frosts of winter, in streaming rain and deep mud. Silently, uncomplaining, they pulled and dragged their heavy burdens of guns and wagons for hundreds and thousands of kilometers until they collapsed in harness from exhaustion, lay dying along the road, and a merciful bullet put an end to their suffering.

Horses – they galloped in fear, whinnying under enemy fire and air attacks, until they had to lay down their equine lives.

Horses – they fell victim to icy cold without sufficient stables, or to hunger because even the most capable and caring drivers could not provide enough fodder.

Horses – to the last of their strength, they were the good, never-failing helpers of the soldiers, their best and truest comrades.

The horses were not forgotten in any of the divisional histories that appeared after the war. Here are a few notable excerpts:

45th Infantry Division, Eastern Campaign:
> "It is certain that we learned to know and appreciate the value and significance of the horse very particularly in Russia. Whether in the sand and swamp or in the deep mud where motor vehicles stuck fast beyond salvation, when motors failed in Siberian cold and wheels could get no grip on ice-covered slopes in uneven country – the horse could always be relied on most to get through and was often our last hope . . . Man and horse were always close friends."

83rd Infantry Division, Eastern Campaign:
> "Our friend the horse shall not be forgotten in our thoughts of our fallen, wounded and missing comrades. Loyal and dependable, it always did its work under the worst conditions and privations."

98th Infantry Division, Eastern Campaign:
> "Without the little, unprepossessing Panje horses and their wagons and sleighs, our whole supply system would have come to a stop in the winter of 1941-42."

The Volunteers

The author considers it an honor to remember soldiers who were actually not soldiers and never appeared in any war news or statistics, whose real names were scarcely ever known, and of whom one heard nothing more after the war – yet their presence and quiet efforts later relieved the hard-fighting troops, especially of the supply trains and back-line services. We do not speak here of the various armed local units and so-called eastern troops. We speak here of the Russian volunteers in the service of the German Wehrmacht, as they were called officially, known less impressively but concisely and familiarly as "Hiwi" to the soldiers. They were not recruited, not ordered, not forced into service – they simply came and were there, as prisoners, turncoats or civilians. What they had in common was that they all had their nose full of the Red Army, and since men were lacking throughout the troops as early as 1942, one or another of these Russians were put to work carrying ammunition, bearing stretchers, etc. They stayed and received food and lodging, which was most vital to them in the war. How such a thing came about is recorded in the history of the 198th Infantry Division:

"Many prisoners volunteered for service with our troops, partly from bitterness toward the Soviet government that had driven them into the fire, partly to get out of prison camp. These volunteers were a help to our troops. They had suffered heavy losses in the last days and weeks, and once again men had to be drawn from the supply trains. Now 'Hilfswillige' could perform supply services, bringing rations forward and taking wounded men back. And a remarkable thing happened: These shaggy ex-Red Army men, who had fought bitterly against us just a short time ago, generally proved to be capable helpers. As long as they were treated decently, they behaved reliably, with scarcely any exceptions, and gained our respect and recognition."

At the beginning, the volunteers usually went on wearing their Soviet uniforms, and sometimes civilian clothes, but gradually they received parts of German uniforms. Their only identifying mark was at first a white armband with the lettering "Deutsche Wehrmacht."

This presence of Russians necessarily became more and more familiar in the German units as their shortage of their own personnel increased, so that after some initial misgivings from "above", these former Russian soldiers and civilians became recognized helpers who voluntarily agreed to perform service within the framework of the Wehrmacht, and without weapons at that. They now became officially used interpreters, drivers, horse and wagon tenders, stretcher bearers and helpers of other kinds, thus making more combat soldiers available for the troops. This use of volunteers slowly took on definite form. The basis of it was set by the Org. Abt. of the OKH in the spring of 1942. The volunteers also received particular emblems gradually. On the usual German uniform they wore dark green collar patches of Russian type with a white central stripe, as well as dark green shoulder patches with red borders, and a blue and red cockade without a national emblem on their caps. There were also appropriate lower ranks corresponding to the German ones.

What sort of a role these volunteers played in the later years of the war is emphasized, for example, by a strength report of the 18th Army on June 1, 1944, in which a specific reference to the volunteers was made – Actual strength: 195,303 soldiers, 13,560 volunteers – Lacking: 3269 soldiers, 10,659 volunteers.

There was, though, no predetermined, organized integration of the volunteers into the infantry divisions. The only factors were the initiative of the individual unit commander and the developing feeling of mutual trust. In the end there was scarcely a division that did not include several hundred volunteers in its ranks. No precise numbers were available during the war, though the total number must have been between 150,000 to 200,000.

With very few exceptions, the "Hiwis" were capable, dependable, willing, honest, satisfied and often touchingly thankful for any recognition. In contrast to the armed "eastern troops", where there were often mutinies, front changes and the like, volunteers very seldom left the troop with which they felt increasingly at home. Typical of so many of them is this quotation from an open letter which the Russian volunteer Nshan Mraktschian wrote to the Chief of the 9th Company of Regiment 98 in the summer of 1943:

"Herr Chef! I, an Armenian war prisoner, have now worked in your company for quite a long time. I want to thank you for the friendship with which I have been treated, as have the other Russian war prisoners (in the Company the men call me Nathan) . . ."*

The German soldiers and the Russian "Hiwis" developed a notably good relationship to each other, and the Ivans, Feodors, Pyotrs, Vassilis and whatever their names were always felt like part of the unit and remained loyal to it to the end. Nothing is known of their further fate. As soon as they fell into Soviet hands at the end of the war, liquidation or at least prison camp and forced labor were certain.

The Division Chaplain

Those who were never mentioned in Nazi propaganda and press reports should likewise have a chapter dedicated to them.

There were already Wehrmacht chaplains in peacetime, plus civilian pastors as local chaplains of various large garrisons and bases. Every active infantry division officially had two military chaplains of different denominations to serve the troops spiritually. With the constant new founding of divisions once the war began, the number of pastors naturally was no longer sufficient, and numerous pastors from civilian life were called into service as chaplains, particularly for the field army.

By order of the OKH on October 24, 1939, there were separate service instructions for chaplains. According to them, the work of field chaplains was to be done from then on by so-called "*Kriegspfarrer*" (war pastors) of the Catholic and Protestant faiths. The previously active Wehrmacht chaplains who served as war pastors among the troops retained their peacetime title of "*Wehrmachtsgeistliche*." The civilian clergymen entering the field army were officially designated "Kriegspfarrer" and were given this position as Wehrmacht administrators for the duration of the war, unless revoked.

An infantry division at war strength thus received two war chaplains, one Catholic and one Protestant. The division commander, to whose staff the war chaplains belonged, was their only direct military superior officer. Officially, all war chaplains were subordinate to the Wehrmacht field bishop of their denomination in Berlin as their direct superior.

The war chaplains of the army, generally called "division pastors" by the troops, wore the same uniform as the troops in the field. It consisted of long field-gray trousers or riding breeches and an officer's jacket though without shoulder patches or insignia of rank, but with embroidered silver collar panels with violet backgrounds. They did not wear the Schiffchen or field cap, but rather the peacetime peaked cap with silver cord and violet piping on the edge. On the cap, between the national emblem and the rosette, was a small cross in Gothic style for Catholic

---

*A copy of the original is in the author's possession.

and in simple form for Protestant chaplains. There was also a red cross armband on the upper left sleeve of the jacket or coat (like that of the medical units), but with a violet middle stripe and a large silver cross in the denominational form, hanging on a chain around the neck, normally placed between the buttons of the jacket, and only worn hanging on the chest for official acts and other clerical occasions. A belt of the officers' type completed the uniform.

The only parts of the uniform that gave an indication of rank were the collar panels and the silver uniform buttons or piping (up to Heeres-Oberpfarrer). The forms of the crosses differentiated the two denominations. For special events such as services, masses, etc., the Catholic chaplain put on his vestment and surplice over his jacket or coat. The chaplain's only equipment was a gas mask, or in special cases also a steel helmet. The war chaplains were the only fully unarmed soldiers in the entire division; they were not allowed to carry any weapons.

The Catholic war chaplain was equipped with a field pack, the Protestant with a field case, to carry the mass and altar objects needed for services. And since everything had to be in order for war chaplains too, each was officially supplied with 100 field hymnals. Uniform supplying of the troops on the front with religious texts was done through the field bishops according to lists issued by the OKH.

According to war strength instructions, an acolyte stood beside a Catholic chaplain and a sexton beside a Protestant to assist them, but soldiers from the troops often volunteered to serve as acolytes and helpers in religious services. For mobility, the two chaplains shared a car, or when possible, two saddle horses or motorcycles with sidecars. The IIa of the division was responsible for all their needs (*see also* section "The Division Staff").

The two war chaplains were also the only members of the whole division who made their plans of action, did their duties and spent their time without being ordered, though they naturally followed instructions from the division commander or the wishes of the various unit commanders in particular situations, but otherwise they were responsible and obligated only to their faith and conscience. The chaplains were usually at the division staff quarters, where news, instructions and requests could reach them. Beyond that, they could do their job better the more fully mobile they were and the more often they could go to the troops and share their lives on the march, at rest, in the trenches, before attacks or wherever else the troops were, and this was basically the same for both chaplains. It was only natural that despite their different beliefs, the best understanding prevailed between them and they helped each other when they could. For example, it was customary that, on days of major combat, the division chaplains would agree mutually that one of them would be at the main dressing station of the 1st medical company and the other at the 2nd medical company or the field hospital.

The originally negative attitude of many division commanders and other officers and men toward the chaplains changed more and more as the burdens of the war, physical and spiritual alike, grew ever heavier, especially as the two war chaplains, as happened in almost all cases, took their manifold activities in the large realm of the division very seriously, often under the most difficult conditions and situations.

Their activities began with the larger solemn occasions, with masses and general absolution as well as communion before major battles, in which whole troop units – although participation was always voluntary – often appeared almost to the last man, down to the spiritual care of individual small units, wounded and sick men. Religious services with confession and communion or prayer meetings were also held behind the front when the opportunity appeared, and the soldiers took part, to the extent that it was possible for them, particularly in back-line dwelling areas, hospitals and the like. In addition, the chaplains brought their spiritual and humanitarian services to the foremost lines, sought out the soldiers in their trenches, support points and bunkers, to talk and pray with them in their deep sorrows, cares and fears. At the main dressing stations and field hospitals they offered physical help as well as moral support in the treatment and care of the wounded and sick, sent letters home for them, provided bibles for them (this was expressly stated in their service instructions), spoke words of consolation and hope, and sent letters of sympathy to the loved ones of the dead (after official notice had been sent). Not the least of their services was the sad duty of officiating at the burials and funerals of those who had fallen, when circumstances allowed. and often of working together with the graves officer of the division and assisting him in his duties. Later the office of the graves officer was fully united with that of the two war chaplains. They now had the tasks of uniting individual graves to form larger military cemeteries, planning and setting up cemeteries along with their assistants and detailed soldiers, and particularly of keeping precise information as to grave locations and lists of the fallen. Certain forms had to be filled out by each unit for each fatality, including not only personal information on the dead man but also precise data as to the date, location and cause of death. These reports were sent to the division chaplains, registered, and sent on to the Wehrmacht information office in Berlin.

Despite all the Nazi writings with which the troops were supplied, as well as the later Nazi command officers, more and more soldiers recognized the selfless help, the consolation and support afforded by the war chaplains during the course of the war, and the news that "our chaplain is coming!" always ran through an army position like wildfire. Or if his head suddenly appeared in the low doorway of a smoky bunker. He did not merely bring his prayer books and hymnals along, but also a few cigarettes, packages of tobacco or chocolate.

The war chaplains regarded themselves as part of the troops and members of their divisions. They shared victory and defeat with the soldiers and served the officers and men not only as spiritual clergymen but likewise as understanding and helpful comrades, gaining great respect and gratitude. They were underway in their cars or motorcycles on hot, dusty roads in midsummer marches, they rode their horses through the deep mud of country lanes in the spring and fall, and drove their Panje sleighs through the icy air of winter. They were present in attack or retreat, stayed with the troops in pockets or encirclements, and often enough went with them into imprisonment, never to return.

Those who had survived everything returned after the war had ended and returned to their civilian clerical work, silent and unnamed.

The Division Staff

The division staff "ruled" over all the previously named units. The division commander (originally a general of the infantry or a lieutenant general, later in the war also a major general) was the leader of the division within the framework of the superior command area (army corps) that gave him his orders, instructions and assignments, and was responsible for the total condition of his division.

The division staff consisted of individual specialists who were responsible to the division commander in all their areas and subjects.

The whole division staff had a complement of 98 officers and men. With 29 motor vehicles, 2 buses and 17 motorcycles, it was (except for saddle horses) fully motorized, but only armed with handguns such as pistols, rifles and two light machine guns.

The staff was composed of three main groups:
1. *Command Unit*
(Command Ia, deputy Ic), with the Ia, Ic, O1, O3, 1st and 2nd interpreters.

– The Ia, at the rank of *Oberstleutnant* i.G. (in the General Staff) was the 1st General Staff officer in the division. He dealt with everything that involved the individual units in command and tactical terms, including troop leadership, training, organization, transport, housing, air-raid protection, evaluation of experience, etc. He presented possibilities of battle conduct to the division commander, worked out commands, and represented the commander in his absence.

– The O1 (1st Assistant Adjutant), usually a Major or *Hauptmann*, was the assistant to the 1a. Among his duties were the preparation of maps and the war diary. He was also responsible for structuring and strengthening all units in the division, and for contact with neighbor units.

– The Ic, at the rank of Hauptmann i.G., was the 3rd General Staff officer. As defense officer he handled all matters that concerned the enemy and, on the basis of interrogation of prisoners, surveillance of enemy radio and other communications, information from local inhabitants, etc., and evaluation of all information, provided the necessary data on the strength, structure, movements and intentions of the enemy. These data, as exact as possible, and important information formed the foundation for evaluation of the enemy, tactical considerations and decisions by the division commander and Ia. The Ic was likewise responsible for providing maps of enemy positions, defensive actions (espionage, sabotage, enemy propaganda), surveillance and secrecy in the division area, particularly in the telephone, radio and field postal services, and finally for the discipline and spiritual guidance of the troops.

    – The O3 (3rd Assistant Adjutant), at the rank of *Oberleutnant*, and one or two interpreters, were provided to assist the 1c. Subordinate to the above were the division map unit, under the command of an *Oberleutnant*. The map unit included a printing platoon for map production and duplication, utilization of captured maps through German overprints, production of shot tables for the artillery, etc.

Attached to the command unit were the division artillery leader (commander of the artillery regiment), the division engineer leader (commander of the engineer battalion), and the division intelligence leader (commander of the intelligence unit) for the action and use of their units within the framework of the division. During marches, attack and retreat fighting, the command unit formed an ad hoc command echelon that was located as far forward as possible (the motto was: "Command from the front"). It consisted, for example, of the division commander, the O1 and artillery leader in a personnel car, a radio truck and several motorcycle messengers.

2. *Adjutanture* (Command IIa, deputy IIb) with IIa, IIb, III, registration, commandant of the staff quarters.

    – The IIa, at the rank of Major, was the division adjutant. He and his personnel handled matters of replacements, personnel matters of the officers (promotions, decorations, furloughs, punishment) as well as war rolls and rosters, and lists of losses.

    – The IIb, at the rank of Hauptmann, had the same duties, but as applied to non-commissioned officers and enlisted men. He was also in charge of activities in the orderly room and supervised secretaries, clerks, etc.

    – III consisted of the division court-martial with a judge advocate and a notary. Also taking part in court cases as assessors were an officer of the division staff, usually IIa or IIb, and another of the same rank as the defendant. An officer of the division staff with legal training was made available for the defense of the accused. The court-martial, sometimes criticized during the war out of ignorance, often deliberately after the war, was responsible for trying all serious crimes, misdeeds and punishable acts that could not be handled by superior officers in the usual disciplinary manner, and this applied to all soldiers and officers up to the rank of *Hauptmann* (higher ranks had to answer to higher courts). These crimes and punishable offenses included unauthorized absence from the troop, military disobedience, refusal to obey orders in the face of the enemy, neglect of duty, self-mutilation, theft of Wehrmacht property, treason, sabotage, plundering, rape, robbery and murder of civilians. Punishment ranged from imprisonment (detention for officers) or prison camp (punishment companies) to death. The lighter penalties imposed by the courts-martial were usually served as front duty within the division, the more serious cases in field correctional facilities. The court also had the power to try the civilian population of the division area, who could be charged in particular with espionage, sabotage, hostile acts, support of partisans, etc. How infrequently the courts-martial imposed and actually carried out sentences of death, as opposed to reports that appeared in postwar times, is shown by official statistics:

In the entire German Army, from September 26, 1939 to January 31, 1945, 12,245 death sentences were passed and about 6000 were carried out. This amounted to 0.2% of the field army's average strength of some three million men. Crass examples from the last months of the war are not typical of the whole war, nor are their numbers known.

– The registry, with notaries for incoming and outgoing commands, secret command matters, keeping records, obtaining office supplies, etc.

– The commandant of the staff quarters was a Hauptmann of the division staff. He was responsible for the establishment of the division staff quarters (to which the entire command unit normally belonged), lodging and food for the members of the division staff, security by staff sentries, camouflage, cover and air-raid protection, maintenance of staff cars, assignment of duty officers, etc. As company chief, he was responsible for the supervision and welfare of all non-commissioned officers and men on and off duty, including the motorcycle messenger platoon of the staff. The command unit and adjutanture had a combined strength of seven officers, three administrators, 29 NCO and men, with 18 motor vehicles (two of them buses, one for the Ia, one for the map unit) and 14 motorcycles.

3. *Quartermaster Unit* (Command Ib, deputy O2) with Ib, O2, Ib/WuG, Ib/Kfz, IVa, IVb, IVc, IVd, IVz, with a complete strength of twelve officers, eight administrators, 29 non-commissioned officers and men, with 13 motor vehicles and 3 motorcycles. It included:
　　– Ib with 5 officers, 5 NCO and man, 2 cars

– IVa with 5 administrators, 3 NCO and men, 2 cars
– IVb with 2 officers, 3 NCO and men, 1 car
– IVc with 2 officers, 2 NCO, 1 car
– IVd with 2 administrators, 2 men and 1 car. Half the staff of the division supply leader was detailed to it.

The quartermaster unit was the division's supply center. It was commanded by Ib.
– The Ib, at the rank of a Major i.G., was the second General Staff officer in the division. He was responsible for supplying the whole division, as well as for sending supplies such as munitions, rations, fodder, clothing, etc. forward and sending wounded men, prisoners, leftovers, etc. backward. He always had to be informed of the position and intentions of the division command, in order to make anticipatory suggestions for supplying the troops and utilizing the back-line services. Also, among his duties were the deployment and movement of the supply trains, construction of facilities, traffic regulation and air- raid protection in back-line areas, production of maps for use in supplying, etc.
The Ib was responsible for informing the division commander of all important matters. With the quartermaster of the superior corps and, when necessary, the chief quartermaster of the army, he handled all permanent supply problems directly. At his side stood the so-called "*Fachbearbeiter*", who – regardless of their ranks – received their instructions from the Ib. These specialists always had to stay up to date in their areas and give the Ib anticipatory suggestions for the utilization of their services and for supplying. They gave their instructions in the form of suggested commands for the Ib, who harmonized them and gave the "special instructions" for the division.
– The O2 was the second assistant adjutant and assistant of the Ib. Above all, he handled the organization of back-line services.
– The Ib/WuG (Waffen und Geräte = weapons and equipment), at the rank of *Hauptmann*, was responsible for the replacement, supply and maintenance of weapons, ammunition and equipment of all kinds, with the exception of engineer, intelligence, medical and veterinary equipment (here the appropriate commanders or IVb and IVc were in charge). There were further duties such as moving weapons and equipment that needed repair, removal of empty containers, establishment of ammunition and captured materials distribution centers, testing new weapons, ammunition and equipment for field readiness, and instructing the troops in the use of newly introduced items.
– The Ib/Kfz was the division engineer, at the rank of *Hauptmann*. His field of responsibility included the replacement and supply of motor vehicles, tires, spare parts and fuel, removal of motor vehicles in need of

repair and old materials, setting up fuel distribution centers, utilization of the workshop company and the fuel column, traffic regulation and discipline.

– The IVa as the division assistant adjutant, at the rank of *Intendantur-rat*. He was the superior troop officer of all administrative and supply services. His work area included the supply of all troop units with rations, fodder, clothing, equipment, housekeeping needs, canteen goods, etc. Also among his duties were the purposeful use of administrative services, the establishment of distribution centers for food and other needs and of field post-office collection and distribution centers, obtaining and efficiently using commissary articles from the country, movement of commissary supply trains, etc.

– The IVb, at the rank of *Oberfeldarzt* or *Oberstarzt*, was the division surgeon. He was simultaneously the troop commander of the medical services and superior officer of the medical personnel in the whole division. His area of duty included the movement and focal-point deployment of the medical companies, the ambulance platoons and the field hospital facilities for the supplying and transport of wounded and sick men in the entire division area, further transport of the wounded to the rear, health regulations and hygienic measures for the troops as well as the civilian population, action against epidemics, supervision and checking of the health situation, replacement of medical materials and equipment.

– The IVc was the division veterinarian, at the rank of *Oberstabsveter-inä*. He was the superior troop officer of the veterinary services and the specialist in charge of the whole division's veterinary and blacksmithing personnel. His realm encompassed the most practical use, movement and deployment of the veterinary company, horse replacement and, when necessary, transport, health services for the animals and proper shoeing (especially important in the winter), action to avoid and combat epizootics among troop and civilian animals, and veterinary treatment and hygiene. He was also responsible for the supply of veterinary equipment and medicine, and finally for supervision of the butcher units' work and checking of foodproducts of animal origin.

– The IVd were the Catholic and Protestant war chaplains (*see also* section "The Division Chaplains"). Their work was done according to instructions from the division commander or their own estimation, in line with their spiritual duties.

– The IVz was a staff paymaster with accounting office and field cashier's desk. All payment of all division members was done via the field cashbox, as were (through the individual units) the payment of service pay, financial transactions, sending of funds to families at home, etc.

An example is the field cashier's desk of the 12th Infantry Division.

Between June 22, 1941 and December 31, 1941 it paid out 5,312,450 Reichsmark and received 1,715,964 Reichsmark. It lost 33,400 RM to enemy action.

The Quartermaster Units Structure:
– The division supply leader, at the rank of Major. He was the troop leader of supply services and was in charge of regulating their use, movements and activities along with the specialists, and to obtain knowledge of supply routes.
– The field postmaster was the leader of the field post office and was responsible for the operation of field mail pickup and delivery stations, postal limitations, and replacement of equipment.
– The leader of the commissary supply train, usually a *Hauptmann*, was responsible for the movement and use of the food supply trains according to the commands of the Ib.
– The leader of the pack train had the same duties.

The entire division staff was not drawn together into one place, but rather divided according to location. The command unit occupied the division command post some 10 to 15 kilometers behind the front. Here, covered as well as possible by patches of woods, ravines, etc., the division commander, Ia, Ic, etc., worked in the so-called command bus, in tents or, in static warfare, also in large bunkers. The adjutanture and quartermaster unit were located 15 to 20 kilometers behind the front, usually in permanent buildings and structures, so as to be able to carry out their duties as undisturbed as possible.

Particular attention should be given to the military police, who were much decried in postwar days as "dogs on a leash"; within the division, what with their small numbers on the one hand and their manifold tasks on the other, they were certainly not in a position to commit the oft-cited excesses against their own troops and civilian population. Military police with their orange service-arm color existed only in wartime. They wore the usual army uniform plus, as a particularly visible identifying mark, a ring collar on a chain with the national emblem and inscription "Feldgendarmerie", the emblem of the general police on their left upper arm, and a brown band with the lettering "Feldpolizei" on their left lower arm.

The military police troop was directly subordinate to the division commander. Its complement was one officer (*Oberleutnant* or *Leutnant*) and 36 men (lowest rank at least *Unteroffizier*), with 7 cars, 1 truck, 6 solo and 2 sidecar motorcycles. It was armed with pistols and machine pistols.

The service of the military police was performed in individual small troops in the rear of the division area. Their duties included keeping order, providing security and directing traffic. To keep order, they used patrols to observe the disciplined behavior of the soldiers when they were active to the rear, detached from their units, kept order in furlough traffic by patrolling railroad stations, intervened in punishable behavior against the civilian population, searched for deserters, acted to minimize loss of discipline and panic, directed retreating troops along withdrawal routes, set up gathering stations for scattered units, etc.

Among their security duties were keeping watch for suspicious civilians (spies, saboteurs and partisans), searching prisoners for important information, and setting up prisoner gathering centers in the battle zone. In crisis situations they also acted to defend the division staff. An important area of duty was their work in directing traffic. In addition to generally maintaining discipline and keeping traffic in order on the roads, one of their main duties was the planned regulation of traffic at narrows, bridges, etc., as well as during major advancing or retreating troop movements.

The military police were given special powers for all of these tasks, and their powers were considerable. All Wehrmacht personnel, including officers, had to identify themselves to military policemen of lower rank on request. The police could search persons, possessions and places, check vehicles and baggage, had the right to arrest any non-commissioned officers and enlisted men (in the case of officers, though, only when they were apprehended in the act), and in special cases even the right to use firearms.

Without the action of the military police, the vast technical achievements of moving military traffic would have been impossible. In the back-line area, they were valuable helpers of the troops fighting up front.

Just as the troop units coalesced during the course of the war, particularly in the east, the strength of the division staffs decreased, either from personnel decreases or losses. As the war grew wider and harder, there could be no more talk of a feudal life for the staff. While the staffs were a favorite target of Allied bombers in the west, the division staffs in the east had to defend themselves against the land and weather as well as the enemy.

From victorious campaigns (Poland 1939) . . .

. . . to the bitter end (prisoner-of-war camp, Italy 1945).

Ammunition

Ammunition was the general, all-inclusive term. There were cartridges with bullets and cases, cartridge ammunition with shell and case, grenades with inserted charges and separately loaded ammunition with shell and cartridge. Also ranking among ammunition were hand grenades, lighting and signaling devices, explosives, hollow-charge shells, etc. They were spoken of, counted and reported in "rounds."

Cartridges

The cartridges consisted of a case with percussion cap, a charge of powder and a bullet. The last tapered conically to the rear in order to decrease the airless space in its trajectory. The bullet consisted of a jacket and a core.

The pistols and machine pistols used the same cartridge of 9mm caliber, with a total weight of 12 grams and measuring 29mm long. The bullet was made of lead with a steel jacket, and weighed 8.09 grams. On account of the shortage of lead, the new 08 (mE) cartridge was introduced in February of 1941; it had a bullet of cast steel with a steel jacket and lead base, plus a steel cartridge.

The same cartridges, with a caliber of 7.92mm, were likewise used for rifles, light and heavy machine guns. There were the sS cartridge (the standard type) and special cartridges. They had the same steel cases and manufacturing processes, but different bullets and powder charges.

The special cartridges could be told apart externally by the color of the bullet and of the ring groove near the base of the cartridge.

– The sS cartridge had a heavy full-point bullet and a hard lead core. The length was 79mm, the bullet diameter 8.2 mm, the bullet weight 12.8 grams, the powder charge 2.85 grams, the total weight including case 23.75 grams. See illustration for size. Marked with a green ring groove. This cartridge was replaced as of the autumn of 1940 by the Sm-E cartridge, with a bullet comprising a cast steel core and a lead jacket. Marked with a blue ring groove.

– The SmK cartridge had a pointed bullet comprising a steel core surrounded with lead (armor-piercing, with a penetrating power of some 10mm at 100 meters). Marked with a black bullet tip and red ring groove.

– The SmKH cartridge had a pointed bullet comprising a tungsten carbide core surrounded with lead (armor-piercing), marked with a black bullet and red ring groove.

– The SmKL'spur cartridge was a tracer cartridge with a pointed bullet of steel core surrounded with lead and a flare at the base. Marked with a yellow bullet tip and red ring groove.

– The SPr cartridge had a pointed bullet with core and steel jacket, and a white phosphorus flare at the point of the bullet. Marked with a chromed bullet tip, black ring groove. This cartridge, also called the B cartridge (for Beobachtung = observation) was used particularly to observe shot ranges.

The cartridge for the Panzerbüchse 39 antitank gun also had a caliber of 7.92mm, but was considerably longer and stronger than a normal rifle cartridge and had five times the charge. The length of the cartridge was 114mm, it weighed 98.7 grams, of which the bullet weighed 14.5 grams. The armor-piercing bullet was pointed and had a hardened steel core and a flare.

The 43 (hurz = short) cartridge was a new 7.92 mm caliber cartridge; it had a full-point bullet with a lead core in a short steel jacket, measuring 47mm long and weighing 7.8 grams, with a powder charge of 2.1 grams and a total weight, including the case, of 16.29 grams. This cartridge could be fired only from the new 44 assault rifle.

All bullets had a tombac-plated outer steel jacket.

Ammunition Packaging
– sS or SmE cartridges iL (in Ladestreifen = in charger, rifle cartridges), 1500 rounds in wooden boxes, weight 48 kg.
– sS or SmE cartridges oL (without charger, machine gun bullets), 1500 rounds in wooden boxes, weight 46.4 kg.
– Stick hand grenades with igniting fuse and detonator, 16 rounds in wooden boxes, weight 25 kg.
– Hand grenades with igniting fuse and detonator, 30 rounds in packing boxes, weight 9 kg.
– Launching grenades, 50mm, for light grenade launcher, 10 rounds in sheet metal boxes, weight 12 kg.
– Launching grenades, 81mm, for medium grenade launcher, 3 rounds in sheet metal boxes, weight 40 kg.
– Launching grenades, 120mm, for heavy grenade launcher, 2 rounds

in boxes, weight 40 kg.

– Explosive shells, 37mm, for antitank gun, 12 rounds in sheet metal boxes, weight 21.5 kg.

– Rifle shells with propellant charge, 30 rounds in packing boxes, weight 8.9 kg,

– Panzerfaust (antitank shells) ready to use, 4 rounds in packing boxes, weight 32 kg.

– Panzerschreck (antitank shells), 6 hollow-charge rockets in shot boxes.

First Ammunition Supplies

As the basis for large-quantity shipments of ammunition of all kinds, a so-called "first ammunition supply" for each weapon was established. It consisted of a certain number of cartridges and shells and was the quantity that the troops carried with them on their combat vehicles, in light columns and in the space provided for it in the storerooms of the division supply services. This supply of ammunition was calculated per weapon and 48 hours and was thus the ration that could be fired in two normal combat days. The total weight of the first ammunition supply for an infantry division, for example, amounted to some 60 tons at the beginning of the eastern campaign.

**First Ammunition Supplies of an Infantry Division in 1941
in Individual Statistics for Light and Heavy Infantry Weapons**

Weapon	Total	per man	in Vehicle	in Column	Stored
Pisto	12	8	–	2	2
Rifle	90	45	15	20	10
MP	768	192	320	128	128
Light MG	3750	–	2500	750	500
Panzerbüchse	145	20	105	20	–
Heavy MG	6750	–	4750	1250	750
Lt. launcher	165	–	90	45	30
Hvy. launcher	140	–	96	24	20
Lt. Inf. gun	180	–	120	40	20
Hvy. Inf. gun	80	–	40	20	20
37mm Pak	220	–	180	24	16
50mm Pak	210	–	164	28	18

In order to maintain a continuing awareness during a running battle, the units were required to report their ammunition consumption, supply and needs, in rounds, to their command posts daily at a prescribed time, usually toward evening. These reports eventually went to the division, section Ib/WuG, which gave the superior corps a complete report and requested what was needed.

New Infantry Division 43

To improve the proportion of combat soldiers to supply-train men in the infantry divisions and keep the divisions smaller in numbers, a new type of infantry division was ordered and defined in terms of wartime structure as of October 2, 1943 (except for divisions in Norway, at home in Germany, etc). The former basic structure had proved itself and remained essentially the same; the lower number of men was to be balanced by better and stronger weapons. But since weapons and materials could not always be prepared in the planned quantities, what really occurred was usually a decrease in combat strength. This restructuring was also introduced only gradually.

War Structure of Infantry Division 43
Division staff with map unit including printing troop (motorized), traffic control platoon (motorized) and music corps.

3 Grenadier Regiments, each with:
1 staff company with intelligence platoon, engineer platoon, mounted or bicycle platoon (6 light machine guns in all).
1 staff company with staff, 3 grenadier companies each (each with 16 light machine guns, 2 81mm medium grenade launchers) and 1 heavy company (12 heavy machine guns, 6 81mm medium grenade launchers or 75mm light infantry guns).
1 infantry gun company (12 81mm medium grenade launchers, 4 120mm heavy grenade launchers or 150mm heavy antitank guns).
1 antitank company (1 platoon with close-combat weapons, 1 platoon with 50mm medium antitank guns, 1 platoon with 75mm heavy antitank guns motorized).
1 fusilier battalion (instead of reconnaissance unit) with staff, structured like a grenadier battalion, but with one company equipped with bicycles and therefore capable of being used for reconnaissance.
1 Panzerjäger unit with staff, 1st company (6 37mm light antitank guns, 6 50mm medium antitank guns), 2nd company (12 75mm heavy antitank guns motorized), 3rd company (12 20mm light anti-aircraft guns on self-propelled mantelets).

1 Artillery Regiment with:
Staff and staff battery
2 light units (each with staff, staff battery and 3 batteries, each with 4 105mm light howitzers, horsedrawn).
1 heavy unit (staff, staff battery and 3 batteries, each with 4 150mm

heavy howitzers motorized) (sometimes also 1 unit with 2 batteries of 88mm anti-aircraft guns, motorized for ground combat).

1 engineer battalion with staff, 1 horsedrawn company, 1 company with bicycles, battle gear echelon.
1 intelligence unit with staff, 1 telephone company, partly motorized, 1 radio company, motorized, 1 light intelligence column.
1 division combat school.

Medical Services with:
1 medical company, horsedrawn
1 medical company, motorized
1 ambulance company

Administrative Services with:
1 administrative company, motorized, including commissariat
1 bakery company, motorized
1 butcher company, motorized
1 veterinary company, horsedrawn
1 field post office, motorized

Supply Services with:
Staff division supply leader (Dinafü)
2 wagon columns, horsedrawn, with total potential load of 90 tons
1 truck company with potential load of 30 tons
1 supply company, partly motorized
1 motor park troop company with 2 repair-shop platoons and 1 armorer platoon

Noteworthy differences between this new structure and the old type are: The 3rd battalion of every regiment was disbanded, likewise the regimental band and the light infantry columns, the supply trains were strongly reduced. The reconnaissance unit was turned into a fusilier battalion, corresponding to a grenadier battalion, the Panzerjäger unit was armed with fewer antitank guns. The artillery regiment lost its third light unit and horsedrawn column, and the engineer battalion was also strongly reduced. The field replacement battalion was also cut. In the medical services, the field hospital had been largely eliminated since 1942 and transferred to the army medical units. But field hospitals could be requested in cases of special need. In addition, the supply services were reduced.

At first glance, the reductions in supply trains and services do not appear very great. But the decisive feature was that a large number of these soldiers could now be replaced by volunteers who were now an organized part of the army (*see also* section "The Volunteers") and added to the combat troops.

These new-type divisions were supposed to have, as of December 1, 1943, a total strength of 13,656 men, of whom 9652 men (71.6%) belonged to the combat groups, 2245 men (16.4%) to the supply trains and 1759 men (12%) to the back-line services. In the supply and back-line services, several hundred volunteers (the number was not officially set, but left up to the division) often worked.

The armaments were: 2128 pistols, 7980 rifles, 103 rifles with telescopic sights, 302 grenade-launching rifles (Schiessbecher), 681 machine pistols, 128 light and heavy machine guns, 72 81mm medium grenade launchers, 21 120mm heavy grenade launchers, 12 75mm light infantry guns, 6 150mm heavy infantry guns, 6 37mm light antitank guns, 24 50mm medium antitank guns, 18 75mm heavy antitank guns, 12 20mm light anti-aircraft guns, 24 105mm light howitzers, 12 150mm heavy howitzers. Later there were also 600 assault rifles, 108 Panzerschreck and a great number of Panzerfaust antitank weapons.

Despite better arms and "weeding out" of the supply trains, the training of whose members left much to be desired, the restructuring of the infantry divisions did not lead to much progress, what with the constantly decreasing combat strength; on the contrary, for no less was expected of the now smaller divisions that previously when they had been at full strength.

The losses of manpower, horses and material suffered since the beginning of the eastern campaign could not be made up during the uninterrupted heavy fighting, even by restructuring the divisions. Retired General Kurt von Tippelskirch writes in his standard work, *History of the Second World War*:

"The failed German offensive at Byelgorod-Orel in July of 1943 and the subsequent months-long battles that had spread to an area of 1000-kilometer width between the Black Sea and Smolensk had been very costly for the German units. The following statistics give an idea of their extent: Of some 100 divisions (mostly infantry divisions) that were in the three army groups (center, south and A) hit by Russian attacks since July, more than a third were so weakened that they were only marked as division groups on the position maps. That meant that they had sunk to the level of a few week battalions. Only part of them could be refilled. Many were either disbanded or combined in so-called corps units of two divisions each, though they only had the strength of one division and were so designated for purposes of disguise. The other divisions had also suffered heavy losses, and scarcely a single one still had its intended strength.

How much the fighting strength continued to decrease is shown by the examples of a few divisions in the southern sector of the eastern campaign, north of the Dniestr, in March of 1944:

1st Infantry Division: 2 battalions, 1 light battery, 1 heavy battery, no antitank guns.

75th Infantry Division: 3 battalions, 1 light battery, 1 heavy battery, no antitank guns.

82nd Infantry Division: 3 battalions, 3 light batteries, no heavy battery, 21 antitank guns.

96th Infantry Division: 9 battalions, 5 light batteries, no heavy battery, 9 antitank guns.

168th Infantry Division: 6 battalions, 6 light batteries, 3 heavy batteries, 6 antitank guns.

208th Infantry Division: 8 battalions, 2 light batteries, 2 heavy batteries, 9 antitank guns.

254th Infantry Division: 2 battalions, 2 light batteries, no heavy battery, 20 antitank guns.

291st Infantry Division: 5 battalions, 6 light batteries, 2 heavy batteries, 6 antitank guns.

371st Infantry Division: 7 battalions, 4 light batteries, 3 heavy batteries, 3 antitank guns.

These were no longer divisions, but only more or less weak battle ground – and these conditions prevailed almost everywhere on the eastern front."

New Infantry Weapons

Since the previous weapons of the infantry divisions had proved themselves fully, with few exceptions, comparatively few improvements and further developments took place, unlike other types of units such as armored divisions. In order to be able to maintain strength despite their own steadily decreasing combat strength and the growing numbers of the enemy, rapid-firing weapons as well as antitank weapons were urgently needed.

Pistol 38

This pistol did not offer much that was new, even though it possessed a few unusual technical characteristics. Unlike most self-chargers, its hammer did not need to be cocked completely in advance in order to be ready to fire. It could also be carried without danger when the hammer was let down slowly. Despite that, many soldiers still swore by their "08" pistols.

Technical data:

Caliber	9 mm
Weight (unloaded)	960 grams
Weight of holster	530 grams
Length	21.3 cm
Other data	same as the 08 pistol.

Assault Rifle 44

The breakthrough to a modern, rapid-firing machine weapon that could replace the rifles, quick-charging rifles and machine pistols and was envisioned as a uniform weapon for the entire infantry took place only very late. This development began with the 42 machine carbine, the first of which reached the eastern front in the winter of 1942-43. This machine carbine still used the normal sS rifle cartridge. The next development was the 43 machine carbine, which was then designated 43/1 and only given the designation of Assault Rifle 44 on its introduction to the troops in the autumn of 1944.

The 44 assault rifle likewise functioned as a gas-pressure charger with hinged breech and hammer bolt, and consisted, aside from the barrel and breech, almost exclusively of stamped parts with a minimum of fittings. The rifle, which could be used for both single shots and sustained fire, had an arched, inserted staff magazine holding 30 rounds, and each man carried twelve magazines. The use of a rifle grenade device was possible. A special advance was the new 43 short cartridge (*see also* section "Ammunition").

Technical data:

Caliber	7.92 mm (short)
Length	93 cm
Barrel length	41.8 cm
Weight	4.62 kilograms
Sight range	100 to 800 meters
Optimal range,	single shots to 600 meters
Optimal range,	sustained to 300 meters
Initial velocity (V_o)	650 meters per second
Rate of fire	500 rounds per minute

The 44 assault rifle blended all the advantages of a modern infantry weapon: high, efficient rate of fire, good target accuracy, sufficient range, easy maintenance and servicing, and last but not least, an inexpensive manufacturing process. The recoil was bearable and controllable, the individual bursts of fire could be held on target quite well. This weapon, though heartily welcomed by the troops, came to the front much too late and in too-small numbers. Only a few infantrymen made its acquaintance a few months before the war ended, and it was first issued to special units (Waffen-SS, etc.). As of October 1, 1944 only 110,000 of them were on hand.

Rifle Grenade Device ("Schiessbecher")

As of about the middle of the war, the rifle squads were issued, in addition to the light machine gun as a flat-fire weapon, their own "steep-fire weapon" in the form of a rifle grenade-firing device, also called a "Schiessbecher" (literally "shot beaker" or "shooting cup") with sufficient hand-grenade launching range to allow attacking an enemy in or behind cover. This simply designed device, introduced as of 1942, was an additional firing apparatus that could be attached to any rifle to fire rifling-stabilized, shrapnel-effect or armor-piercing small grenades. Such a rifle grenade device consisted of a short barrel with rifling turning to the right, a sight, and a bracket that was fastened to the muzzle of the rifle barrel behind the foresight by two swinging hooks. The rifled barrel itself had to be screwed into the front of the bracket with its own wrench. A grenade sight mounted on the left side of the rifle had markings from 50 to 250 meters.

The grenades, inserted in the front of the barrel by hand, were propelled by cartridges of varying strength (small rifle cartridges with 1 to 1.9 grams of powder, according to the grenade used), which were loaded into the chamber of the rifle like ordinary cartridges.

Technical data:

Caliber	30mm
Weight	2.5 kilograms
Length	27.3 cm
Barrel rifling	8 riflings
Range, flat fire	to 250 meters (max. 400 meters)
Range, steep fire	25 to 75 meters
Initial velocity (V_o)	50 meters per second
Shrapnel effect area	ca. 30 meter diameter (approx. = a light 50mm grenade launcher)
Grenade wgt. (explosive)	288 grams
Grenade wgt. (large antitank)	387 grams

The ammunition consisted of various types of small grenades, including explosive types, small and large antitank types and liquid-filled smoke grenades, which could also be used for antitank combat, plus fog, light and propaganda grenades. The explosive grenades, equipped with a rip-cord igniter, could also be used as hand grenades. All these grenades were delivered ready to fire. In every rifle squad, one man was detailed for rifle grenade fire, and carried, in addition to his rifle with Schiessbecher, a double carrier with, normally, ten explosive and five antitank grenades. He could fire it lying down, kneeling or standing.

Machine Gun 42

The new MG 42 was developed from the earlier MG 34 and fully introduced to the troops by 1943. Except for the long cooling louvers in the jacket, the MG 42 was hard to distinguish from the MG 34 externally, and in principle it was also a recoil charger with a movable barrel and roller breech, air cooling, changeable barrel and belt feed, but with a different barrel bolt and 0.5 kg lighter. From the start, this weapon was planned for production under wartime conditions; for example, the earlier milled parts were extensively replaced by stamped sheet metal. Barrel changing was improved and simplified so that it could be done quickly without touching the hot barrel. The rate of fire – the MG 42 was made only for sustained fire – was so great that individual shots could not be distinguished, blended into each other and produced a constant sound. The MG 42 was less sensitive to dirt and dust and did not fail in the Russian winters; it could be used, just like the MG 34, on a mantelet as a light or heavy machine gun.

Technical data:

Caliber	7.92 mm
Weight	11.6 kilograms
Length (barrel length)	1.22 meters (53 cm)
Sight range	200 to 2000 meters
Maximum range	3000 meters
Effective range	to 1500 meters
Initial velocity (V_o)	820 meters per second
Rate of fire	1300 to 1400 rounds per minute
Maximum range as heavy MG	to 4000 meters

When used as a heavy machine gun, the weight was decreased to 29.7 kilograms.

The MG 42 was an excellent weapon that has maintained its importance, with minor improvements and changes, to the present day. Along with it, the reliable MG 34 was still in use to the end of the war.

Heavy Grenade Launcher 43

When a new 12-centimeter grenade launcher was introduced at the end of 1943, it was designated a heavy launcher, and the previous 81mm type was called a medium launcher.

The 120mm grenade launcher was and remained the infantry's heaviest launcher. It had the same superstructure with barrel, baseplate and bipod with aiming gear, and likewise the same firing principle, but this launcher, since it was much too heavy to be carried by manpower, could no longer be disassembled and carried into position in one-man loads. Thus it was carried, assembled, on a two-wheel chassis and towed by a vehicle. To fire, the launcher had to be slid off the chassis and moved into position. The towing vehicle was either a truck or an Ost (RSO) caterpillar tractor, which also carried the crew and ammunition.

Technical data:

Caliber	120mm
Weight ready to fire	281 kilograms
Weight ready to march	420 kilograms
Barrel length	1.52 meters
Elevation arc	45 to 80 degrees
Traverse arc	3.5 degrees to left and right
Shot range	300 to 6050 meters with 6 charges
Rate of fire	6 rounds per minute
Grenade weight	16 kilograms
Effect	Shrapnel to 40-meter diameter
Crew	1 leader, 6 men

The effect of the 120mm grenade launcher was much greater than that of the 81mm launcher, but as of October 1, 1944 only 3510 of the heavy launchers were in service, and none before that.

Light and Heavy Panzerfaust

The infantry's constant plea for an effective, portable one-man antitank weapon, so as not to be compelled constantly to defend themselves in close combat against masses of enemy tanks in the east and west, and also to be independent of the numerically insufficient and not always or universally available heavy antitank guns of the Panzerjäger, was answered much too late.

Such a weapon finally reached the troops, introduced in small numbers as of September 1943: the so-called "fist cartridge", popularly known as the "Panzerfaust." This was followed by additional larger and more effective versions. The Panzerfaust was developed in 1943 on the hollow-charge principle and was actually nothing more than a hollow-charge grenade at the end of a steel pipe, with a high penetration effect, that could easily be carried, operated and prepared for firing by a single man.

The Panzerfaust weapons were used for antitank action at an effective range of 30 to 80 meters. They consisted of two parts – the oversize "head" with the hollow-charge shell at the front, to be fired, and the long barrel of steel. In the shell were an impact fuse that automatically became live after flying two meters; in the front of the barrel were the wings of the shell and, behind them, a propellant charge of 186 grams of black powder in a cardboard case (with which the barrel always remained loaded) as well as empty space for delayed-action apparatus and igniter. On the barrel was a folding sight, under the barrel a simple trigger.

Before firing, every Panzerfaust had to be made live like a hand grenade, by removing the "head" and loading a propellant charge and igniter. Then the sight was folded up, the safety catch moved forward to "released" and the lever marked with "fire" (the trigger) pulled. On firing, the black-powder charge in the barrel was ignited. A part of the resulting gas pressure drove the shell out the barrel by its winged end, while the other part of the pressure escaped backward out the open end of the tube and thus eliminated most of the recoil (thus a recoilless weapon). This plume of fire, shooting one to two meters out of the end of the barrel, was the weapon's great disadvantage, for it could be lethal to a distance of three meters. Thus a Panzerfaust user had to be especially careful that nobody was standing behind him, and also that no walls, earthworks, trees, etc., were in the way, which could have caused danger for him. Finally, of course, the plume of fire and heavy smoke betrayed the shooter's position, which required a quick change of position after firing.

Aiming at a tank was done as with other weapons, by backsight notch and foresight. In practice, all firing positions – standing, kneeling or lying – were possible. The Panzerfaust could be fired only once.

There were four variations of the Panzerfaust:

At first, in 1943, the Panzerfaust 30 "small" appeared (fist cartridges 1 and 2), which were almost identical, though version 2 had a higher weight. The overall length was 1.03 meters, the weight 3 kilograms, the barrel diameter 4.5 cm, sight 30 meters, penetrating power 14 cm of armor at 30 meters. Fist cartridge 2 weighed 5.1 kg and penetrated 20 centimeters.

Since the penetrating power and range of both types were still too little, an improved Panzerfaust 60 "large" followed in 1944, with a length of 80 cm, weight 6.1 kg, barrel diameter 5 cm, sight markings 30, 60 and 80 meters, penetrating power 20 cm of armor at 60 meters.

Since this type's performance was not fully satisfactory either, the Panzerfaust 100 was developed, length 1.15 meters, weight 6.8 kg, barrel diameter 6 cm, sight markings up to 150 meters, penetrating power 20 cm of armor at an initial velocity of 40 meters per second. For the Panzerfaust 60 and 100 the hollow-charge shell had a diameter of 15 cm and a weight of 3 kilograms.

The Panzerfaust soon became the most frequently used means of antitank warfare and, thanks to its simple operation and great effect, remained very popular among the soldiers from mid-1944 to the end of the war. The Panzerfaust was mass-produced after its introduction; here are some production statistics:

Panzerfaust	July 1944	January 1945	February 1945	March 1945
"small"	75,000	6,500	7,000	525,000
"large"	120,000	1,250,000	1,200,000	430,000

Panzerschreck

As of 1944, much smaller numbers of another antitank weapon were introduced, bearing the designation "Raketenpanzerbüchse 42." This "rocket antitank gun" was a recoilless weapon from whose barrel fin-stabilized hollow-charge projectiles with rocket propulsion were fired – the infantry's only rocket weapon. The improved model, the "Panzer-schreck" ("tank terror"), became known to the soldiers as the "Ofenrohr" ("stovepipe") and was likewise a portable weapon with a barrel, a trigger apparatus below, and a small shield to the left of the barrel. Unlike the Panzerfaust, this weapon had to be loaded from the rear and operated by two men. Since it likewise gave out a heavy plume of fire from the rear, it too was no ideal weapon.

Technical data:

Caliber	88mm
Weight	9.5 kilograms
Length	1.64 meters
Shot weight	3.3 kilograms
Initial velocity (V_o)	130 meters per second
Range	to 400 meters
Penetrating power	15 cm armor at 60-degree impact angle

By enlarging the caliber to 10 centimeters and lengthening the barrel to two meters, the range was increased to 500 meters. But sure targeting, especially on moving tanks, was only possible up to 200 meters.

Operational Reports

(Extracts from Divisional Histories)

Infantry Marches and Battles

44th Infantry Division, Polish campaign, 1939:
The division traveled some 540 kilometers in 18 days of marching and fighting, which meant an average daily march of 29 kilometers.

45th Infantry Division, Polish campaign, 1939:
Large-scale quick marches were demanded of the foot troops. In lasting oppressive heat, terrible dust and miserable thirst, the men showed in these days with bitter energy what marching performances they could give. In thirteen days 400 kilometers were covered from the border to the Lubaszov area, an average of over 30 kilometers a day.

56th Infantry Division, western campaign, 1940:
From May 10 to 15, 1940, thus in six days, the division covered 140 to 180 kilometers, in sometimes very heavy fighting with many river and canal crossings.

45th Infantry Division, western campaign, 1940, south of La Malmaison, crossing the Aisne on June 9, 1940:
At 5:00 our artillery suddenly opened fire. Over the river bottom at this hour there still lay heavy fog, unfortunately, which made reliable observation impossible. The artillery had to move their fire forward, which compelled the infantry to open its own path over the river for the first jump. In the process, it met a wakeful enemy, fully prepared to defend himself, who threw a murderous fire at it. Enemy riflemen and machine gunners lay unseen in cover on the other shore, firing from bushes, trenches and sandbag bunkers, or were posted in trees along with their

machine guns. The French artillery, to provide a full measure, fired from their gun positions all the way back to the fortifications of Rheims on all our advance positions with shells of all calibers up to 28 centimeters, with destructive effect.

At first it appeared that every attack would end in bloody defeat. A part of the first infantry wave fell dead or injured into the Aisne along with their shot-up rubber boats, or the boats floated on downriver out of control, with their crews dead. But the attackers did not give up. More and more rubber boats were launched, and when one squad was shot down, the next, tough and bitter, sprang into the boat. Others plunged into the water fully equipped and managed to swim to the other shore.

The first shock troops of Infantry Regiment 133, led by *Leutnants* Wolfinger and Schweitzer, reached the south shore during the crossing despite heavy losses, but met heavy enemy defense there, that wiped them out almost completely as they stormed forward. Lt. Schweitzer died of a shot in the abdomen.

6th Infantry Division, eastern campaign, northern sector, July 1, 1941:
The 260-kilometer march from the preparation area in Memell and to Riga was covered in ten days on very bad roads and while fighting . . .

98th Infantry Division, eastern campaign, central sector, toward Korosten, summer 1941:
On July 30, 1941, the march of the division (previously OKH reserve), which saw service at the front from then on, ended in the woods south of Malin after daily marches of 40 to 50 kilometers (since July 9) in oppressive heat and humidity and penetrating dust.

45th Infantry Division, eastern campaign, southern sector, during the conquest of the Brest-Litovsk fortress, June 22-30, 1941, excerpt from a firsthand account by Hans Teuschler, who received his doctorate and became a school professor after the war:
June 22: A heavy machine gun near me was in a bitter fight with these cursedly unpleasant Russian sharpshooters. Suddenly the Gunner 2 standing behind me screamed: "Hit the dirt!" No sooner had I done it than an enemy bullet penetrated my chest. After spinning almost twice around, I collapsed. When I regained consciousness after a long time, I saw a terrible scene: At the front edge of the position, half erected, was the mantelet of the heavy machine gun; behind it lay Gunner 1, badly shot through the lung, on his last legs and groaning with pain and thirst. "Do you have something to drink, comrade?" he asked me. Laboriously I handed him my field flask. To the right of me crouched the leader of the heavy machine gun, who did not move when I spoke to him. Farther away I heard from all sides the mournful cries of helpless wounded men:

"Medic . . . Medic . . ." The enemy sharpshooters had done a thorough job. With my last strength I was able to turn onto my back, so as to lie more comfortably and not on top of my ammunition case. My chest was as heavy as lead, my jacket and short soaked in blood. At first I began to look for the wounded spot, until I finally found a small hole under my left collarbone. I pressed a bandage onto it so that a scab would form. The exit wound was already scabbed over from my having been lying on my back. Gradually the miserably hot day died away and a wretched night began . . .

Note: Since the squad was cut off, the wounded men could not be rescued until the third day.

98th Infantry Division, eastern campaign, central sector, August 23, 1941:
Burned bridges and Russian roads in steady rain slowed the marching speed. The mass of the division plodded through sand or mud toward the Dniepr. Small villages were the stations on this wretched march, in which 10 to 20 horses a day died in their traces of complete exhaustion. Worn out and dead tired, the infantry found a few small places that were already overflowing with fast troops. The men scarcely had the energy to eat their food.

198th Infantry Division, eastern campaign, southern sector, advance into the Donets Basin, mid-October 1941:
The advance was continued without interruption, but despite all their efforts, the troops could no longer cover any great distance in a day. The further march of the motorized units came to an almost complete stop on account of fuel shortage. High marching performances were just as impossible for the groups on foot, which were slowed by many collapses of men and horses, exhaustion and the lack of replacements for torn and worn-through boots. They (the marches) even decreased more. And the troops only seldom found quarters in the already overfilled villages. Three quarters of the men and all the horses had to spend the nights, which were already noticeably cold, outdoors.
    Firsthand report of a member of Infantry Regiment 326 of October 17, 1941:
    Toward morning a radio broadcast ordered a further advance. We set out, greeted by a cloudless sky. During the course of the morning, though, a storm came up. The wind blew over the bare steppe, and light raindrops began to fall. Soon it began to pour steadily. Around noon the wagons gathered at a hay barn to the right of the road, so as to have at least a little shelter from the rain and wind, and hot food was given out at the field kitchen, which we ate immediately and eagerly, a blessing for

the hungry and freezing men. For two hours the advance route had to be kept open for the motorized parts of the division, which rocked by laboriously through the morass . . . The waiting time ended. Marching was hard and harder, and the horses had to strain harder and harder to set the wagons in motion. In a cloudburst the heavens poured their masses of water on us. The tent cloth wrapped around me had been soaked through long ago, my coat too, and even my jacket and trousers no longer had a dry thread. Small streams of water ran over the horses' hair . . . Again twilight sank over the land and we had not yet reached our goal. The road became bottomless and the weather raged on endlessly. The mud, which ran into the tops of our boots, made every step misery. If only we hadn't been so damned exhausted . . .

45th Infantry Division, eastern campaign, central sector, battle around Tula, December 4, 1941:
From the border (Brest-Litovsk) via Kiev to Jelez on the Shossna, 2100 kilometers were covered in marching and fighting from June 22 to December 8, 1941.

Then during the night the temperature dropped again to 37 degrees below zero . . . The 43rd Army Corps now moved the focal point to the right, to the 31st Infantry Division. The division attacked in bitter cold, broke through the first enemy position and came to a stop there. The losses were tremendous. Infantry Regiment 82 counted 100 fallen and 800 frozen on one day.

98th Infantry Division, eastern campaign, central sector, winter retreat from the Nara (before Moscow) as of December 24, 1941:
Excerpt from the diary of *Obergefreite* Huber:

About 2;00 A.M. we reached our first destination . . . Gradually Christmas morning dawned. Now we had to go to the edge of the forest to occupy an intermediate position. Thirty emaciated forms, in summer uniforms and tattered coats – it was more than thirty degrees below zero – with torn gloves and boots, many in laced shoes. With thin head protectors, chalk-smeared steel helmets and an empty feeling in our stomachs, we set out. With two operating light machine guns and a few functioning rifles. The path led through deep snow that lay on the fields and meadows. Then came the position at the edge of the woods – a few holes drifted half-full, over which a bitter wind blew and soon covered us from top to bottom with a thin layer of ice. In the afternoon the wind grew to a single lashing snowstorm in which you could no longer see the man next to you.

45th Infantry Division, eastern campaign, central sector, winter retreat in the direction of Orel, as of December 8, 1941:

With patient determination the division fought its way westward step by step in icy cold, with meager food, poor clothing and sometimes insufficient supporting fire. The enemy brought more and more new forces from the south and tried with unbelievable stubbornness to stop our march. Thus our troops constantly had to fight with the front to the south and simultaneously continue to move westward, so the enemy found no time to establish himself in front of us with great masses of troops . . . One of our most urgent problems was turning over our wounded whom we had been able to bring this far, and sending them on. Whoever had any means of transportation at his disposal in these critical days – be it a truck, a sled or anything else – naturally took wounded men along. Leaving them behind would have meant their sure death, either by freezing or liquidation by a merciless enemy. Poorly bandaged, wrapped in a few blankets and bedded on straw, these poor fellows often suffered unspeakably on the long cross-country marches. So it was really a relief to be able to hand them over for further care to the rear at last.

The dead had to be left behind. In most cases it would have been impossible to bury them; either enemy action left us no time, or we lacked explosives to penetrate the ground, which was usually frozen over a meter deep. At times we still tried to take fallen comrades along on sleds for days, in the hope of soon coming to rest. Finally we had to abandon the sled along with the dead to drag ourselves along . . .

The December retreat was finished (on December 30, 1941), the result was staggering. The division was hit bitterly hard. The supply services had been able to save some of their vehicles, but the combat troops had lost practically everything that they could not carry – more than half of the guns, the greater part of the vehicles and almost all personal belongings had been lost. But the losses were even more painful – about 400 dead were left behind in these days. The number of those who were lost to wounds or freezing was more than that.

6th Infantry Division, eastern campaign, northern sector, 1941-42:
Infantry Regiment 18 of the division had covered 1645 kilometers from June 22, 1941 to January 2, 1942 in 76 marching days, with frequent battles. From January 1 to March 31, 1942 every man in the company stood watch for 360 hours and also put in 450 hours of work (position building, etc.).

198th Infantry Division, eastern campaign, southern sector, Mius position, February 1942:
In the heaviest snowstorms we ever experienced, and in icy cold, the men stood unsheltered in the open up to 40 hours without relief and food and fought off enemy attacks.

56th Infantry Division, eastern campaign, central sector, north of Orel, February 1942:

On January 2, 1942 the division attacked again . . . By February 17, in ceaseless heavy fighting, it reached a line 5 kilometers southeast of Krapivna, which meant a distance of about 20 kilometers in nine days under the worst weather conditions (temperatures to 40 degrees below zero and deep snow, in which one sank up to his abdomen off cleared paths). In the process, the regiments had to wage frequent forest battles. What with a lack of winter clothing, a considerable number of the losses were caused by frostbite of first to third degree.

370th Infantry Division, eastern campaign, southern sector, Crimea, 1941-42:

In November the peninsula of Kertsch was conquered in hard fighting, in which the division took part, ending on November 16, 1941. On November 19 the men of the division began the march back to Sevastopol in ice and snow, in order to join the battle against the fortress as the severe winter set in. Meanwhile the enemy landed in Feodosia. Now the division had to return to service there. The march back toward Feodosia took place early in January 1942, again over ice-covered mountain roads in the Jaila Mountains, and in heavy snowstorms. Tremendous demands were made on men and horses, many horses died of exhaustion. By January 18, 1942 the city and harbor of Feodosia were taken again.

In the meantime the enemy had occupied the entire peninsula of Kertsch again. After hard defensive fighting at the Kertsch isthmus, the division had to set out to win back the peninsula at the beginning of May 1942. By May 20, 1942 Kertsch was taken again. A few days later, the division marched back again on the path to the front before Sevastopol, to take part in the attack and storming of the fortress.

Thus the division had to cover over 800 kilometers in repeated back-and-forth movements on the Kertsch peninsula.

290th Infantry Division, eastern campaign, northern sector, pocket of Demyansk:

On May 1, 1942 two officers, 14 non-commissioned officers and 62 men defended the support point of Szomshino until the last of them fell.

198th Infantry Division, eastern campaign, southern sector, attack over the Mius, summer 1942:

In the period between July 19 and August 12 the division covered some 500 kilometers in advancing and fighting . . . Now the division stood before the western Caucasus. The slowly flowing Kuban still separated the division from the mountains and the wooded foothills. It was tropically hot, with temperatures up to 40 degrees. In the few hours of rest that the troops were allowed, they could hardly think of sleeping. The humid heat did not let up, even at night . . . August 18: by about midday it had become unbearably hot again. Again and again men and horses collapsed from heatstroke . . .

11th Infantry Division, eastern campaign, northern sector, summer 1942: To clean out an enemy breakthrough position in the Kirishi bridgehead, in the night of July 22-23, 1942 the I./Infantry Regiment 2 was moved into the bridgehead. In bitter fighting against a splendidly armed and stubborn enemy, and in a swampy brush country completely flooded by pouring rain, where any taking of cover, any fast moves forward, were impossible, sinking in swamps to above their knees, the infantrymen suffered heavy losses but pushed the enemy back from the captured territory step by step on the early morning of July 23.

17th Army, eastern campaign, southern sector, advance into the Caucasus, summer 1942:
It was a 700-kilometer advance into the new battle area. Gigantic clouds of dust hung over the advance routes. The few sources of drinking water in the Kuban steppes were constantly thickly surrounded by men and animals, and a heat of up to 40 degrees prevailed. The infantry covered up to 50 kilometers a day under the burning sun.

198th Infantry Division, eastern campaign, southern sector, western Caucasus, end of August 1942:
The III./Infantry Regiment 308, under *Hauptmann* Niess, continued to hold its attained positions on Lyssaya Mountain, though the heavy enemy raids were repeated every day. In the pauses in fire, oaks were cut down with captured timber saws and the positions were strengthened. Then the Russians cut the supply lines and telephone wires to the rear; the battalion was surrounded. Despite strict rationing of food and drinking water, the supplies shrank to nearly nothing. Ammunition also became scarce.

Day and night, nerves were strained to the utmost. Again and again the hoarse shouts of the attacking Russians were hurled at the defenders, again and again the enemy was thrown back in close combat, often with cold steel. The wounded were gathered in the center of the position in hopes that relief would come soon and supplies would be available.

198th Infantry Division, eastern campaign, southern sector, Novorossisk, February 1943:
On the morning of February 9, Grenadier Regiment 305 was ready to drive the Soviets out of the southwestern part of the city. The attack in the early afternoon went off successfully at first. The poor visibility of the

terrain in the suburb of Stanichka offered the advancing companies welcome cover. Soon the battalions moved over the city line, when an impenetrable barrage fire came at them. Coast batteries of the largest calibers, artillery, twin anti-aircraft guns and air attacks caused very heavy losses . . . In the evening the regiment had to be taken back to the starting point.

61st Infantry Division, eastern campaign, northern sector, Volkov bridgehead, spring 1943:
The division had a frontal breadth of 19 kilometers to defend. The disadvantage of such an extent was that it allowed no depth and did not permit the separation of reserves. Just the most vital securing duties and building of positions, in view of the meager trench strength – the squads had decreased to 5 to 7 men – demanded constant service, so that the infantrymen could get no more than five to six hours of sleep in narrow, damp foxholes, in which conditions were made still worse by storms and vermin.

6th Infantry Division, eastern campaign, central sector, crossing south of Orel in the Hagen position, summer 1943:
During further crossing over the Kroma near Kromy in the night of August 2-3, 1943, the Russian night bombers were especially active with bombs and weapon fire. Although Grenadier Regiment 18 marched well separated, it suffered considerable losses in this night. It was a bad night, it rained. Only a person who knows the black soil in this area, which is like walking on soap when it rains, can imagine how exhausting a march is in the dark of night, while being bombed and fired on. Men and horses were soaked through, lost their footing, waited in the mud. At every moment a vehicle got stuck, whether a truck or a horsedrawn wagon, a motorcycle or a gun. In desperation, the company chiefs and commanders stumble through the darkness, trying to keep their units together. "Hauruck!" Drive the horses, dig out the vehicles – fall down, collapse, be ridden down, run into others . . . how is the next line of resistance to be met? At 3:00 it became light; by then the new line had to be set up and occupied. And it was done. At 3:00 the division stood at its new main battle line, ready to defend itself. Dead tired, every man slumped in his foxhole, prepared his rifle and machine gun for firing, or still worked on his position. Unwashed, unshaven, without sleep, with inflamed eyelids, with torn uniforms, emaciated and overstrained without rest, the infantryman stood here – marched, prepared and fought against overwhelming superiority. After weeks of fighting, this was the situation of the division, which was to be maintained until August 5. As soon as it was light, the first T 34 tanks, along with the enemy infantry, moved against the HKL.

98th Infantry Division, eastern campaign, southern sector, Kuban bridgehead, summer 1943:

On July 22, 1943 the fourth battle began at 5:30 A.M. with drumming fire that made the bunkers shake in the ground like boats in a storm, and in minutes the air was so filled with dust and smoke that visibility was only good for 15 meters. Between 6:00 and 6:45, salvos of the "Stalin organs" (Russian rocket salvo launchers), firing 84 rockets every 30 seconds, roared down on the division's sector. All phone lines were destroyed in no time, 20 minutes after the enemy fire started, the radios also went dead. In the time between 7:00 and 8:15, low-flying planes swept over the trenches again and again, usually in groups of three, and hit them with bombs and weapon fire; their attacks were repeated at 8:00, 11:00 and 4:00. The air was full of noise, cracking, pounding, rattling, with flashes of light, dust and smoke.

At 8:00 the first report reached the division. In almost the whole division sector, with focal points at Infantry Regiment 282 and the division battalion, close combat was already raging. The enemy was attacking with two rifle divisions, 80 to 100 tanks and 150 to 200 fighter planes, supported by a mighty artillery overly rich in ammunition. The battlefield looked like a horrible, hellish scene. Without a pause, the impacts sent up fountains of earth. With a dark, almost black cloud of smoke, a tank exploded here and there, a fighter plane burst into flames and smoke and fell to earth like a comet. Through it all the machine guns barked and the hand grenades exploded dully . . .

The night sank down over indescribable destruction and exhaustion. But the enemy had not succeeded in breaking through . . .

The fourth battle at the Kuban bridgehead, from July 18 to 27, 1943, cost the division, in ten days of the hardest defensive fighting, the loss of 42 officers and 1725 NCO and men, an average of 176 men per day.

24th Infantry Division, eastern campaign, northern sector, near Novgorod, Grenadier Regiment 102 fought its way out on January 19, 1944:

Shortly before arrival, the critical situation was known to all. Every man now knew that everything depended on the success of the breakthrough. The first contact with the enemy took place along the railroad line. With "Hurrah!" the first battalion overran the enemy to a depth of one to one and a half kilometers. With cold steel the battle group, which also included other units, cut its way through. Again and again attacks were made amid the movement. The bravest and least frightened fighters among the officers, non-commissioned officers and men stormed forward and pulled the others along with them. Thus another three kilometers of enemy positions, already set up, with their front along the railway embankment to the south, were rolled up. When the attacking power of the first battalion was exhausted, the next one moved to the front. So ground to the west was quickly won in ruthless advancing. The other battalions and units, following close behind, fought off heavy enemy counterattacks from the north. And yet the breakthrough seemed to be failing when the forefront met heavy Soviet opposition at the railroad station in Naschtschi. Turning away into the enemy-free but trackless and snow-covered forest to the south would have been the end. So it was a matter of pulling all our strength together again, and it succeeded: The final breakthrough was accomplished.

On the morning of January 20 the troops, now completely scattered, reached enemy-free territory. A few troops that had been separated to the south joined the new line on January 21 and 22. The losses were high. The wounded were brought along on the reliable Akjas. Only those who could not be transported were assembled and went into imprisonment with the staff surgeon, Dr. Theissen and medical *Oberfeldwebel* Maurer, who stayed with them voluntarily.

198th Infantry Division, eastern campaign, southern sector, relief attack against the pocket of Cherkassy, February 12, 1944:
Grenadier Regiment 326 was given the command to march, when replaced by Grenadier Regiment 308, immediately to Vinograd and retake this important point. The men of Regiment 326 were still fully exhausted from the last night attack. For weeks there was no roof over their heads, they just marched, fought and marched again and again. The roads were in an unimaginable condition. And now too there was no rest.

24th Infantry Division, eastern campaign, northern sector, west of Novgorod, January 31, 1944:
The further retreat of Grenadier Regiment 31 through the deep snow of the swamp meant tremendous exertion for the troops. They moved forward only very slowly, fighting a rear-guard action almost without pause. Every delay made the fully exhausted men fall into a deep sleep, so that the leaders had to use all their energy to get them to march farther. Every few minutes the leading squad had to be changed, because breaking a path through the heavy, wet snow exhausted them again and again. All heavy equipment was lost.

17th Infantry Division, eastern campaign, transfer and breakthrough fighting west of Nikopol, February 1944:
Report of a regiment leader of the division (name not given), written on February 15, just as the weather worsened and cold, snowstorms and new suffering began:

"Since about February 4 achievements have been demanded of every single man that left all previous demands far behind. Since the transfer in the bridgehead (Nikopol), the men have marched or lain outside in holes. Most of the grenadiers have chills or a fever of more than 38 degrees. The soldiers have had no sheltered place to stay for about two weeks and are fully exhausted. During the last march out of the position at height 100.1 into the present area, the grenadiers, during short rests from marching, collapsed into the muddy retreat route and fell asleep in the snowdrifts. Every one had to be awakened before they could march farther. The men have been without supplies for many days, their underwear has been worn for about four weeks, is completely filthy and infested with lice, their socks are torn to pieces. No replacements are at hand.

The felt winter boots are one of the grenadiers' worst burdens, wet, heavy as a log of wood, falling to pieces. All their winter clothing is threadbare and soaked through, no chance to dry it, stiff with frost at night, giving hardly any warmth.

The grenadiers' feet look especially bad. Wounds give off pus or blood. The men no longer march, they "shuffle" (about one kilometer per hour). Even the best men and marchers in the regiment are in despair at the marches that are ordered again and again, because they simply can't keep it up any more. Along with that, the regiment no longer has a doctor since the loss of the *Oberarzt*, Dr. Teusch.

The food is in short supply, corresponding to the conditions, more cold than warm . . . no hope of reestablishing fighting strength through bearable fighting conditions.

. . . The men see no chance of improving their conditions, they are constantly exposed to the bad weather. The mass of the grenadiers, even the best fighters, are fully apathetic. The desire to be wounded becomes stronger and stronger, so as to be freed at last from the misery that borders on torture . . ."

360th Infantry Division, eastern campaign, northern sector, battle zone southwest of Narva, April 19, 1944:
It began to rain. The roads disappeared, the paths were afloat somewhere in the swampy woods. But the army group's order to attack prevailed (counterattack against a Russian bridgehead on the Narva). The division was successful to a breadth of only one kilometer on each side of the "Petersen Lane." In the morning twilight the fire of our own artillery began, and the heaviest fire of the Russian artillery also began, the grenade launchers and "Stalin organs" (Russian rocket salvo launchers) pounded the companies who had taken their positions on the HKL (main battle line). In Grenadier Regiment 401, attacking to the right of the "Petersen Lane", the commander of the first battalion and the flamethrower squad of Engineer Battalion 240 fell, as did all the radiomen with their

radios. To the left of the lane, Grenadier Regiment 391 attacked, and their losses were no lighter. At the Russian fortifications, the leader of the first battalion fell with a bullet in his head during the first new minutes. In the first unit of Grenadier Regiment 399, which was supposed to follow Grenadier Regiment 401, not even half the men were unwounded. Trees crashing down caused the heaviest losses. Wounded men drowned when they got into the funnel of the flooded swampy woods . . . Then messengers reported that the enemy had cut his way in again and occupied his old main battle line. The companies of Grenadier Regiments 391 and 401 had to withdraw fighting again in order to break through the Russian lines again in the evening of the same day, this time from behind.

98th Infantry Division, southern sector, final battle at Sevastopol, May 9, 1944:
Oberst Faulhaber, Commander of Grenadier Regiment 282, pulled the retreating, scattered men of the regiment together near Dumski. Under the Ia clerk, *Feldwebel* Ssymank, they were sent into defensive action again. Scout troops reported the "Engineer Ravine" to be in enemy hands. The enemy advanced frontally too. With the last antitank gun, heavily laden enemy infantry was attacked. Until about 1:00 P.M. the defenders held on in Dumski, almost surrounded. Their ammunition was almost exhausted. At the last minute *Oberst* Faulhaber ordered them to move out through the "Tank-trap Ravine." With two squads he covered the withdrawal. In the process the colonel was badly wounded by two machine-gun shots. Later he lost his right leg.

24th Infantry Division, eastern campaign, central sector, summer 1944:
An extraordinarily difficult withdrawal of the division, which had begun west of Vitebsk on June 22, 1944, ended in Riga on October 10. The men had achieved an incredible lot, the losses had been heavy, and the division that had supported the right wing of the entire Army Group North near Obol-Polozk during the collapse of the Army Group Center was a different division from the one that now, decimated, tired and fought out, crossed the Düna the last time. And yet the Soviets had never been able to destroy the division.

198th Infantry Division, western front, midsummer 1944, breakthrough north of Montélimar against American troops:
It was now high time for the division marching back through the Rhone valley to connect with the retreat movement of the 19th Army toward the north, but this was not possible without breakthrough fighting. On the Rhone Valley road, jammed with troops and supply trains, the division could not break through; connecting with the 85th Army Corps and the Army was no longer possible. The situation was unclear. So the division

commander made the decision that on August 29, 1944 the mass of the division would break through along the side road that led through the hilly country several kilometers east of the Rhone Valley.

The fact that the enemy (the 36th US Division) had occupied this hilly land with strong forces a few hours before the beginning of the breakthrough was to be fatal for the division.

At the first light of dawn on August 29, the division moved out to lead the breakthrough with Grenadier Regiments 308 and 326. Soon the foremost battalions ran into heavy enemy resistance, and the following parts of the division came under heavy enemy artillery fire. The division had to split up into separate battle groups. The losses of the leading battalions were heavy, and the following units also lost the greatest part of their vehicles. During this breakthrough fighting, the division commander and a part of his staff were taken prisoner. Among the many who fell on that day were the division surgeon, who had treated the wounded in disregard of the heaviest artillery fire, until he himself was hit by a fatal splinter. On the evening of August 39 it already appeared that the division had lost about 1500 men during the breakthrough. The regiments were reduced almost to company strength. Fortunately, some soldiers of the division who had become separated and were also able to fight their way through turned up.

44th Infantry Division, eastern front, northern sector, retreat fighting along the Düna west of Dünaburg, August 7, 1944:
About noon a firestorm of enemy artillery and launchers broke loose. The whole main battle line was enveloped in smoke and dust when the tanks set out shortly afterward. Numerous enemy fighter echelons steadily attacked any targets in the depths of the main battlefield, especially the battery positions and the command posts of the staffs. It was again a scene of large-scale battle . . .

Despite the destruction of at least eight tanks by the 75mm antitank guns of the 14th company of Grenadier Regiment 102 and a few 88mm anti-aircraft guns, a strong pack of tanks broke through the main battle line. It was followed by twenty more tanks, that fought down the individual nests on the battle line with their tank guns and machine guns. Although the crews of the light infantry guns of the 13./102 held on bravely and, with their guns, mowed down the infantry brought in by some tanks of the third wave, in the end they, like the antitank-gun crews, were rolled over or shot down. The tanks broke through to the division command post but were turned back there by the antitank reserve of the 1st Company of Panzerjäger Unit 24 and spirited individual fighters, despite losses. The enemy infantry that followed the tanks had already established itself on the "Windmill Heights" near Midceni. The chief of the staff battery, *Oberleutnant* Wettengel, located nearby with the supply trains and parts of the intelligence platoon of the I./Artillery Regiment 60, pulled his men together, drove the enemies from the dominating heights in bitter fighting and held them, although the enemy brought up reinforcements in one countermove after another, and although he himself was already wounded, until additional German forces were on the scene.

The commander of Panzerjäger Unit 24, *Hauptmann* d.R. Christ, intervened in this battle with' men of his staff and the division staff and formed an important center for the scattered parts of Grenadier Regiment 102. Here *Oberst* Apelt, after fighting his way through to the division command post with his staff, formed a new line of defense, that was held until the planned withdrawal in the evening. The II./102 was nearly wiped out, its commander wounded. The I./102 was rolled up from the left and pushed into a swampy forest, but was able to pull itself together to some extent by evening.

In Grenadier Regiment 32 the enemy tanks had overrun the main battle line in their first attack and even passed the regimental command post and moved into the artillery positions . . . Meanwhile our own artillery had had a hard fight to maintain their firing positions. Battery officers, gun leaders and gunners fought so bravely that a large number of tanks were destroyed and the majority of the guns that were still able to fire could be saved by the exemplary action of the drivers. Several guns were destroyed, only a very few had to be blown up for lack of ammunition or opportunity to remove them from their firing positions.

Although the division was scattered by this large-scale attack on August 7, it was already fully ready to defend itself on August 11.

11th Infantry Division, eastern campaign, northern sector, withdrawal to Lake Peipus, winter 1944:
The German numerical inferiority placed indescribably high demands on the commanders and the troops; one makeshift solution followed another. the "poor people's war" reached its continuing high point . . . In icy cold, the troops often went without warm food for days, their winter clothing was wet or frozen stiff. In their pockets they had only crumbs or frozen pieces of bread, in their field flasks frozen tea. Sleep was counted in minutes.

56th Infantry Division, eastern campaign, East Prussia, January 1945:
On January 13, 1945 the enemy storm broke. The main thrust hit our 56th, the 69th and 1st Infantry Divisions. After a murderous hail of fire and under unending heavy air attacks, they were overrun by massed Soviet infantry and tanks. Deep penetrations into their own positions were the unavoidable result. The few reserves present were soon used up, and the few reserves of the Corps and the Army could not restore the

situation. Driven back step by step, the brave resistance of the defenders succeeded in holding the front to some extent for three days. Then their strength was crippled, the dam broke and fate took its course.

17th Infantry Division, eastern front, central sector, Pulavy bridgehead west of the Vistula, mid-January 1945:
On January 14, 1945 the great enemy attack broke loose in unbelievable power. After several hours of steady fire that began before the first morning light, the Russians stormed against our positions . . .

On this day of battle, with all forces working together, some 100 tanks and armored vehicles were shot down by antitank guns and, above all, Panzerfäuste . . .

The other parts of the division fought for five more days, in battles that swung back and forth, after the beginning of the withdrawal movement ordered by the Corps. The troops attacked automatically as soon as they came upon enemy units catching up with them, often singing the national anthem . . . In two tangles with strong enemy units, the whole division, which still numbered in the thousands, was caught up in cries of "Hurrah!" and singing the Deutschlandlied . . . Shouting and singing continued over long periods of time, in which the men stormed against the enemy again and again.

198th Infantry Division, western front, Bad Kreuznach area, mid-March 1945:
In the night of March 18-19, the division built a new line of defense north of Tiefenbach, in which they awaited the morning in widespread support points with Regiments 305 and 308. Loud battle noise to the west, and soon to the southwest too, hinted at bad things to come.

Early in the morning of March 19, strong enemy tank units attacked the division front behind a wall of artillery fire and with pursuit bombers in action, and pushed through between the individual support points. An unequal battle flared up with individual cut-off support points. The losses were shockingly high, the front was penetrated. The power to push the enemy farther back was lacking.

On the next day the division consisted of nothing but ruins. With oppressive superiority, the enemy (3rd US Army) moved toward the southeast, toward the Rhine. Mercilessly the fighter-bombers even dived on single men. Since almost all vehicles had been lost, along with all the heavy weapons and equipment that had been used at the front, the rest of the division flowed back, mainly on foot, toward the rescuing Rhine. In the process, they were caught again and again by enemy tanks. Many soldiers did not survive this chase. They fell, were taken prisoner wounded, or surrendered, fully exhausted and beaten. In this fighting, the capable Commander of the I./Grenadier Regiment 326, *Hauptmann*

Dressel, holder of the Knight's Cross, also fell. Despite this deadly whirl-wind, the division leadership was always able to make contact with units fighting alone or reunite scattered ones, draw back to the Rhine, and cross it on ferries between Speyer and Germersheim in the night of March 23-24.

98th Infantry Division, Italian front, area around Senio near Lugo, early April 1945:
Early in the morning of April 9, great bomber units suddenly flew out of the Apennines heading southeast. The enemy squadrons flew over the division sector and dropped their heavy bombs on the artillery posi-tions. An uncanny roaring and thundering followed. Then a gigantic cloud rose high over the ground, out of which wood, stones and clumps of earth were constantly flung down. The carpet bombing was followed immediately by pursuit-bomber attacks on individual targets to the fore-most foxhole. As of 3:20 P.M., the enemy artillery fired five waves, each lasting 40 minutes, with ten-minute pauses between them, in which pur-suit bombers swept over positions and barriers and fired on or bombed anything that still moved or looked in any way suspicious. Then they gave the infantry the signal to move in (two New Zealand divisions). In the area where each enemy battalion was pushing forward, six flame-throwing tanks led the way against our barricades, which had been evacuated since 3:00 P.M. The glowing bursts of fire were poured on them. At almost the same time, the New Zealand infantry crossed the barricade.

11th Infantry Division, eastern campaign, northern sector, the end at the Courland bridgehead:
On May 7, 1945 the division commander received the command from the Supreme Commander of the Army to rescue as many soldiers of the division as possible from Courland by sea. The Russian Air Force had already attacked the advance route and now ceaselessly bombarded the harbor of Libau. In the harbor there were still a number of small ships; their capacity could not hold anywhere near all the soldiers who gath-ered here as the hours passed. Yet a discipline that was amazing for this situation prevailed. With cheers for troop and Fatherland, for command-ers and battlefields, the men took leave of hotly contested Courland, the site of bloody battles and of many graves that they left here. Tests of true loyalty to one's own unit were seen in scenes where, for example, officers or men turned away from the quay in order to look for their units, which had not yet reached the harbor and share with them the fate of surren-dering their weapons and going into Soviet imprisonment. The former division commanders, General Thomaschki and General Boege, also re-mained behind, as did the Commander, *Generaloberst* Hilpert.

The Close Antitank Combat Troops

98th Infantry Division, eastern front, northern sector, before Gorki, October 25, 1941:
The crews of the two following tanks surrendered after they had been brought to a stop by the 4./Infantry Regiment 282 with concentric charges.

11th Infantry Division, eastern campaign, Kirishi bridgehead, June 1942:
All armor-piercing weapons were smashed by the heavy fire on June 5. So the enemy was able, almost unhindered at first, to push into Novinka and Kirishi as well as the positions between them, and roll over or enclose positions and command posts one after another. The enemy infantry followed the tanks only when the greatest number of the defenders had been put out of action. The encouraged men of the 1st and 2nd Companies of Infantry Regiment 23 tried to go at the tanks with concentric charges. *Unteroffizier* Olschewski of the 2./23 wiped out four tanks singlehandedly in a short time . . .

. . . *Leutnant* Nötzel, leader of the 14./23, tried with a few men to attack the tanks with rifle grenades and fell in the process . . .

. . . five or six tanks had pushed past Plavitzny to the regimental command post. Here too, all the men were gathered together for resistance. *Oberleutnant* Germann, Assistant Adjutant of Infantry Regiment 23, had makeshift explosive charges prepared and formed antitank troops. Several tanks, one of them right in front of the command post, were destroyed by hollow charges, others got stuck in the swamp or the trenches and were blown up.

From June 5 to July 8, 1942, 100 enemy tanks were destroyed, most of them in close combat.

6th Infantry Division, eastern campaign, summer fighting around Rshev, 1942:
Close-combat troops in and behind the main battle line attacked the enemy tanks whenever the opportunity presented itself; for example, on August 5 *Gefreite* Schulte-Strathaus blew up two tanks in the main battle line with mines. *Leutnant* Herber destroyed two T 34 and, on August 7, another T 34 in close combat.

56th Infantry Division, eastern campaign, withdrawal fighting near Orel, July 1943:
In the same way, the previous battles had also decimated our division's antitank weapons, so that our grenadiers and engineers, had to make do primarily with close-combat weapons in battle against the Russian tanks.

V. Corps, eastern campaign, fighting at the Kuban bridgehead, 1943:
On May 26, in the heavy withdrawal fighting there, 21 tanks were destroyed in the areas of various units through the use of close-combat weapons.

30th Infantry Division, eastern campaign (place and time not given):
A Feldwebel of the III./Infantry Regiment 46, smashed two T 34 tanks with 3-kilogram charges within a few days.

6th Infantry Division, eastern campaign, after the attack in the direction of Kursk had failed, summer 1943:
There was another hard fight on July 17, before the old main battle line of July 5, out of which we had moved to attack. At first 40 enemy tanks rolled out, followed by infantry, in the end there were 70 tanks moving against the division. Our own artillery and mortars detailed to us fired all their barrels could stand . . . *Unteroffizier* Scherz of the 10th Company of Grenadier Regiment 58 first went with two men against a KW I standing before the main battle line, knocked down the infantry securers (machine-gun crew) of the tank with concentric charges in close combat, and destroyed the tank with a T-mine that he threw into the turret. Some two hours later he destroyed a penetrating T 34 with a hollow charge.

24th Infantry Division, eastern campaign, northern sector, after evacuating the Luga bridgehead on February 13, 1944:
The first field attack with tanks was turned back, although four tanks crossed the main battle line. *Feldwebel* S. of the 13th Company of Grenadier Regiment 32 climbed onto one of them and shot down the tank commander with a pistol when the hatch opened.

335th Infantry Division, eastern campaign, end of March 1944, on the retreat from the Bug to the Dniestr:
Since it no longer had any usable weapons, the 14./Grenadier Regiment set up five antitank troops. On March 31, more than 70 T 34 tanks attacked the regiment's sector. At 1:00 P.M. the 1st Battalion reported that the Russian attack had been beaten off. In all, eight destroyed T 34's, some of them burning, were counted in the battalion's area. Of these, the antitank troops of the 14th Company had chased six penetrating tanks between the houses of the village and destroyed them.

Western Front, Normandy war zone, summer 1944:
On June 13, 1944 *Unteroffizier* Brasche of the 1st Company of Grenadier Regiment 901, who was detailed with his squad as a close-combat troop, destroyed five British tanks within the shortest time near Villers Bocage,

two of them with the "Panzerschreck" ("Stovepipe") close-combat weapon.

The Reconnaissance Units

24th Infantry Division, Polish campaign, 1939, before the Warthe on September 4, 1939:
Here three still undestroyed bridges leading over several arms of the river to the opposite shore. The enemy machine-gun nests on the east shore were so well camouflaged that they could not be aimed at by our own fire. Yet the foremost parts of the I./Infantry Regiment 102 and Engineer Battalion 24 worked their way forward on both sides of the causeway, though suffering losses. One bridge after another was taken. Some of the men courageously set out to make the explosive charges, that were ready to be ignited, harmless, while others were already storming on to the next bridge. In the process the company chief of the 1./102 was wounded, the company chief of the 3./102 fell, a *Hauptmann* of the engineers was hit fatally, and many men bled with him. Then an antitank gun of the 14./102 drove through the Polish machine-gun fire and fired on enemy tanks that were firing from cover. A little later an armored scout car of Reconnaissance Unit 24 pushed over the causeway and the bridges to the very front and brought help and relief to the heap of infantrymen and engineers. By evening all the bridges were taken.

17th Infantry Division, Polish campaign, 1939:
The Reconnaissance Unit 17 supplied its division with meaningful and clear results of its reconnaissance, which guaranteed a fast advance. Here too, in the typical reconnaissance manner, the enemy lines of resistance were felt out and determined by luring them to fire. After that the battle groups of the division moved in to attack, driving the enemy out of his positions and forcing him to retreat. The job of the scouts was now to keep contact with the weakening enemy and regain it where it had been lost . . . On September 3 the mounted squadron of Reconnaissance Unit 17 had already shown a particular cavalry spirit – it recognized a Polish battery that was changing position to the rear. The riders went in to attack with drawn sabers, the battery was blown up and several guns and ammunition vehicles were captured.

6th Infantry Division, western campaign, 1940:
The mass of Reconnaissance Unit 6, which turned off the road to Les Andolys toward Courcelles on its own initiative near Corny (before the Seine), was not able to take possession of the bridge there unharmed either. The enemy blew it up after a short firefight. Making a quick decision, the mounted squadron turned away toward Mousseaux. Scout

troops under their squadron chief, Baron von Boeselager, swam across the Seine around 2:30 P.M. under weak gunfire. More or less equally strong units of the bicycle squadron also crossed the river by swimming or in rubber boats and formed a small bridgehead with the riders.

5th Infantry Division, eastern campaign, central sector, near Mosty, summer 1941:

On June 27 the advance unit of the division moved forward, after brief fighting near Zoludek, to the Niemen near Orla. The big wooden bridge was unharmed. A bridgehead was quickly formed on the south shore. Then this bridgehead of Orla was taken over by the advance unit of the 35th Infantry Division, while the advance unit of the 5th Infantry Division, under *Rittmeister* Niemack, was to form a new bridgehead.

Rittmeister Niemack decided, despite strong enemy attacks against the Orla bridgehead, to move out from it with a squadron of Reconnaissance Unit 5 to the south shore of the Niemen, break through to the southwest and thus form a bridgehead at Piaski.

The mounted squadron, which received this assignment, broke out without delay, crossed a tributary of the Niemen at a ford that evening and advanced into the area northeast of Piaski during the night . . . Thus strong enemy units could be cut off here from withdrawing from the big pocket of Bialystok and Grondo on the roads leading eastward from here.

56th Infantry Division, eastern campaign, late June 1941:

Reconnaissance Unit 56, strengthened to serve as an advance unit by Panzerjäger and a light howitzer battery, was located 10 kilometers before the left wing of the division on the evening of June 27, after various fights against enemy rear guards, in order to reach the railroad line leading from Kovel to the northeast during the night and follow it 2 kilometers to reach the Turya crossing (11 kilometers northeast of Kovel). Capturing this crossing undamaged was of great importance to the future course of the operation. After back-and-forth fighting in the early morning hours of June 28, with critical hours for the advance unit, attacked by superior enemy forces on both wings in places, it was finally possible to capture the bridge unharmed.

198th Infantry Division, eastern campaign, southern sector, summer 1941:

On the afternoon of June 27, *Oberstleutnant* Zimmermann and the remainder of his advance unit also rejoined the division. After a very costly battle, the unit had not been able to hold the dominating Hill 229, and was able to get away from the enemy only by abandoning almost all its motor vehicles, antitank guns and bicycles, which were stuck fast in deep mud. Their extraordinarily high losses on July 26 added up to: 2 officers, 5 non-commissioned officers and 21 men dead, 5 officers, 17 NCO and 52 men wounded, 1 officer, 4 NCO and 36 men missing.

168th Infantry Division, eastern campaign, southern sector, 1942:
In May of 1942 parts of the mounted squadron of Reconnaissance Unit 168 rode successfully into an attack of withdrawing Russian troops at the Donets crossing.

And finally, the fate of a mounted squadron:
On August 25, 1939 a squadron taken from the former Cavalry Regiment 8 joined Reconnaissance Unit 18 and took part in the Polish and western campaigns as part of the 18th Infantry Division. After the end of the western campaign, the mounted squadron was detached from Reconnaissance Unit 18 again and, when the new 123rd Infantry Division was formed, used as the 1st Squadron of Reconnaissance Unit 123. Here it took part in the eastern campaign from the start, moved across the Volga to the Seeliger Lake in the northern sector, and then joined in the withdrawal to the Denyansk pocket, where it was surrounded for 14 months. After leaving the pocket in March of 1943, the squadron was detached from Reconnaissance Unit 123 through restructuring and became part of the newly founded Cavalry Regiment North.

The Panzerjäger

24th Infantry Division, western campaign, 1940, south of Sedan, on May 23, 1940:
For more than seven hours, Infantry Regiment 102 had fought off all French counterattacks. *Leutnant* Müller of the 14th Company of Infantry Regiment 102 was particularly successful, shooting down five enemy tanks on Hill 275 with two 37mm antitank guns and the last nine shells, and forcing six more to turn back.

56th Infantry Division, western campaign, 1940:
On May 11, 1940 the division reached the Belgian-Netherlands border in fast-moving pursuit fighting. When French tanks advanced into the open right flank, *Gefreite* Lehmann of Reconnaissance Unit 25 shot down four enemy tanks.

61st Infantry Division, eastern campaign, northern sector, advancing through Lithuania toward the Vindau, summer 1941:
Repeated counterattacks of enemy tank units were beaten back on June 26. On this day the enemy lost 36 tanks (light Russian T 26 type) before the sector of Infantry Regiment 151 alone, and *Gefreite* Heinze of the 14./

Infantry Regiment 151 shot down ten tanks within twenty minutes.

98th Infantry Division, eastern campaign, winter retreat before Moscow:
On January 13, 1942 before Medyn, the Panzerjäger survivors from *Leutnant* Seyler's Platoon numbered one officer, one medical NCO, six men and three 37mm antitank guns.

31st Infantry Division, eastern campaign, central sector, Suchinitzki zone, breakthrough of the von Gilsa battle group, winter 1941-42:
At the beginning of January 1942 the fighting in the Yuchnow area went on with the greatest bitterness and with no pardon. Panzerjäger Unit 31, for example, defended the village of Kostino as rear guard. On January 21, 1942, at 2:55 P.M., the last radio report from it came in: "Right side of town lost . . ." Then nothing more was heard from the unit.

6th Infantry Division, eastern campaign, fighting around Rshev, summer 1942:
Of the many fights against enemy tanks, the fight of *Unteroffizier* Bode can be cited particularly. In the heaviest enemy artillery fire, he shot down three T-34 tanks with his 75mm heavy antitank gun, one of them at a range of 50 meters. Though wounded, he remained at his gun, and two days later he shot down two tanks again. Despite being wounded again, he continued to command his gun. After destroying the two tanks, he and his crew took cover in a nearby dugout, was caved in there by a direct artillery hit, and he and his men could be dug out only in the coming night. The next morning he destroyed another tank and shot two more afire. In the process he was wounded a third time, this time severely.

98th Infantry Division, eastern campaign, during the "buffalo" withdrawal action, mid-March 1943, southwest of Wyasma near Lasini:
On March 18, 1943 a large-scale Soviet tank attack of some 100 tanks moved against Grenadier Regiment 282 . . . In it, there took place, among others, an unequal battle between the crew of a 37mm antitank gun of the 14./Grenadier Regiment 282 and a T 34. Without any cover, the gun crew sent shot after shot against the oncoming tank, which likewise spat fire and came nearer and nearer despite being hit several times. Two men of the gun crew fell. The two survivors jumped to the side. The one made the effort to stick a hand grenade into the muzzle of the tank's gun; the other tried to fire one more shot from the gun. Then the tank caught up with them and both were shot fatally.

24th Infantry Division, eastern campaign, fighting before Leningrad at Krassny Bor, mid-March 1943:

In this battle, one of the greatest difficulties was fighting enemy tanks. It was astonishing how capably they operated in the swampy woodlands. The commander of Panzerjäger Unit 24 used all his energy to bring at least one 37mm antitank gun to the foremost line personally, with which at least six tanks were brought to a stop.

56th Infantry Division, eastern campaign, withdrawal action from the Orel area, July 1943:
The whole Panzerjäger Unit 156 still had only four 37mm and two 75mm antitank guns.

On August 16, 1943 eight of 27 attacking tanks were shot down by *Obergefreite* Mühling of the 14th Company of Grenadier Regiment 244 alone.

198th Infantry Division, eastern campaign, battle of Byelgorod, summer 1943:
Scarcely had the new positions been taken by Grenadier Regiment 326 in the early morning of August 5, 1943 when a strong enemy tank attack took place along the big road toward the regiment. Obviously the enemy wanted to penetrate into Byelgorod in one stroke. But the Panzerjäger of the 14./Grenadier Regiment 326 and Panzerjägerabteilung 235 shot down 13 tanks in a short time. Thereupon the enemy drew back again.

6th Infantry Division, eastern campaign, south of Orel, August 1943:
The crew of a single 75mm antitank gun of Panzerjäger Unit 6 shot down seven T 34 tanks in Glinki on August 6 . . . Eight enemy tanks moved against the gun of *Unteroffizier* Heise, destroyed it and knocked out the crew. Heise was covered over in his foxhole, so that he could not move. But scarcely had the tanks rolled on than comrades jumped in and dug him out.

98th Infantry Division, eastern campaign, defensive fighting against Soviet landings on the Crimea peninsula near Kertsch, early December 1943:
On December 4, 1943 Grenadier Hefter of the 14th Company, with his heavy antitank gun, shot down four of ten T 34 tanks driving through his own main battle line.

370th Infantry Division, eastern campaign, mid-January 1944:
On January 15, 1944 a large-scale Soviet attack began, proceeding from Leningrad, with heavy fire, tank attacks and fighter-plane action . . . Until the evening of January 17, 69 tanks were shot down, 20 of them by the division's Panzerjäger, 19 by the antitank guns of the 14./Grenadier Regiment 399 and four by the infantry guns of the 13./Grenadier Regiment

399, the rest by the artillery, in close combat, etc.

24th Infantry Division, eastern campaign, withdrawal fighting along the Düna in the Dünaburg area, July 1944:

The withdrawal in the night of July 18, 1944 took place under considerable pressure from the enemy. The retreat extended into the late morning hours and the heat attacked the men viciously. Thus it remained until 9:00, when the new position was occupied . . . About 10:00 the enemy again made his way forward and began to attack with infantry and tanks . . . In the first breakthroughs into the main battle line, several tanks were shot down by the antitank guns of the 14./Grenadier Regiment 32 and Panzerjäger Unit 24, and others were set afire during exploratory advances into the hinterland by heavy antitank guns and artillery fire, especially by the III./Artillery Regiment 24. The tank battle reached its high point when subordinate assault guns went on a tank hunt. These battles dragged on into the sinking night and brought the enemy further heavy losses. *Stabsgefreite* Unger of the 1./Panzerjäger Unit 24 alone shot 11 T 34 tanks afire with his 75mm antitank gun, while *Hauptmann* Schüssler destroyed ten enemy tanks with his assault gun. The last came when he got out of his assault gun, the barrel of which had been rammed and bent by a T 34, and set a hollow charge on the sidewall of the Soviet tank, so that it was blown up. In all, 55 tanks were destroyed in the division area on that day.

81st Infantry Division, eastern campaign, northern sector, south of Polosk, June 28, 1944:

The Soviets came, battalion after battalion moved forward. The II./ Grenadier Regiment 161 could not stop, it had to move back to the antitank positions. Another hour passed. Then the first of the Soviet regiments attacked again. As if on the drill field, the rows of riflemen came over the hill. When they were about 400 meters from their own positions, *Leutnant* Haupt gave his antitank platoon the command to fire. The three 75mm guns still intact fired more than 100 rounds in five minutes. The enemy attack came to a stop some 100 meters in front of the guns.

370th Infantry Division, eastern campaign, near Molodetchno, early July 1944:

In Molodetchno parts of the hurriedly advanced division were unloaded in order to build up a first organized opposition in the great hole torn by the enemy between the Army Groups North and Center . . . 88mm antiaircraft guns performed valuable defensive service against the heaviest air attacks on the railroad station and in ground fighting . . . Bitter fighting raged around Molodetchno, which was completely in flames . . . Near Losk the battalion set up for defense. Ceaselessly, Russian tanks attacked the positions; the antitank guns of the 14./Grenadier Regiment 391 shot down nine of them.

Artillery Firefights

6th Infantry Division, eastern campaign, central sector, defensive fighting on the Tma, winter 1941:
The battle at Bukontovo on December 25 had become hopeless; the Soviets were too strong numerically. Therefore *Oberleutnant* Dunker and his remaining men moved back to the west and occupied a new securing ling before the firing positions of the 4th and 6th Batteries of Artillery Regiment 6. At once the unit commander, *Hauptmann* Stiewe, aimed his guns directly at Bukontovo. Standing upright between his guns, he gave his commands to the crews operating in the midst of enemy fire and prevented the enemy from continuing his attack.

6th Infantry Division, eastern campaign, winter 1942:
The I./Artillery Regiment 42 beat off 26 enemy attacks and preparations from January 24 to 31, 1942 with 3284 rounds, that had to be brought forward through deep snow under the most difficult conditions.

370th Infantry Division, eastern campaign, northern sector, south of Lake Ladoga, January 1942:
On January 17, 1942 strong Russian tank forces, accompanied by infantry, pushed into the firing positions of the I./Artillery Regiment 240 and occupied them after hard close combat, in which a number of the attacking tanks were destroyed. In defending his positions, the commander of the 1st Unit fell. *Leutnant* Volkmann of the 2nd Battery then moved into the lost positions during the night of January 18, along with engineers, and organized the rescue of the wounded and fallen artillerymen and the guns there.

11th Infantry Division, eastern campaign, northern sector, Volkov area, spring 1942:
Artillery Regiment 11 had a special share in the successful defense, as despite the unusual division breadth of nearly 40 kilometers, it always supplied dependable fire support and smashed several attacks in their very beginning phases. The self-sacrificing action and the personal bravery of the VB, radiomen and telephone men in the foremost line have likewise led to success in the defense and to overcoming all the batteries' difficulties in changing positions and providing ammunition.

6th Infantry Division, eastern campaign, central sector, defensive fighting near Rshev, midsummer 1942:

Our artillery supported the units in action ahead in a way that could not be excelled. Concentrations and changes of fire were carried out with the greatest precision and speed, and the artillery fire fell where it was wanted and ordered. The success of the defensive fighting was gained to an outstanding degree by the artillery that, with its fast action and precise aim, smashed a great number of enemy attacks, often just as they were beginning. *Obergefreite* Schmitzer of the 4th Battery also excelled at the B position on the main battle line. When his battery chief was severely wounded and out of action and all other officers had been detailed to infantry action in the defense of an enemy attack supported by tanks, he led the fire of his battery. When he recognized that it was only possible to fight off the strong enemy attack by concentrating the fire of several batteries, he requested further fire support by radio. With the greatest calm and sang-froid, he finally directed the fire of three artillery units and used this well-situated fire to smash the attack of three Russian battalions, observing, shooting and radioing under heavy enemy fire.

LIV. Army Corps, eastern campaign, southern sector, attack on the Soviet fortress of Sevastopol, May 1942:
The artillery fire of the Corps with its five infantry divisions used over 700,000 shells in five days, of which, for example, Artillery Regiment 22 of the 22nd Infantry Division fired 100,000 shells.

6th Infantry Division, eastern campaign, central sector, withdrawal movement south of Bryansk, mid-August 1943:
B-positions, gunners and drivers did their duty without exception under enemy artillery fire.

24th Infantry Division, eastern campaign, northern sector, winter retreat to Lake Pleskau, January 25, 1944:
Parts of the II./Artillery Regiment 24 had also gotten into a very difficult situation when the enemy had overrun the battalion z.b.V. 454. Partially in close combat, the gunners had to open a retreat route out of their positions south of Chernaya Rechka. Despite the constant threat of enemy infantry, the limbers made a path to the firing positions and back to the road to Pogi. Here again, the drivers did their duty most bravely and, through their ability and tenacity, did the seemingly impossible on roads that the wet weather turned to morasses and, along with the gunners, saved the guns, except one howitzer that stuck fast and then was blown up.

17th Infantry Division, eastern campaign, southern sector, withdrawal fighting to the Bug, late March 1944:
At the position some 60 kilometers northeast of Rasdelnaya a serious crisis developed again, especially for Infantry Regiment 55. But it was

mastered by Artillery Regiment 17 which, holding its positions unshakably despite the lack of infantry fire, smashed all Russian attacks, sometimes by direct fire.

56th Infantry Division, eastern campaign, central sector, fighting around Vitebsk at the beginning of the enemy offensive on June 21, 1944:
Despite steady enemy air attacks against the battery positions of Artillery Regiment 156, the regiment was able to support the hard-fighting infantry effectively again and again by capably directed fire concentrations.

24th Infantry Division, eastern campaign, northern sector, area northwest of Dünaburg, August 17, 1944:
Batteries of Artillery Regiment 24 were frequently in serious danger of being overrun on this day. The 2nd Battery had the enemy just 200 to 300 meters in front of its gun barrels three times, fired straight at them and used parts of its crews in infantry action. Later the battery was able to change its position to the rear.

56th Infantry Division, eastern campaign, East Prussian war zone, February 1945:
As long as the artillery still had a supply of ammunition, it formed the backbone of the defense. Often enough, when the infantry was pushed backward during the course of the day, it remained undisturbed in its old positions, which now had become "open" firing positions, and fired directly on the enemy before it made position changes to the rear during the night.

6th Infantry Division, eastern campaign, Varka bridgehead on the Vistula, January 14, 1945:
After the infantry positions had been shattered completely by heavy enemy fire and mass assaults by infantry and tanks, the enemy also pushed into the positions of Artillery Regiment 6. The commander of the 1st Unit fell, the commanders of the 2nd and 3rd units were wounded, eight battery chiefs were dead or missing. Of the crews of the B and VB positions, only a few returned. The mass of the artillery regiment were wiped out in their firing positions, sticking to their guns to the end. In the process, the gunners destroyed at least 25 enemy tanks at short range and caused the enemy heavy losses. On the evening of this day only one or two guns remained of the three light units, and of the 4th Heavy Unit, situated farther back, only seven heavy field howitzers remained.

The Engineers' Work and Warfare

98th Infantry Division, western campaign, crossing the Oise-Aisne Canal on June 5, 1940:

With artillery fire ahead of them, the first rubber boats were launched at 5:30 A.M. Defensive fire began at once. The engineers sprang into the boats, the infantrymen behind them, and now the engineers laid to the oars. In mighty strokes the coverless surface was crossed, and the first boats quickly reached the enemy shore . . . Slowly the attack moved forward. Meanwhile the engineers' second task had begun – building a bridge. At first it was under heavy enemy artillery fire. At a gallop, the heavy pontoon wagons thundered through Bichancourt. Direct hits struck the columns. Losses of men and horses brought temporary confusion and stoppages. But there was no engineer without the most extreme desire for action . . .

31st Infantry Division, western campaign, 1940:
Six engineer companies of Engineer Battalions 31 and 45, plus a company of Engineer Battalion 2, bridged the Loire near Ancenis on June 22-23. In 22 hours, using the equipment of 14 bridge columns, a 375-meter 16-ton bridge was erected.

70th Infantry Division, southeast campaign, 1941:
Engineer Battalion 70 excelled in rebuilding blown-up mountain roads so much that, in the final parade in Athens on May 5, 1941, parts of the battalion were allowed to march at the head for special recognition.

56th Infantry Division, eastern campaign, 1941:
The engineer battalion of the division had proved to be an indispensable helper of the troops in the first weeks of the campaign. First of all, the engineers had to build military or makeshift bridges over numerous rivers, including the Styr, Horyn and Slucz, to name only a few. On account of the usually wide swampy banks, these bridges often reached a considerable length, such as the Horyn bridge near Horodziec, 600 meters long. Of that, 400 meters of swamp had to be bridged. Even when our engineers found the substructure intact, the desolate and destroyed superstructure had to be replaced. Within five hours, thanks to good organization and active cooperation of all the engineers and officers, plus the help of Russian prisoners, this job was finished. In addition, countless bridges over brooks, suitable only for Panje wagons, had to be reinforced so they could at least carry heavy howitzers. There was often work to be done seeking and removing mines as well.

6th Infantry Division, eastern campaign, southeast of Polozk, July 1941:
On July 16 the 5th Company of Infantry Regiment 18 crossed the Düna in rubber boats in the evening. Under the protection of this bridgehead, as yet small and weak, Engineer Battalion 6, with the 3./Engineer Battalion 129 subordinate to them, built a 154-meter military bridge that was us-

able by all vehicles by 3:30 A.M., an astoundingly short time.

Engineer Battalion 6 had built or replaced a total of 80 bridges, including small ones, between June 20 and July 31.

What heavy losses the engineers suffered in infantry action is shown by a report of December 28. According to it, the 2nd and 3rd Companies of Engineer Battalion 8 each had only one officer, 4 NCO and 25 man left.

Army Engineer Regiment 690, eastern campaign, bridgebuilding over the Dniepr at Berislav in the night of September 2-3, 1941:
Subordinated to the engineer regiment in command for this task were Engineer Battalions 46, 40, Geb. Engineer Battalion 54 and a Rumanian engineer company, as well as eight bridge columns with 116 German pontoons from Bridge Equipment B and 22 Rumanian pontoons, which were linked to form a total of 43 ferries. Despite storm, waves and fast current, after a bridgehead was formed on the far shore, at which minor fighting still took place, bridge construction was begun at 5:00 P.M. on September 2. Despite enemy night bombers and some fire from a Soviet 21cm battery, the work was continued at night. At 3:30 A.M. on September 3 the last units of the bridge (pontoons) were put in place, and at 4:00 the 450-meter 8-ton military bridge was opened for crossing. At 4:20 A.M. the first artillery units were already crossing the river, which was almost 500 meters long. Two armies crossed the Dniepr on this bridge. Despite frequent enemy air attacks, in which parts of the bridge were destroyed and 25 engineers fell or were wounded, the damaged parts of the bridge were always repaired immediately and the pontoon bridge kept in service.

35th Infantry Division, eastern campaign, central sector, withdrawal fighting before Moscow, December 1941-January 1942:
From the Rusa on it was possible to slow down the enemy's movement. This was attributable mainly to the barricade command of the engineer battalion, which worked tirelessly with the rear guard to barricade the retreat routes effectively. This allowed the division to reach and develop the Gshatsk position without further enemy pressure.

61st Infantry Division, eastern campaign, spring fighting near Ssinyavino, 1942:
After the heaviest losses to date, the whole Engineer Battalion 161 numbered only one officer, 3 NCO and 33 men.

11th Infantry Division, eastern campaign, April 1942:
The engineers of Engineer Battalion 11 had tirelessly taken a hand in the defensive fighting of the infantry at the Volkov pocket, often side by side with them or serving as antitank troops. 2314 mines were laid, 389 Rus-

sian mines removed, 125 blockhouses and posts, 8086 meters of corduroy road and 38 bridges and crossings, measuring 277 meters in all, had been built, plus 4130 meters of firing aisles.

24th Infantry Division, eastern campaign, southern sector, fighting at the fortress of Sevastopol, June 1942:
On June 18 the taking of the northern fort still had not been achieved despite repeated attacks. The command of this attack group had been transferred to the commander of Engineer Battalion 24. The works were surrounded by a three-meter-deep walled trench that could be crossed only with assault ladders. Then unexpectedly, in the night of June 21, shock troops of the 2./Engineer Battalion 24 were able to penetrate into the fort from the northeast. Everything had been prepared in the most careful way. At a signal, bundles of hand grenades lashed together flew over the ditch and put the crews on the slopes out of action. What happened then took place in seconds. Conquering the trench, breaking into the position. Then came the forward movement of units to the rear, rolling up the enemy trenches and smoking out the dugouts with mines, concentric charges and flamethrowers. Any and all opposition was broken in close combat, and after three hours the big fort was firmly in the hands of the engineers.

370th Infantry Division, eastern campaign, southern sector, attack on the Sapun heights in the area of the Sevastopol fortress, June 1942:
The German attack began at 2:30 A.M. on June 29. At the head of the infantry, the engineers removed the enemy minefields.

58th Infantry Division, eastern campaign, northern sector, after the battle at the Volkov in June of 1942:
The fighting strength of Engineer Battalion 158 on June 26 was down to: 1st Company, 1 officer, 1 NCO and 2 men; 2nd Company, 1 officer, 2 NCO and 22 men; 3rd Company, 1 officer and 9 men.

6th Infantry Division, eastern campaign, central sector:
Engineer Battalion 6 built approximately 1500 meters of 8- to 11-ton bridges from June 22, 1941 to June 21, 1942, laid 33.6 kilometers of German mines and removed 5400 Russian mines.

6th Infantry Division, eastern campaign, central sector, front at Rshev, autumn 1942:
Position construction by the engineers: In the period from October 11 to November 28, the 2nd Company of Engineer Battalion 6 had prepared 1777 Spanish rider obstacles, moved them forward and set them up before our own lines in 25 night actions. 791 T- and 107 S-mines were laid,

wood for 23 protective bunkers was cut and installed in the main battle line at night, 7 tank positions were prepared, 625 S- and K-rolls unrolled and 675 meters of connecting trenches dug.

During the entire summer and autumn fighting around Rshev, the battalion, despite the constantly necessary infantry action, had laid a total of 6800 T- and S-mines and built 8 kilometers of barbed-wire obstacles before the main battle line.

98th Infantry Division, eastern campaign, central sector, defense at the Vorya position near Gshatsk, September 1942:
A week's accomplishments for Engineer Battalion 138: construction of 1.06 kilometers of trenches, laying and preparing of 112 rolls of barbed wire and 427 Spanish rider obstacles, preparation of tripwires with booby-traps, 750 meters of runners for muddy trenches, building of 750 meters of road obstructions to obscure enemy view, clearing 700 square meters of forest for firing field, laying 216 T- and 35 tripwire mines, laying of 650 meters of corduroy road, building of a 14-meter 8-ton bridge.

305th Infantry Division, eastern campaign, southern sector, battle for Stalingrad, autumn 1942:
During the heavy close combat in the assembly halls of the tractor factory and Hall 4, the engineer battalion of the division stood out in particular.

98th Infantry Division, eastern campaign, central sector, "Buffalo" withdrawal movements, southwest of Vyasma, March 1943:
Even more than in the other types of combat, the success of this shortening of the front was owed to the tireless engineers. No ford or crossing remained unmined, no bridge fell unharmed into the enemy's hands, and no mine barricade was completed until the last man in the rear troops – often at the last moment – had passed through the gap.

In the new position after the withdrawal movement: Engineer Battalion 198 was in constant action before the front. Even in the night of March 20-21, two platoons of the 2nd Company laid 500 T-mines under difficult conditions. While laying another 950 mines, the 3rd Company suffered under heavy enemy fire before Dyuki – at times the work had to be stopped completely – 29 men were lost. In the following night, 1444 T-mines were installed before the main battle line. In the hinterlands, building roads and bridges kept the engineers breathless.

61st Infantry Division, eastern campaign, northern sector, Volkov area, summer 1943:
The engineer battalion of the division had suffered severe losses in the past battles and numbered only one officer, three non-commissioned offi-

cers and 33 men. The battalion was refilled again.

Note: In the withdrawals that took place on all fronts beginning in 1943, the engineer units often saw service as infantry.

Achievements of the Intelligence Units

Polish Campaign, 1939
From September 9 to 20, the radio unit of a division staff sent and received 739 orders and reports, making a daily average of 65.

61st Infantry Division, eastern campaign, northern sector, Baltic area near Narva, summer 1941:
In order to bridge the great distances between the battalions and make cohesion and command possible, the radiomen worked with their portable radio sets day and night without relief. From July 28 to August 6, among others, several thousand encoded radio messages were exchanged by the 16 ultra-short-wave transmitters of Infantry Regiment 151. Since the beginning of the campaign, the troops of the horsedrawn telephone company of the division's intelligence unit had installed, prepared for use and then removed more than 2000 kilometers of lines, mostly on foot.

24th Infantry Division, eastern campaign, southern sector:
In the battles on the Sevastopol front that began in mid-January of 1942, the listening service of Intelligence Unit 24 performed valuable services. Here enemy telephone and radio messages were listened to.

35th Infantry Division, eastern campaign, central sector, withdrawal fighting before Moscow, December 1941-January 1942.
Hard pressed by the enemy, it succeeded in getting away from the enemy, holding the ordered intermediate lines and staying together. The intelligence unit, which maintained telephone connections in every situation through ceaseless action, including connections with neighbor units, played a decisive role in the orderly course of the withdrawal.

56th Infantry Division, eastern campaign, winter fighting, 1941-42.
In the very same way, Intelligence Unit 156 and the troop intelligence units accomplished incredible things that made possible the successful leadership of the division. Without the first-class intelligence unit, commanding the division would have been impossible, not only in this instance, but in the whole eastern campaign.

6th Infantry Division, eastern campaign, central sector:

Intelligence Unit 6 installed a total of 4600 kilometers of telephone lines and removed them all again from June 22, 1941 to June 21, 1942.

Near Rshev, summer 1942:

And the trouble-shooters . . . ? – "Connect me with X! . . . Is X there? . . . Is X there?" . . . "Do you finally have a connection with X?" – "I'm trying steadily. The line must be down . . ."

Two have already stood up and picked up their intelligence pack with their tools and the field phone. "So long," they both say quietly, and "Good luck" goes with them. They leave the intelligence bunker. Outside is a thundering artillery fire, punctuated with the detonations of "Stalin organs", grenade-launcher strikes and machine-gun clattering. One jump at a time, the two trouble-shooters rush along the line, throw themselves down, dive into shell craters for cover against tank fire, until suddenly the line lies there, torn apart. Yes, but where is the other end? Search, creep, jump, till finally the other end is found. Then it is fixed quickly . . . And so it went day after day, night after night, weeks and months long, until one or the other was hit.

6th Infantry Division, eastern campaign, southern sector, attack fighting at Kursk, July 1943:

A trouble-shooting troop with *Obergefreiten* Lux and Dehle and Gunner Freimann of the 3rd Company, Artillery Regiment 6 mended the shot-up lines between the advanced B position at Hill 257 and fire control twenty-five times in one day, under endless artillery and infantry fire.

198th Infantry Division, eastern campaign, southern sector, battle at Byelgorod, midsummer 1943:

The former telephone connections from the division command post to Byelgorod had become unusable, since they led through an area that had meanwhile fallen into enemy hands. The radio connections had also been interrupted at times. The division could expect heavy fighting in the coming night and wanted in any case to assure the conduct of the combat action. For that reason the Brachert telephone construction troop of Intelligence Unit 235 was given the assignment of installing a new line over the ridge that ran southward from Byelgorod. Nobody knew whether the road leading over the ridge to the city was still free of enemies. In any case, enemy tanks could be expected anywhere in the country. It seemed like a miracle to the construction troop that it could drive over the deserted ridge and carry out its so important task. Only shortly before Byelgorod was it fired on by Soviet tanks from west of Krassnoy. But the construction troop was lucky and reached Byelgorod unharmed. In the evening twilight it reported to the command post of Grenadier Regiment 326. The telephone connection with the division was reestablished . . . On the way back, a wagon of the construction troop took a direct hit from a tank, one man fell, one was wounded.

6th Infantry Division, eastern campaign, central sector, withdrawal movement southeast of Bryansk, July 23-August 15, 1943:
The telephone and radio men of the troop intelligence units and Intelligence Unit 6 worked without rest and almost without pause in heat, dust or rain to provide the necessary connections, repaired them in machine-gun, antitank, artillery or tank fire, kept them in order and thus created the conditions for conducting the battle.

Difficulties of the Administrative and Supply Services

45th Infantry Division, eastern campaign, central sector, advance through the Pripyet Marshes, summer 1941:
It went on for four weeks, through swamp, dirt and dust, in the direction of Gomel . . . This was no longer an "advance", but literally a miserable crawling through 40- to 50-cm-deep sand, bottomless morass, thick woods and overgrown brush. In places long corduroy roads first had to be built to make any progress at all. The motor vehicles had inconceivable engine troubles, for the fine sand got into everything and damaged pistons and cylinders. In addition, they were much too low-slung for this terrain, their chassis often hit bottom and they could be moved only with a lot of help on both sides, often enough with a broken axle or fenders, mufflers, brake lines, etc., torn off . . .

The column drivers in particular did everything humanly possible to move ahead.

97th Light Division, eastern campaign, southern sector, summer 1941:
After Vinniza had been reached and taken in mid-July, the enemy resistance stiffened again. The Slovakian Brigade was overrun by the Russians and only brought to a stop again by energetic action from the bakers and drivers of the division.

6th Infantry Division, eastern campaign, central sector, during the battle at Vyasma-Bryansk, 1941:
Early in October the division's advance was slowed by swampy, bottomless and narrow woodland paths and the developing shortage of fuel on account of supply difficulties. A period of bad weather beginning at the same time (Russian autumn mud season) did its best to make most of the motor vehicles get stuck in the swampy forest lanes. One truck after another got stuck from October 7 on. These vehicles stood all along the division's line of march until the frost began, watched only by their drivers, many of them in the woods. It would fill a whole chapter to tell what

the dutiful, loyal men did, left on their own, to maintain the division's motor vehicles and feed and defend themselves. This loyalty was rewarded. In November, the vehicles could be driven after the division on the now-frozen roads with the first arriving supplies of fuel.

198th Infantry Division, eastern campaign, southern sector, advance toward the Donets Basin, October 1941:
Every heavy rain or snowfall turned the deep soil into impassable mud that could hinder, indeed cripple any marching movement. Then the troops always had to get by without supplies, because the supply trains themselves necessarily ran out of rations and war materials and could often be gotten underway again with the necessities brought in on light Panje wagons. Added to this, in the region that the division had to pass through there were only bitterly salty springs with water that was scarcely usable for drinking or cooking. This also caused commissary problems. The lack of raw fodder was especially hard on the horses, who constantly had high demands made on their strength.

The organizational work of the division quartermaster, *Hauptmann* i.G. Müthen, the industrious and inventive division commissary chief, Dr. Hermann, the energetic supply columns under the command of Dinafü Major Honold, all his loyal supply units as well as commissary officers, paymasters and foddermasters of the troops, including the bakery and butcher companies deserved our thanks that ways were found again and again to overcome the supply problems.

198th Infantry Division, eastern campaign, southern sector, in the Donets Basin, late october 1941:
The scene as concerned the division's motor vehicles at that time was rather hopeless. The workshop company was swamped with work. Replacement parts from home could hardly be obtained. Instead, broken-down vehicles had to be stripped and completely abandoned in hopes of later repairs.

The motor vehicle breakdowns on this long 380-kilometer march were especially high, adding up to 21 solo motorcycles, 10 sidecar motorcycles, 18 cars, 17 trucks, one bus and four ambulances. The shortage of motor vehicles in the division to date totals 61 solo motorcycles, 87 sidecar motorcycles, 24 cars, 66 trucks, 2 buses and 10 ambulances. There was no hope of improvement in the motor vehicle situation.

98th Infantry Division, eastern campaign, central sector, on the Nara, still during the advance toward Moscow, December 4, 1941, evening:
The temperature sank to 30 degrees below zero . . . Even while underway, the motor vehicles' radiators froze despite the Glycantine in them, the radio batteries, even the oil in the weapons froze. Then too, the spare-

parts situation was so bad that only a tenth to a fifteenth of our needs could be met.

To cite just one example: In this cold of 32 degrees below zero, *Gefreite* Ulsenheimer drove his truck from Yuknov to Maloyaroslavets. On the way the drive belt of the captured Russian truck broke. His companion removed another one from a broken-down truck along the road and got the truck going again. It got so much colder that Ulsenheimer thought his feet would freeze. Once the two of them warmed up in a Russian shed, and then the motor would not start. Warm the water, take out the spark plugs, pour gasoline into the openings from the canister . . . In spite of that, the motor froze again immediately and could not be turned over any more, all the cables were gone. Then light gasoline under the motor, it got warm again and the truck started. Until the next breakdown . . .

45th Infantry Division, eastern campaign, southern sector:
The cold winter of 1941-42 had a destructive effect on motor vehicles. One vehicle after another had to be abandoned and destroyed as the result of severe frost damage or because of a lack of fuel, and in spite of all the drivers' efforts.

6th Infantry Division, eastern campaign, central sector, 1941-42:
The 45-truck pack train of the regiments covered some 59,400 kilometers from June 22, 1941 to June 1, 1942 and moved 123 tons of baggage and 2380 tons of food supplies.

6th Infantry Division, eastern campaign, central sector, defensive fighting at Rshev, summer 1942:
The city of Rshev was constantly under the heaviest enemy artillery fire and rolling bomb attacks. What was accomplished by the supply trucks and ambulances, the supply and food services in this hail of bombs and shells, which also had the Volga bridges as its particular goal, to keep up the supply of weapons, ammunition, food and materials was an outstanding achievement for them all. Quietly and unnoticed, they carried out their difficult tasks, on which the life and combat of the troops depended, and seldom gained recognition or honors.

98th Infantry Division, eastern campaign, central sector, southwest of Vyasma, March 1943:
When the division's supply services ran smoothly despite all the difficulties of the mud season, it was attributable to the small, mobile horsedrawn wagons. All alone, they supplied all the division's needs in ammunition, food, equipment and engineering supplies through day and night action. All the motor vehicles, on the other hand, were silent.

6th Infantry Division, eastern campaign, central sector, withdrawal movement southeastward of Bryansk from July 23 to August 15, 1943:
The motorcyclists, the supply-train drivers and services assured the supply of the division in ceaseless, tireless service, day and night, under the most difficult and primitive conditions.

3rd Mountain Division, eastern campaign, withdrawal from the Nikopol bridgehead, early February 1944:
After the breakthrough of the 30th Russian Army Corps had taken place, the leader of the 6th truck column, *Oberleutnant* Peer, was charged with the defense of the village of Pereviskiv on February 2. He had at his disposal two truck columns, the workshop company and, along with various other supply units of the division, some groups made up of assorted men . . . The town was held until February 10. In the process *Kriegsgerichtsrat* Bramer, who gathered men from scattered units together throughout that time and made them into battle groups, fell . . . and the Protestant division Chaplain May was badly wounded too.

98th Infantry Division, eastern campaign, southern sector, defensive fighting in the peninsula of Crimea, October 1943:
Two hundred men from the supply trains and back-line services were chosen and trained for front service. Emergency companies were also formed from staffs and administrative and commissary companies, without exception, and trained daily. Their leaders were administrators and older non-commissioned officers, all of whom did not lack for tough combat experience and fought well. Yes, many of the paymasters and others unaccustomed to combat stepped in as front officers and gave their lives in action.

The Work of the Medical Services

254th Infantry Division, western campaign, before the encirclement fighting at Dunkirk, May 1940:
At the preparatory ward and operating room of the 1st Medical Company there were thick crowds. The stream of incoming patients continued to swell. As the *Oberarzt* reported, the surgeons were already working in two groups. Physicians and dentists assisted. The chief pharmacist and his assistants all had their hands full supplying the needed medical supplies. The medical *Gefreite* in charge of sterilizing received assistance from the 3rd Platoon. All the men who had already been operated on were doing well. Except those who died in transport, there were no dead . . . The medics went from stretcher to stretcher, from the treated to the untreated wounded men. Many of them – pastors in civilian life – not only took care of physical needs, drinks, bedpans, etc. They also helped

those who were facing eternity, gave faith, consolation and confidence, and took last messages to those back home or wrote letters to loved ones.

98th Infantry Division, eastern campaign, central sector, near Korosten, mid-August 1941:
Both main dressing stations – that of the 2nd Medical Company in Jusefovka and that of the 1st Medical Company in Chepovichin – were working to exhaustion. The 1st Medical Company treated 1253 wounded men in 12 days.

198th Infantry Division, eastern campaign, Dnjepropetrovsk bridgehead, September 1941:
A surgical group of the 1st Medical Company in an advanced position in the bridgehead came through splendidly. It had set up its main dressing station in a cellar, where the numerous wounded men could be treated immediately. Although the building above the cellar and the nearby houses had been destroyed by enemy grenade fire, even difficult operations and treatment of wounds went on without interruption. In these days many soldiers owed their health and life to the medical skill, the calm and strength of the *Oberarzt* Dr. Runge.

98th Infantry Division, eastern campaign, withdrawal from Moscow to the Istya, December 27, 1941:
That exemplary, caring, loyal comrade, the regimental surgeon of Infantry Regiment 282, *Stabsarzt* Dr. Schievelbein, was taken by surprise by enemy snowshoe troops while treating wounded men, was wounded and then died for the soldiers entrusted to him.

The medical support point in Medyn treated 1640 men from November 4 to 11, in seven days, 1241 of them wounded and 299 sick, mostly with frostbite.

24th Infantry Division, eastern campaign, southern sector, in winter combat during the first attacks on Sevastopol, 1941-42.
The medical and veterinary services of the division also had one hard winter behind them. The high number of wounded men in the days of fighting before Sevastopol and the constant care of sick men in difficult positions made the highest demands on the medical officers and their assistants. Much silent heroism was experienced here. A *Feldwebel* of the regimental band of Infantry Regiment 31 stayed in a crudely covered hole in the ground on the edge of the slope above a rocky cave for four months. He voluntarily declined to be relieved and constantly transported the patients from the dressing stations near Mekemsia to the ambulance station with his vehicle, a light Panje wagon drawn by two Panje horses . . . At the main dressing stations of the two medical companies in

Salankoy and Cherkes-Kermen they operated, bandaged and treated patients day and night; they were always ready to help.

The field hospital of the division had been set up in Baktchissaray.

98th Infantry Division, eastern campaign, withdrawal from Moscow, early January 1942:

Often it was only possible to transport the wounded away from the front under enemy fire. *Gefreite* Winckler, driver of an ambulance – himself already wounded – rescued five wounded men by inspired driving, disregarding enemy fire at the southwest exit route from Mayolaroslavets. Wounded again while breaking through the fire, he nevertheless brought the five safely to Medyn.

Scherer Battle Group, eastern campaign, northern sector, Cholm pocket, spring 1942:

The wounded (2200 in all) were operated on by the *Stabsarzt* Dr. Ocker (the ranking surgeon in the pocket), *Oberarzt* Dr. Muck and their assistants in a low, unprotected room that was penetrated five times by Russian antitank shells. A wooden sled on blocks served as an operating table. The doctors worked in day and night shifts, often only by flickering candlelight.

56th Infantry Division, eastern campaign, southern sector, spring 1942:

With great dedication, the division surgeon, *Oberfeldarzt* Dr. Klein, devoted himself to completing the medical facilities. Bathing and delousing facilities were set up near the front, and the main dressing stations, which took on a more hospital-like character, made it possible for sick and slightly wounded men to stay close to the division until they were discharged.

918th Infantry Division, eastern campaign, southern sector, attacking toward Tuapse (West Caucasus), summer 1942:

Stabsarzt Dr. Stochdorph and *Stabsarzt* Dr. Oeding, like all other doctors, were tirelessly treating the wounded during these weeks. Under the most difficult conditions they and their helpers did their duty.

78th Infantry Division, eastern campaign, central sector, 1943:

Here, for example, a battalion surgeon who – severely wounded himself – kept on doing his duty at the troop dressing station of his battalion for several hours, until the last wounded man was treated. Only then did he allow himself to be taken to the main dressing station.

11th Infantry Division, eastern campaign, northern sector, summer fighting on the Volkov, 1943:

Here too, all the doctors and medical officers worked to the last again, including Dr. von Wiek and Dr. Krause. *Oberarzt* Dr. Nolte had served a sector with his helpers all alone since the loss of two battalion surgeons. *Stabsarzt* Dr. Beck and his assistants ran the main dressing station at Kelkovo.

56th Infantry Division, eastern campaign, central sector, defensive fighting around Orel in July of 1943:
The numbers of losses give eloquent testimony to the hardness of the battles and the focal-point action of the division in the very first days of the fighting. At the two main dressing stations of the division, 1229 wounded men were treated from the beginning of the battle on July 11 to July 15. The self-sacrificing activity of our medical services is particularly worthy of honor. In the fateful month of July they lost 6 medical officers wounded, 15 medics fallen, 57 wounded and 12 missing.

198th Infantry Division, eastern campaign, southern sector, battle at Byelgorod, summer 1943:
In addition, Assistant Surgeon Dr. Rüdiger stood out for his unselfish treatment of the wounded despite the heaviest machine-gun and rifle fire; he was one of the last to leave the position and was then wounded by a shot in the chest while going back.

24th Infantry Division, eastern front, northern sector, withdrawal fighting at the Luga bridgehead, winter 1943-44:
On January 31, 1944 a firefight developed at close ranges, in which two company leaders, the battalion surgeon and many engineers of Engineer Battalion 24 fell . . . Meanwhile, the enemy was attacking from the east in steady streams against the rear-guard, so that the few vehicles had to be blown up in order not to fall into enemy hands . . . The survivors of Engineer Battalion 24 made their way in. The less wounded men were brought along. The division surgeon took care of the seriously wounded, hitching up 32 Akjas with the help of the mounted platoon. In the process he was surprised by the Soviets, and the rescue work no longer succeeded. The unit surgeon of the intelligence unit fell into enemy hands, along with several medical officers. The division surgeon fought his way through the woods alone and reported back on February 2.

198th Infantry Division, western campaign, breakthrough north of Montélimar on August 29, 1944:
Among the many who fell that day was the division surgeon, who cared for the wounded, ignoring the heaviest American artillery fire, until a fatal splinter hit him.

The Veterinary Services

45th Infantry Division, eastern campaign, pocket battle near Kiev, September 24, 1941:
A line set up in great haste on the west bank of the Szupoy prevented the greater part of a penetrating enemy group from breaking all the way through. Only individual parts got across the river, meeting sections of the division lying there, such as Veterinary Company 45 in Lisogubova-Sloboda, who fought off the attack under *Stabsveterinär* Dr. Kirchmair but suffered bloody losses.

198th Infantry Division, eastern campaign, southern sector, Mius area, November 1941:
What with overexertion, coldness and lack of fodder, the condition of the horses worsened from day to day, and with it the division's mobility decreased more and more, although the commissary centers, veterinary services, foddermaster and drivers gave the greatest care to helping their four-legged comrades. Of an intended complement of 4600, only 3100 army horses were still alive, and fully 1200 of them could scarcely stand up and were completely out of the question as draft horses. They could have been saved if they could have been sent to an area with good fodder and kept in good stables for eight weeks. Such a place had to be found. This question was taken up by the division veterinarian, Dr. Priebus, with energy and success. and a long, slow column of exhausted animals set out in the direction of Stalino to find better fodder places in the area between Stalino and Dnyepropetrovsk. Thanks to the good organization of the march by the veterinary services and their careful treatment by the horse handlers, the great majority of the horses survived to reach their new quarters, where they were properly restored to health. For the time being, 1600 Panje horses had to take over as draft horses. Splendidly recovered, the horses rejoined the troops in mid-June, just at the right time for the summer advance of 1942.

24th Infantry Division, eastern campaign, southern sector, before Sevastopol, winter 1941-42:
Our four-legged comrades also suffered severely. They scarcely saw oats for months at a time. Under the greatest difficulties, raw fodder at least was brought in from the country, though never in sufficient quantities. Every piece of wood they could reach was taken as food. It could not be avoided that the division suffered additional considerable losses of horses, although the veterinary officers, foddermasters, blacksmiths and drivers did everything imaginable for them.

Activities of the Chaplains

24th Infantry Division, western campaign, during fighting around Mont Dieu south of Sedan, May 1940:
Our comrades who fell near the enemy could not be rescued at first. At night it was attempted, and wounded men were searched for, but no more were found. Then on May 19 a wounded man was seen dragging himself back. A first attempt to draw him into our lines was stopped by French fire. But when the division chaplain Sch. walked out openly onto the meadow with a Red Cross flag, the enemy held his fire so that this wounded man and two more could be rescued.

83rd Infantry Division, eastern campaign, central sector, area northeast of Vitebsk, January 28, 1942:
Only now did we learn that our beloved Protestant division chaplain Brinkmann had fallen. He wanted to drive his ambulance to Kryest to be with his suffering and wounded comrades of the 3rd Battalion of Infantry Regiment 257. "I am needed there, there at the front," he always said. He proved his loyalty with his death.

198th Infantry Division, eastern campaign, southern sector, during fighting to relieve the Cherkassy pocket in the Vinograd area, February 12, 1944:
Amid the attacking soldiers there appeared, as so often before, Pastor Fischer, to be with the wounded and dying in their last hour.

5th Infantry Division, in a report from Protestant Chaplain Kühn:
When I was transferred from the 5th Army Corps to the 5th Infantry Division on August 20, 1941, I met the Catholic division chaplain there, the Wehrmacht chaplain Grosse-Schanze, already decorated in World War I for bravery before the enemy, whose sense of humor and experience of life made his company very pleasant. At that time the division came to a stop for the first time during the eastern campaign and prepared itself in the area east of Dukovchina for the pocket battle of Vyasma. Thus it was possible for me to get acquainted with many officers and men in peace and hold services. These took place here, as they did during the entire war until April of 1945, within closed groups. The form had been agreed on by us two division chaplains and approved by the commanders of the units, whereby a joint service of both faiths took place with song, prayer and sermon took place first, and the regimental band often took part up to 1943. After the joint service, the Catholic soldiers held mass and the Protestants communion. For services announced in advance, the participants numbered between 80 and 95% of the troops . . . Religious services in the division remained the same until

the Easter services in 1945 . . .

On an average, some 20 to 30 services a month were held by us two division chaplains throughout the war. There were also prayers on the battle line.

Division Staffs

198th Infantry Division, eastern campaign, southern sector, summer advance, 1941:
On July 26, as a result of an unexpected enemy attack near the marching columns pursuing to the east, a defensive front of the division set up to the south was formed with great holes. All dispensable officers and men of the division staff had to occupy the hill south of Beresovka and secure the area to the south and east.

6th Infantry Division, eastern campaign, central sector, withdrawal west of Kalinin to winter positions, as 1941 turned to 1942:
On January 1, 1942 the division staff reached Koledino in the evening. This village now consisted of only two buildings. The two-room house of the division staff had to house 30 to 50 men. And in this building full to overflowing with men we had to work, telephone, write, plan and dictate orders while some of the men snored, others ate their last bit of bread, still others looked for lice and many smoked. The air was so thick you could have cut it with a knife. But outside it was ice cold, 52 degrees below zero was recorded. The division staff had nothing to eat either. And outside on the road, the endless, ceaseless, restless columns of returning vehicles rolled past.

198th Infantry Division, eastern campaign, southern sector, withdrawal from the western Caucasus, January 30, 1943:
Shortly after midnight the Russians attacked. Through a hole 500 meters wide that remained in the defenses of Tugurgoy the enemy was able to move forward to the division command post at 12:30 A.M., under cover of night. By gathering all their strength (division staff, parts of Intelligence Unit 235, etc.) they closed off the location of the breakthrough and pushed some of the enemies back in counterthrusts. Although the Soviets had almost surrounded the division headquarters, the men of the headquarters, under Oberleutnant Breucha, who fell in this battle, held their positions for several hours.

198th Infantry Division, eastern campaign, southern sector, near Uman, March 1944:
On March 10 the division was scattered. In the last days the division staff

was left very much to itself and had to protect itself with motorized and mounted scout troops.

24th Infantry Division, eastern campaign, northern sector, February 1945:
In the new position in the Courland bridgehead near Ciedras, intermediate positions had to be built in the hard, frozen ground. Every man not actually fighting was called in. The officers of the division staff, combat clerks and intelligence men had to dig trenches several hours every day in order to fortify the heights at Ciedras. The Ia and even the division commander pitched in.

83rd Infantry Division, Pillau on Danzig Bay, April 24-25, 1945:
In these two days the already very decimated division was completely smashed by superior Soviet forces. A few survivors were able to cross over to the Frische Nehrung in the night of April 25-26. The division commander, *Generalmajor* Wengler, landed with a few companions from the last boat near Neutief. A little later he, the IIa Major Benz, Staff Commissary Chief Caramanlaki and Senior Paymaster Entorf fell victim to an aerial bomb.

Losses of Individual Infantry Divisions

A few statistics of losses given below will show how the infantry divisions lost more and more men, particularly since the beginning of the campaign in the east.

45th Infantry Division, Polish campaign 1939 (18 days):
Total losses 158 dead, 360 wounded.

5th Infantry Division, western campaign 1940 (6 weeks):
Losses 282 dead, 706 wounded, 17 missing.

18th Infantry Division, western campaign 1940 (6 weeks):
Losses 558 dead, 2030 wounded and missing (ca. 15%).

45th Infantry Division, eastern campaign, attack on Brest-Litovsk fortress on June 22, 1941:

The stubbornly defended fortress could be completely conquered only after eight days. In this time the division lost 482 dead, including no fewer than 32 officers (more than in the entire French campaign).

56th Infantry Division, eastern campaign 1941:

In the first seven days of the campaign the division had already lost 40 officers and about 1020 men in total losses. On August 14 the division attacked over the Mostova sector, with losses on this day alone numbering 10 officers and 389 men.

126th Infantry Division, eastern campaign, end of August 1941 at Staraya-Russa:
By previously applicable standards, the division was at the end of its strength. The combat strength of the rifle companies had sunk to 50 men, the trench strength was even less, but a necessary rest was again not granted the troops.

98th Infantry Division, eastern campaign, advance fighting near Korosten, August 1941:
Eleven days of combat cost the division 78 officers and 2300 NCO and men. On August 12 the 3rd Company of Infantry Regiment 289 lost 48 dead (3 officers) and 148 wounded (6 officers).

198th Infantry Division, eastern campaign 1941:
From June 22 to July 12, 1941 the losses of the division numbered: 19 officers and 274 men dead, 38 officers and 1111 men wounded, 1 officer and 240 men missing. From June 22 to October 31 the total losses were 5096 officers and men, including 1034 dead and 438 missing.

5th Infantry Division, eastern campaign, central sector, area north of Smolensk, summer 1941:
The total losses of the division from July 20 to August 3 were:
Dead: 13 officers, 365 NCO and men. Wounded: 42 officers, 1072 NCO and men, missing: 1 officer, 72 NCO and men. Total in 14 days: 1565 men.

98th Infantry Division, eastern campaign, central sector:
Losses of the division from August 1 to October 31m 1941: 56 officers, 1332 NCO and man dead, 142 officers, 4142 NCO and men wounded, 5 officers, 204 NCO and men missing. This made a total lost in three months of 5881 men = 1/3 of the entire division.

5th Infantry Division, eastern campaign, central sector, summer 1941:
The losses of the division in the period from June 22 to October 20 were:
Dead: 48 officers, 1222 NCO and men. Wounded: 109 officers, 3268 NCO and men. Missing: 1 officer, 161 NCO and men. Total: 1270 dead, 3377 wounded, 162 missing = about 1/3 of the division.

262nd Infantry Division, eastern campaign, southern sector, attack fight-

ing at Korosten from July 17 to August 7, 1941:
The losses of the division in this period were 634 dead, including 29 officers, 1664 wounded and 295 missing.

61st Infantry Division, eastern campaign, northern sector, advance through Lithuania, 1941:
The 1st Company of Regiment 176 lost in the first six and a half months of the campaign, in dead and wounded, 16 officers, 102 NCO and 552 men.

6th Infantry Division, eastern campaign, central sector, withdrawal fighting from Tma into winter position, 1941:
The trench strength of the infantry units show frightening statistics, for example, the 3rd Company of Infantry Regiment 18, on December 12, 1941 had only 7 rifle carriers, 1 machine-gun crew and one light grenade-launcher crew.

Parts of the **123rd and 218th Infantry Divisions** and other units, eastern campaign, northern sector, Cholm pocket, winter and spring 1941-42:
Of about 5000 men of the units in the pocket, 1555 fell before they were relieved.

56th Infantry Division, eastern campaign, beginning of 1942:
Despite several groups of replacement troops, the combat strength was lower than at the beginning of the campaign. In addition, the great losses of the first six months of 1941 had considerably reduced the number of veteran officers, NCO and men with war experience.

198th Infantry Division, eastern campaign, beginning of 1942:
The division had a combat strength of only some 6600 men. Summer advance 1942, attack over the Mius: The division's losses from July 11 to 19 were 83 dead, 429 wounded and 10 missing.

24th Infantry Division, eastern campaign:
The division's losses from September 1, 1939 to March 31, 1943 were 4941 dead, 18,479 wounded 910 missing, total 24,330 men.

98th Infantry Division, eastern campaign, withdrawal during the so-called "Buffalo movement" of 1943:
From March 3 to 21, during this movement, the division lost 40 officers and 1508 NCO and men in dead, wounded and missing in 14 days.

56th Infantry Division, eastern campaign, southern sector, after the Orel battle, 1943:

On August 1, 1943 (set day) the division lacked 129 officers, 2 veterinary officers, 14 administrators and 3608 NCO and men. Replacements gained in the month of July were 17 officers and 182 recovered NCO and men. The losses from July 1 to 31 were 28 dead, 60 wounded and 5 missing officers and 291 dead, 2621 wounded and 184 missing NCO and men.

31st Infantry Division, eastern campaign, 1942-43 period:
A memo of Grenadier Regiment 17 included names of 28 battles. In this period 35 of the regiment's 70 officers fell. The total strength sank from 1400 to 70 men.

198th Infantry Division, eastern campaign, Novorossisk area, 1943:
On March 17, 1943 the 2nd Company of Grenadier Regiment 305 still had a combat strength of 2 officers, 5 NCO and 49 men. The 7th Company consisted of only 1 NCO and one man. The situation in other units was similar.

98th Infantry Division, eastern campaign, retreat from Crimea to Sevastopol, mid-April 1944:
25 to 30 men of the 1st Battalion, the 13th Company with one heavy infantry gun the three light infantry guns, plus 30 separated men–these were now the strengths of the whole Grenadier Regiment 290 . . . The survivors of the three former grenadier regiments escaped their complete annihilation by renewed night marches.

6th Infantry Division, eastern front, Soviet large-scale attack from the Varka bridgehead north of Radom on January 14, 1945:
In the morning hours the commander of Grenadier Regiment 18, *Oberst* Graf, fell at his command post when he tried to shoot down a Russian tank with a Panzerfaust. In the morning hours of the same day the commander of Grenadier Regiment 37, *Oberst* Lütkehaus, had fallen. These were two regimental commanders on one day, in addition to other high losses.

These figures show very clearly how high the losses in the eastern campaign were, and remained to the end, in comparison with other campaigns. In addition, what with the often merciless warfare of the Soviet troops, a great number of the missing German soldiers must be counted among the dead.

Opinions on the German Soldier

Viscount Lord Alexander, British Field Marshal and Commander of Allied troops in Italy, in a Canadian weekly periodical on March 22, 1956:
"When people think they have to bad-mouth the German Army

in World War II, then they do so without me! The German soldier proved to be brave and capable . . ."

And in another public statement:
> "The German soldiers were possessed of a strong sense of duty
> and discipline and fought bravely and tenaciously everywhere.
> They preserved their high military standards to the end."

Speaking to the British Prime Minister Winston Churchill, the Field Marshal said on March 20, 1944:
> "I doubt whether there is a second troop in the world who would
> survive all that and go on fighting with the same bitterness as
> these people" (German soldiers).

J.F.C. Fuller, former British general and well-known military writer,
stated in his "Military History of the Western World":
> "What the German soldier, completely unprepared for a winter
> campaign (1941-42 in Russia), undertook and what he did,
> constitutes–in terms of endurance–one of the greatest heroic
> deeds in the history of war."

Lord Alanbrooke, British Field Marshal and Chief of the British Empire
General Staff, wrote in his diary on May 23, 1941:
> "The German soldiers are without a doubt the best soldiers."

Matthew Ridgway, former US general and commander of NATO forces,
stated in 1965 that the Americans got to know the German soldier in
battle, and though they rejected his Nazi ideology, they nevertheless re-
spected him as a fighter.

George S. Patton, former US general and well-known tank leader during
World War II, developed a growing admiration during the war for the
German soldiers. They fought bravely and held the honor of their profes-
sion high. He had great respect for the German soldiers . . .

George C. Marshall, Chief of the US General Staff during World War II,
wrote:
> "The Germans are natural fighters, we must admit that. They
> were excellently trained, especially as concerned the non-com-
> missioned officer corps. The basis of their discipline was unshak-
> able . . ."

Dwight D. Eisenhower," US five-star general and Allied commander in
Europe in World War II, was obsessed by the idea of a "crusade" and a
keen opponent of the Germans and the Wehrmacht. After the war,

though, he revised his opinion, as seen in the following words:
> "Meanwhile I realized that my judgment of the Wehrmacht and the attitude of the German officer corps at that time did not correspond to the facts, and I am not unwilling to apologize for my former opinion. The German soldier fought bravely and honorably for his homeland ..."

Lattre de Tassigny, former Marshal of France, in April 1946:
> "In our time there have been some very great achievements, for example the Germans in Stalingrad. They stood for a senseless command. But what they accomplished was exemplary ..."

François Mitterand, French President, visited the Soviet Union in January of 1986 and spoke during his meeting with the Kremlin leadership in Moscow of the "millions of brave and reliable German soldiers who later, in June of 1944, were held down in the east by the Soviet major offensive of that summer so that the Western Allies could make progress after the invasion of Normandy ..."

F.O. Miksche, Czech military writer, in his book, "The Failure of Atomic Strategy":
> "Not one of the western powers was capable of accomplishing what the German Wehrmacht went through in the Russian winter campaigns of 1941-1944."

Milovan Djilas, member of the commanding staff of Yugoslav partisans with Tito, in his book *The War of the Partisans*:
> "What surprised me most in the course of all these talks (with captured German officers) was the fact that in the German Wehrmacht neither the Nazi ideology nor the Nazi mentality appeared."

Bibliography

General Histories:
Barker, A.J., *Die deutschen Infanteriewaffen des Zweiten Weltkrieges*, Motorbuch Verlag, Stuttgart, 1974.
Brian, Davis L., *Uniformen und Abzeichen des deutschen Heeres 1933 bis 1945*, Motorbuch Verlag, Stuttgart, 1973.
Bunrin Co. Ltd., Tokyo, Japan, *Graphic Action Series of Blitzkrieg*.
Ellis, Christ, *German Infantry and Assault Engineer Equipment 1939 to 1945*, Headly Brothers Ltd., London, 1976.
Engelmann, Joachim, and Scheibert, Horst, *Deutsche Artillerie 1934 bis 1945*, C.A. Starke Verlag, Limburg/Lahn, 1974.
Haupt, Werner, *Das Buch der Infanterie*, Podzun-Pallas Verlag, Friedberg, 1982-83.
Hoffschmidt, E.J. and Tantum, H.W., *Second World War Combat Weapons* (German), WE Inc., Old Greenwich, Connecticut USA, 1968.
Hogg, Jan, *Deutsche Artilleriewaffen im Zweiten Weltkrieg*, Motorbuch Verlag, Stuttgart, 1978.
Mueller-Hillebrand, Burghart, *Das Heer 1933-1945*, 3 Vol., Verlag E.S. Mittler und Sohn GmbH, Frankfurt/Main, 1956.
Niehaus, Werner, *Die Nachrichtentruppe 1914 bis heute*, Motorbuch Verlag, Stuttgart, 1980.
Pabel Verlag, *Der Landser*, series of brochures on events and experiences of World War II, Rastatt.
Petter, Dietrich, *Pioniere*, Wehr- und Wissen Verlag, Darmstadt, 1963.
Piekalkiewicz, Janusz, *Pferd und Reiter im 2. Weltkrieg*, Südwestverlag, Munich, 1976.
Reibert, W., Dr.jur., *Der Dienstunterricht im Heere*, Verlag E.S. Mittler und Sohn, Berlin, 1940.
Schirmer, F. and Wiener, F., Dr., *Feldgrau*, periodical publications of a research group, Lehrte, 1962.
Tessin, Georg, *Verbände und Truppen der deutschen Wehrmacht und Waffen-SS im Zweiten Weltkrieg 1939-1945*, Verlag E.S. Mittler und Sohn GmbH, Frankfurt/Main.
von Tippelskirch, Kurt, *Geschichte des 2. Weltkrieges*, Athenäum Verlag, Bonn, 1951.
Wagner, Carl, *Heeresgruppe Süd*, Podzun-Verlag, 1971.
Weeks, John, *II. Weltkrieg-Handfeuerwaffen*, Verlag Wehr und Wissen, Koblenz/Bonn, 1980.
Zentner, Rolf-Leonhard, *Deutsche Militärhelme 1895-1975*, Verlag Wehr und Wissen, Bonn, 1980.
Zentralarchiv der Pioniere, *Deutsche Pioniere 1939 bis 1945*, Kurt Vowinckel Verlag, Neckargemünd, 1976.

Division Histories:
Reinicke, Adolf, *Die 5. Jägerdivision (vorher 5. Infanteriedivision)*, Podzun-Pallas-Verlag, Friedberg, 1986.
Grossmann, Horst, *Geschichte der 6. Infanteriedivision*, Verlag Hans-Henning Poszun, 1958.
Buxa, Werner, *Geschichte der 11. Infanteriedivision*, Verlag Hans-Henning Podzun, 1952.
von Metzsch, Friedrich-August, *Die Geschichte der 22. Infanteriedivision 1939-1945*, Verlag Hans-Henning Podzun.
Ring der ehem. 24. Inf.Div., *Geschichte der 24. Infanteriedivision*, Selbstverlag, Stolberg/Rheinland, 1956.
Gschöpf, Dr. Rudolf, *Mein Weg in der 45. Infanteriedivision*, Oberösterreichischer Landesverlag, Linz, 1955.
Arbeitskreis der 56. Inf.Div., *Die Geschichte der 56. Infanteriedivision 1939-1945*, duplicated manuscript.
von Zydowitz, Kurt, *Die Geschichte der 58. Infanteriedivision 1939-1945*.
Hubatsch, Walther, Prof.Dr., *Die 61. Infanteriedivision 1939-1945*, Podzun-Pallas-Verlag, Friedberg, 1983.
Tiemann, R., *Geschichte der 83. Infanteriedivision 1939-1945*, Podzun-Pallas-Verlag, 1986.
Gareis, Martin, *Kampf und Ende der 98. Infanteriedivision*, Podzun-Pallas-Verlag.
Hennecke, Kardel, *Geschichte der 170. Infanteriedivision 1939-1945*, Verlag Hans-Henning Podzun, 1953.
Graser, Gerhard, *Weg und Kämpfe der 198. Infanteriedivision*, Traditionsband der ehem. 198. Inf.Div., Tübingen, 1961.

Files and Documents:
Files and Documents of the Infantry School, Döberitz, 1940-41.
Notes by War School participants, 1942.
Printed and written documents from the troops 1940-1944.
Written reports of former unit leaders, troop members, etc.
Numerous files, documents and writings from the author's 30 years of collecting activity.

Photo Credits:
Pabel Verlag, Rastatt: *Landser-Reihe*.
Davis, Brian, L., *Uniformen und Abzeichen des deutschen Heeres 1933 bis 1945*, Motorbuch Verlag, Stuttgart, 1973.
Hoffschmidt, E.J. and Tantum, H.W., *Second World War Combat Weapons* (German), WE Inc., Old Greenwich, Connecticut USA, 1968.
Niehaus, Werner, *Die Nachrichtentruppe 1914 bis heute*, Motorbuch Verlag, Stuttgart, 1980.
Pawlas, Karl R., *Waffenrevue*.
Division Histories published by Podzun-Pallas-Verlag, Friedberg.

Author's archives.

The Soldiers of an Infantry Division in 5 Years and 8 Months of World War II

From the last peacetime parade in Berlin . . .

. . . into the Polish campaign in 1939.

Advancing into the western campaign, 1940.

And new, exhausting advances in the Russian campaign, 1941.

Rest and sleep along the road.

Then came the defensive battles and position fighting — defending in a shot-up woodland.

A trench was the main battle line, even in winter.

Position sentry on the Russian front, autumn 1942.

In a one-man foxhole on the western front.

As of 1943 the withdrawal battles began in the east.

The rear-guard vacates a burning village in the spring of 1944.

Grenadier. and assaul guns prep for a counterthr on the wes front, 1945

Clothing and Equipment

The Wehrmacht national emblem, the cloth emblem worn on the right side of the chest (upper left, next to it the metal version. Below, the metal rosette, as was worn on the peaked cap.

Field jacket (this one of an Oberfeldwebel) and cloth trousers.

Belt with bullet pouches, bread bag and short hand spade, plus carrier for the assault pack (above). gas cover, opened gas-mask canister, and gas mask (lower left), boots (right).

Steel helmet and officer's field cap.

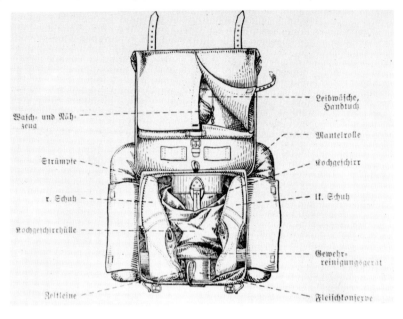

Wasch- und Näh-zeug

Strümpfe

r. Schuh

Kochgeschirrhülle

Zeltleine

Leibwäsche, Handtuch

Mantelrolle

Kochgeschirr

lf. Schuh

Gewehr-reinigungsgerät

Fleischkonserve

Pack with contents packed as prescribed.

Pack without rolled coat, but with rolled blanket.

A machine-pistol pouch in three sections, plus a pouch attached at right for cleaning tools.

A bullet pouch, divided into three sections.

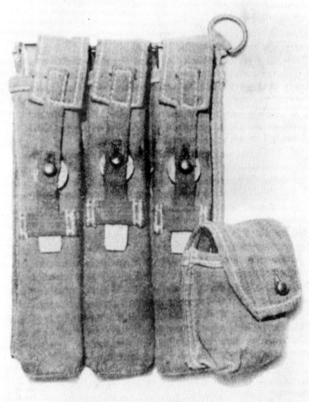

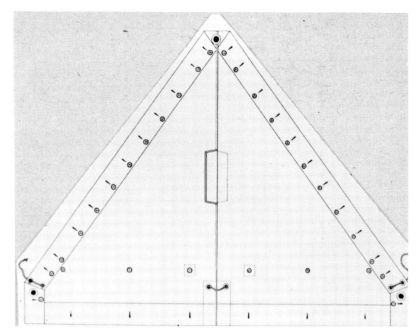

*Always indispensable
— the triangular tent
cloth* (Zeltbahn).

*"Tents for four"
made of four
triangular cloths.*

*The triangular
tent cloth as
protection
against the rain.*

*The service book, carried in
the left breast pocket.*

*The identification disc, worn around
the neck.*

Everyday Military Life at the Front

Thus the soldiers "lived" during peaceful times in the long war years, when the weather allowed.

Deep sleep in hay or straw under a tent roof.

Winter in a Panje hut with a home-made stove.

In position — here one fought, ate and slept.

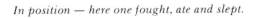

Cover dug in the deep snow.

The front line — a trench with a dugout.

Christmas in the bunker, the main dwelling place.

These four have "organized" watermelon as extra food.

Do it yourself, even darning socks.

The company barber hard at work.

*At rest behind the front —
here one had a good wash,
cooked, and wrote that
long-overdue letter to the
loved ones back home.*

*The "thunder
pole."*

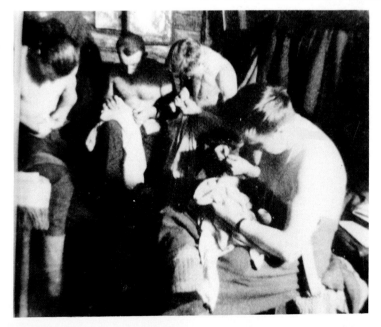

*Daily delousing — the "kills" are
counted precisely.*

214

Drinking and washwater is brought from a Russian village pump.

Wherever time and situation allowed — a card game. Preferable Doppelkopp, Seventeen and Four, or Sheepshead.

15

A letter from home.

The Rifleman

*Loading the 98 k rifle
with a frame of five
cartridges.*

*Ready for
attack —
folding spade
and bayonet
attached to the
belt, the third
man back with
fixed bayonet.*

*Stick and
hand gren
ready for t
shortly be
an enemy
attack.*

Sentry in winter — with rifle and cartridge belt for a light machine gun over his shoulders, stick grenades and opened short spade stuck in his belt between the bullet pouches.

A sip from a field flask with its very worn cover. Camouflage on the steel helmet, held by an auxiliary rubber band.

A machine gunner throws hand grenades in defensive action; on his belt are a holster with an 08 pistol and a bayonet.

The Rifle Squad

The squad leader (Unteroffizier) leads, with an MPi 40, plus stick hand grenades and spade in his belt, binoculars hanging from his neck, behind him Gunner 1 with a 34 light machine gun, bipod folded, and attached belt drum.

On their way (from right to left), squad leader with machine pistol, behind him Gunner 1 with light machine gun, bipod unfolded, followed by Gunner 2 with a machine-gun case and spare barrel holder.

Gunners 1 and 2 in a firefight, Gunner 2 leads the cartridge belt out of the machine-gun case.

Gunners 1 and 2 with light machine gun, bipod folded and attached circular sight, on a tripod for anti-aircraft use.

An attacking row of gunners with fixed bayonets providing covering fire, Gunner 1 with a light machine gun (far left) changes position.

A rifle squad moves out in a row — almost every man carries his usual equipment plus an additional machine-gun case, Gunner 1 (center) has a belt drum on his light machine gun.

A squad in a village — squad leader with a rifle instead of a machine pistol, behind him Gunner 1 with a light machine gun on a carrying strap, then Gunner 2 with a machine-gun case on his back. The men carry small assault packs (tent cloth and cooking utensils on their belts).

A squad in winter camouflage clothing moves out — light machine-gunners 1 and 2 change position to the rear.

A squad after the battle — there used to be ten of them. An infantry cart in the left background.

The Rifle Platoon

Platoon leader (Leutnant with binoculars at right) gives orders to one of his squad leaders (Unteroffizier, carrying, among other things, a gas cover on his chest), both with full steel-helmet camouflage.

Platoon troop in a town (2nd man from left, holding spade, is the platoon troop leader) takes cover from enemy aerial bombs.

Platoon in preparation, 2nd man from left wears a helmet camouflage net, the soldier at the right front has a rolled-up tent cloth on his assault pack carrier.

A platoon attacks, the squads spread out into a "broad wedge."

A light grenade launcher troop moves out — led by the troop leader with an ammunition case on his shoulder, Gunner 2 with the barrel and a case, Gunner 1 with the baseplate.

A light grenade launcher troop in position, Gunner 1 aiming, Gunner 2 ready to insert the first grenade, troop leader (Unteroffizier) with binoculars, ready to observe the firing.

222

A Panzerbüchse troop in position.

The platoon's vehicles: two-horse combat wagons (HF 1), the one in the center covered, the one at left open, and a Panje wagon at right.

A one-horse infantry cart with trailer.

The tried and true Panje wagons with and without covers (2nd vehicle at rear).

The Rifle Company

The company gets ready — company chief, at front, gives written orders to attack to the platoon leaders (Leutnant *at left,* Feldwebel in the middle, Oberfeldwebel *standing in back with telescope). The company troop pays close attention.*

A company troop in winter battle dress before action. Some hoods are pulled over the steel helmet. Front and center, the company leader with pistol and captured Russian map case, at far left the company troop leader with binoculars.

A company marching closed ranks at double time on a sandy road in the Polish campaign, 1939.

224

A company moves forward, the
platoons unfolding into rows of
riflemen, in the western
campaign, 1940.

A company retreats in the eastern campaign during the
winter of 1941-42, still without any winter camouflage
clothing, the company chief mounted.

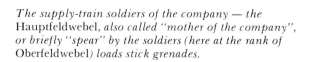

The supply-train soldiers of the company — the
Hauptfeldwebel, *also called "mother of the company",
or briefly "spear" by the soldiers (here at the rank of*
Oberfeldwebel) *loads stick grenades.*

Pay call in the Polish campaign, 1939, at left the writing-room truck, the battalion paymaster sitting in front of it, the company pay clerk sitting at right.

The men of the field kitchen, the two cooks with aprons, plus helpers. At left is the field kitchen, at right the limber with, among others, two pots on it.

Through thick and thin — a small two-horse field kitchen.

Naturally they cooked on the march too — a big four-horse field kitchen.

Food carriers with their squads' utensils.

Food distribution up front among the troops, ladled out of the containers into the utensils (here lidded). The "messboy" puts the company chief's food into a sheet-metal plate (the only special amenity in food service for officers).

For officers, non-commissioned officers (left an Unteroffizier, right a Feldwebel) and enlisted men, the food from the field kitchen in the same.

*The company
shoemaker (left)
and tailor (right)
always have
plenty to do.*

*The saddler also
works outdoors
in the summer.*

*The blacksmith at his light field equipment (belonging
to the battalion supply train).*

Horses and vehicles of the company — a saddle horse, saddled, haltered, with stirrups turned up.

A horse of a two-horse hitch with harness.

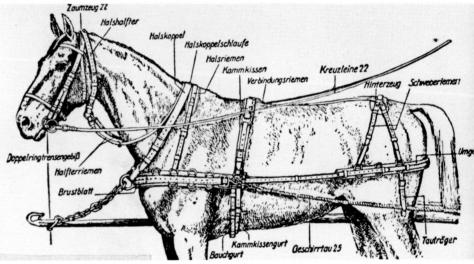

Zaumzeug 22
Halshalfter
Halskoppel
Halskoppelschlaufe
Halsriemen
Kammkissen
Verbindungsriemen
Kreuzleine 22
Hinterzeug
Schweberiemen
Doppelringtrensengebiß
Halfterriemen
Brustblatt
Umga
Kammkissengurt
Bauchgurt
Geschirrtau 25
Tauträger

The left pole-horse of a four-horse hitch with harness.

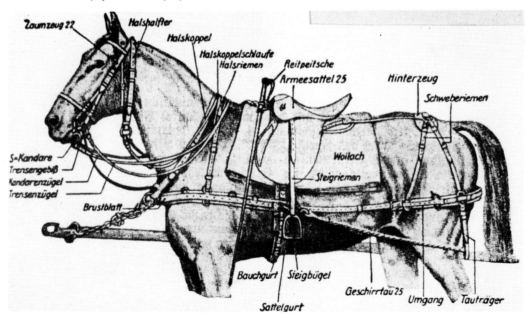

Zaumzeug 22
Halshalfter
Halskoppel
Halskoppelschlaufe
Halsriemen
Reitpeitsche
Armeesattel 25
Hinterzeug
Schweberiemen
S-Kandare
Trensengebiß
Kandarenzügel
Trensenzügel
Woilach
Steigriemen
Brustblatt
Bauchgurt
Steigbügel
Geschirrtau 25
Umgang
Tauträger
Sattelgurt

A company's steel combat wagon (sometimes also used by platoons).

The only motorized vehicles (other than motorcycles) in the company, the three 3-ton trucks.

The supply trains did not have it easy either — the four-horse hitch of an HF 2 in rough country in the eastern campaign, 1941.

Midsummer advance in the dust and heat, in 1942. At left and right on the road are individual squads and platoons, in the middle of the road the combat vehicles (here Panje wagons).

Four-horse hitch in the cold, ice and snow, winter 1941-42.

A four-horse Army Vehicle 2 in the mud near Tuapse, South Russia.

Four-horse hitch in the swamps of the Volkov area, North Russia.

Supply columns wait before a river crossing. In the left foreground, a field kitchen, in the center a four-horse HF 2. Beef cattle are driven along.

Sometimes in winter only Panje sleds can get through.

Supply camp on the South Russian steppes in winter after a snowstorm.

233

Light Infantry Weapons

Stick hand grenade 24 (left) and hand grenade 39 (right).

234

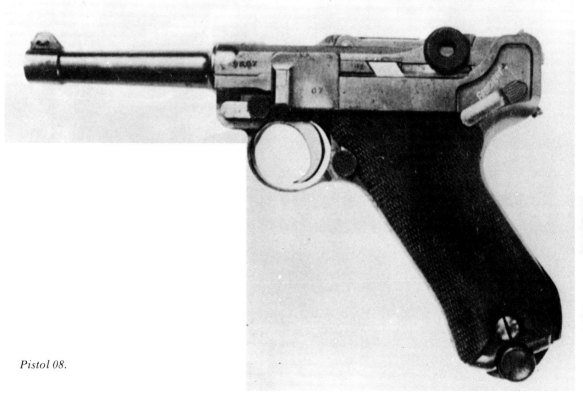

Pistol 08.

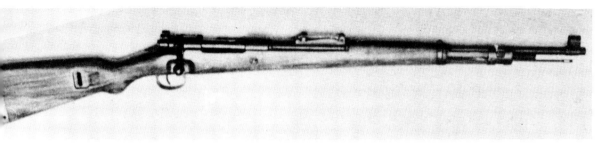

Rifle 98 k.

Self-charging rifle 41.

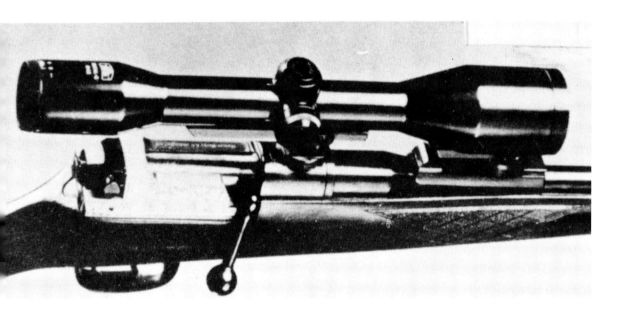

Telescopic sight (Zf 42).

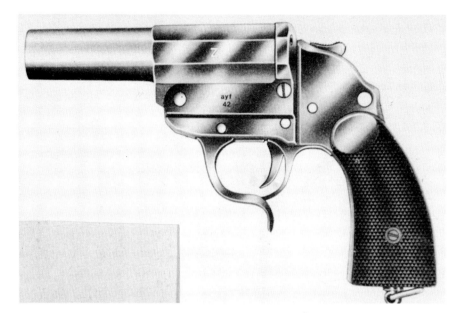

Flare pistol 38.

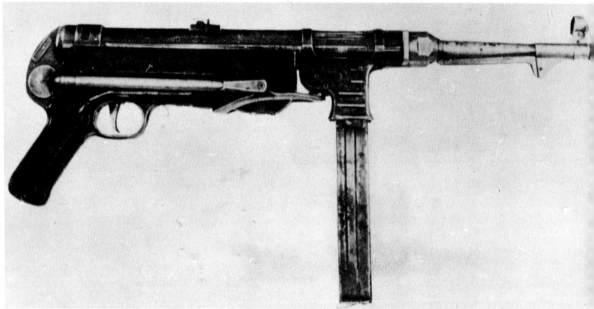

Machine pistol (MPi) 40 (with shoulder brace folded in).

Light machine gun (lMG) 34.

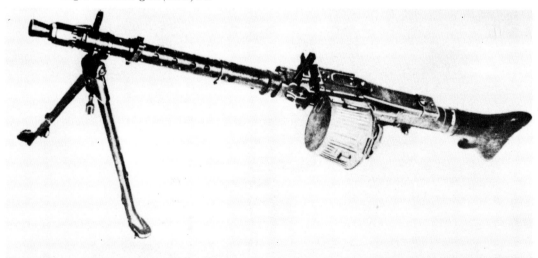

Light grenade launcher (lGr.W.) 36.

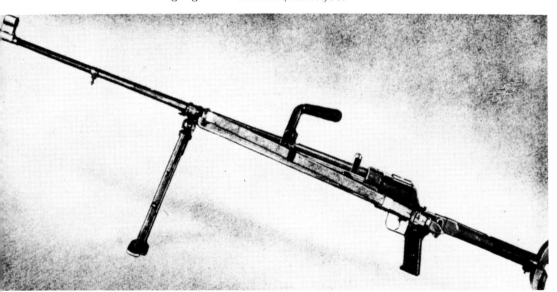

Panzerbüchse (Pz.Büchse) 39.

Heavy Panzerbüchse (s.Pz.Büchse) 41.

The Infantry Battalion — and its machine-gun company

Three times a battalion staff — here in the Polish campaign, 1939. The battalion commander (center) explains the situation.

Battalion staff with understaff and battalion standard taking a rest in the western campaign, 1940.

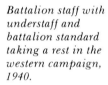

Battalion staff in cover during a battle in the eastern campaign, 1941.

The machine-gun company — observation Unteroffizier *(left) and rangetaker of the company troop with their equipment.*

A heavy machine gun in firing position on a mantelet.

A heavy machine gun — Gunner 1 (with fully camouflaged steel helmet) changing barrels.

A heavy machine gun firing sustained fire, Gunner 2 (left) feeds the cartridge belt.

Two machine guns in twin mounts for anti-aircraft use, pulled behind a four-horse limber.

A heavy (later medium) 80mm grenade launcher, transported dismantled with ammunition on a one-horse combat cart.

240

A grenade-launcher troop carrying their dismantled launcher. At left in a man with the baseplate on his back, in the center a man with the barrel over his shoulder (the barrel could also be carried on the back with a belt), at right a man with the bipod.

A launcher gunner loading an 80mm grenade, with the attached charge clearly visible on the end of the grenade, the launcher is set at its lowest elevation.

A heavy grenade launcher being fired at its highest elevation.

The Infantry Regiment — with regimental units

A regimental commander (center) writes a brief order for a waiting messenger (right), the soldier who has taken off his steel helmet.

A regimental staff in an earthen bunker, examining an order received from the division. From left to right, regimental surgeon (with glasses), commander, adjutant, assistant adjutant. At far right, the intelligence officer takes a troop report on the telephone.

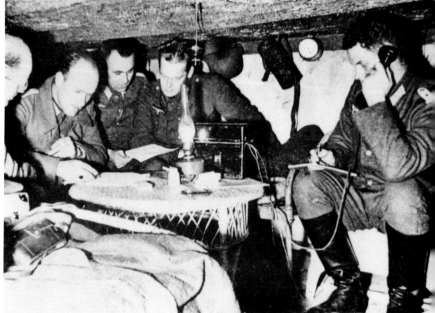

A motorcycle messenger of the regimental understaff in a motorcycle coat, his machine pistol carried crosswise in front of his chest, underway despite a wound.

A regimental mounted platoon during an advance in the eastern campaign, 1941.

The regimental band plays the song of the "good comrade" for the burial of fallen soldiers.

The infantry gun company (13th Company) — bringing a light infantry gun to the front in the Polish campaign, 1939 — the crew has already dismounted.

A light infantry gun platoon on the march in the western campaign, 1940, the crew seated on the limbers.

A light infantry gun, the limber heavily loaded with equipment and baggage, on a muddy village street in the eastern campaign, 1943.

A light infantry gun with its crew in firing position, at the front is the ammunition loader with shells and cartridges on shot baskets.

Heavy Infantry Weapons

Heavy machine gun on mantelet (sMG).

Heavy grenade launcher (sGr.W.) 34.

Light infantry gun (l.IG) 18.

Heavy infantry gun (sIG) 33.

A heavy 150mm infantry gun on the march, the crew partly riding, partly on foot.

246

A heavy infantry gun in firing position, being aimed with a panoramic scope.

An antitank fighter with a concentric charge made of the lashed-together canisters of stick hand grenades.

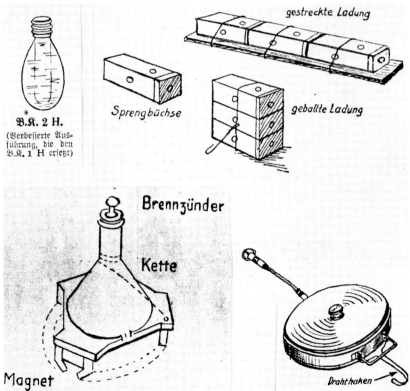

Close-combat antitank weapons: firebomb (upper left), explosive cases (upper right), magnetic hollow charge (lower left), tellermine (lower right).

247

An antitank fighter (Unteroffizier) with a firebomb ready to throw, his steel helmet camouflaged in front.

248

An antitank fighter sets a magnetic hollow charge on the hull of a tank. Over the barrel there already hang two linked smoke bombs meant to prevent the tank crew from seeing.

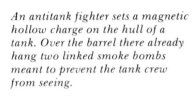

An antitank close-combat troop attacks a Soviet Kv 1 that has been brought to a stop. One man (foreground) covers, the second is already on the tank and throws a hand grenade into the torn-open turret hatch.

Antitank fighters beside an already destroyed Soviet T 34 tank. The troop awaits the explosion of a second tank (background). The standing soldier holds a tellermine by its carrying handle.

The Reconnaissance Unit

A mounted squadron advancing, passing a resting truck column.

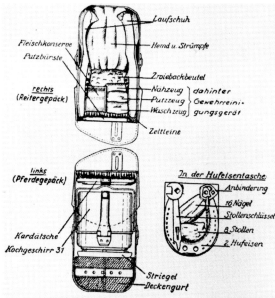

Laufschuh

Fleischkonserve
Putzbürste

Hemd u. Strümpfe

rechts
(Reitergepäck)

Zwiebackbeutel
Nahzeug } dahinter
Putzzeug } Gewehrreini-
Waschzeug } gungsgerät

Zeltteine

links
(Pferdegepäck)

In der Hufeisentasche:
Anbindering
16 Nägel
Stollenschlüssel
8 Stollen
2 Hufeisen

Kardätsche
Kochgeschirr 31

Striegel
Deckengurt

The two saddlebags and their prescribed contents.

249

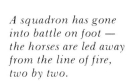

A squadron has gone into battle on foot — the horses are led away from the line of fire, two by two.

A mounted scout troop reconnoiters in the first light of dawn; in the foreground is a vehicle destroyed by mines.

A bicycle company shortly before mounting, their rifles slung over their backs in the prescribed way.

A bicycle company taking a rest, the bicycles leaning against each other in pairs. In the background is the truck carrying spare bicycles and the repair shop.

250

Bicycle riders arriving to serve as reinforcements dismount to go into battle.

The heavy weapons of the reconnaissance unit — here a light infantry gun of a motorized platoon — is stuck in a mudhole (Polish campaign, 1939).

A horsedrawn 37mm antitank platoon crosses a river in the eastern campaign, 1942.

The Panzerjäger Unit

A 37mm antitank gun (from the rear) waiting in place in the Polish campaign, 1939.

A 37mm antitank gun (from the front) with slight camouflage in the western campaign, 1940.

When motor vehicles often could not move during the winter of 1941-42 in the eastern campaign, the 37mm antitank guns had to be set on runners and drawn by horses.

A 50mm antitank gun crew is just loading a shell into the barrel. Additional antitank shells (cartridge ammunition) lie ready in the ammunition containers.

A 50mm antitank gun firing during the eastern campaign, 1943.

253

A heavy 75mm antitank gun behind a heavy Wehrmacht towing tractor with a canvas top, in the western campaign, 1944.

The 37mm antitank gun.

A 37mm antitank gun with a 41 stick grenade in its barrel.

254

The 50mm antitank gun.

The 75mm antitank gun, with an antitank shell standing on end before it.

The Artillery Regiment

At a main B position: the unit commander at the periscope, next to him a battery chief.

B position, equipped with periscopes and telephone connections, under enemy fire.

An Unterwachtmeister *of a VB troop calls for fire by radio.*

A battery officer (wearing the Knight's Cross) uses a whistle to give the gun crews the command to fire.

An ammunition loader brings a 150mm shell to a gun in a shot basket.

The completely exhausted driver of an artillery wagon, asleep in the saddle.

A six-horse hitch with a light 105mm field howitzer, moving at a trot (western campaign, 1940).

Mounted drivers, one in the saddle, one dismounted, drive their team through difficult country (eastern campaign, 1942).

e light 105mm ld howitzer towed hind a limber, th its crew riding.

A light field howitzer is unhitched and the limber is put in its position.

A light field howitzer firing, the barrel recoiling. At right is a gunner with the trigger line.

The 150mm heavy field howitzer, carried dismantled in two horsedrawn wagons, the barrel wagon shown here (western campaign, 1940).

The heavily loaded mantelet wagon. The crewmen have hooked on an Akja with their belongings.

At times, especially late in the war, the heavy field howitzer, its mantelet on a chassis, its barrel drawn back, was also towed by 8-ton towing tractors.

A heavy field howitzer being unloaded from a two-wheel chassis.

A heavy field howitzer battery in firing position.

A heavy field howitzer is loaded.

260

A heavy field howitzer firing.

The light field howitzer (lFH) 18.

The heavy field howitzer (sFH) 18 with mantelet on chassis, ground stake folded in, barrel drawn back (for motorized towing).

*Engineers with power saws remove an obstacle
in the Polish campaign, 1939.*

262   *Engineers bring rolls of barbed wire forward to
build obstacles before the West Wall, in the
winter of 1939-40.*

*Engineers building
dugouts (earthen
bunkers) in the north,
eastern front, winter of
1942-43.*

An engineer NCO observes the effect of an explosive charge on a steel-grid bridge during retreat fighting on the eastern front, 1944.

A small rubber boat lands.

A large rubber boat is taken to the water; the men have taken off their helmets so as not to damage the rubber.

Engineers with a rubber-boat ferry take an infantry platoon across a river; to the left and right are small rubber boats for use in emergencies.

A large rubber-boat ferry with a lFH 18 loaded on it sets out from the shore; in the background is a blown-up bridge.

264

Wounded men are carried over a pontoon footbridge.

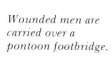

Storm boats bring a shock troop to the enemy shore in the fog.

Building a temporary bridge with the help of large rubber boats.

Bridge Column B carrying half-pontoons on the eastern front, winter of 1941-42.

A half-pontoon is taken to the water after being unloaded (a drill photo from Germany).

A pontoon ferry fully loaded with vehicles just before putting out, a motorboat on hand to push it. In the background, an empty ferry returns.

A company with packs, rifles carried
as in World War I (rarely done in
World War II), crosses a finished
military bridge shortly before the
ramp section.

266

A particularly dangerous job —
searching for mines, 2nd Engineer
with mine-searching pole, western
campaign, 1940.

Yugoslavian
tellermines are
carefully dug up by
hand, southeastern
campaign, 1941.

A mine barrier on an advance route is removed. The engineer at the front carries a long digging pole attached to his belt. Eastern campaign, 1942.

Not only were enemy mines removed, but their own were laid. Engineers prepare a quick barrier, Italian front, 1944.

A deadly weapon of the engineers — a man with a flamethrower moves forward during fighting in a town.

A flamethrower man has ignited the flame and fires bursts of flame at a fortress.

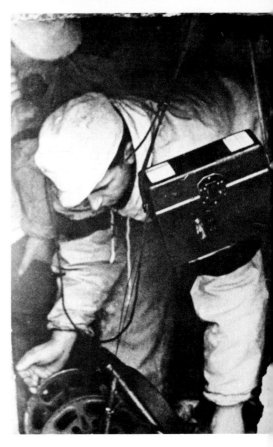

A field telephone is hooked to the wires in a bunker.

Putting up telephone lines in the forests of Karelia, at right the men with the cable drums on their backs, at left the soldier with the pole for high work, eastern front, 1942.

The Intelligence Unit

Trouble-shooters, also called "Strippenflicker", repair a damaged line.

Moving field cable behind the front.

The telephone troop of an intelligence platoon on the front line.

The division switchboard with lines coming in; at left a big telephone truck.

Found everywhere, the hanging red cloth signs with the white "F" and arrow pointing to a phone station, or a white lightning flash for a radio station.

270

A portable radio troop on the march, the soldier at left carrying the opened case with sending and receiving gear, the soldier at right carries the power pack, western campaign, 1940.

A radio troop in a dugout takes a report during the eastern campaign, 1943.

A radioman (note the lightning emblem over the Gefreite's *stripes*) passes on a command from the Unteroffizier *in Morse code.*

A large radio set in operation.

271

A detached power pack for a 30-watt radio station.

A bakery company with camouflaged field baking ovens and piles of firewood before them, heating up.

A bakery company hard at work.

Commissary bread for the soldiers of the division is piled up under big canvas covers, ready for distribution.

The butcher platoon (or company), here with a slaughtering rack, is always busy providing for the troops.

The motorized and horsedrawn supply columns often had a very hard time, as these pictures from the eastern campaign show — a truck column on a dusty "runway" during advance fighting . . .

. . . in the mud season of spring and fall . . .

. . . and on roads swept by snowstorms in the winter months.

274

Ammunition piles at a small Russian railroad station, unloaded from freight trains, await pickup by supply columns.

A horsedrawn column unloads shells.

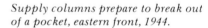

Supply columns prepare to break out of a pocket, eastern front, 1944.

A small unit, but of great importance to the soldiers up front — the men of a field post office at their work.

The mail has come in, is being sorted out and prepared to be picked up by the troop units.

The "spear" (Hauptfeldwebel) personally delivers the newly arrived mail to the men of his company at the front.

The Medical Services

A troop surgeon bandages a wounded man properly on the battlefield, Polish campaign, 1939.

A troop medic (right, with red cross armband) treats a badly wounded man on the front line, western campaign, 1940.

Comrades and an auxiliary stretcher bearer (at right, without a rifle), bring a badly wounded man out of the line of fire on a stretcher.

An improvised troop dressing station, eastern front, winter 1944-45.

Although slightly wounded himself, he marches along with his men — an Oberarzt *during the withdrawal fighting, eastern front, 1944.*

A horsedrawn medical company on the march, with red cross flags hung on the wagons, Polish campaign, 1939.

The advance troop of a medical company arrives on bicycles to set up a gathering place for slightly wounded men.

A main dressing station with tents and an ambulance, wounded men wait to be transported further.

A slightly wounded man helps a badly wounded comrade at a main dressing station.

278

An ambulance platoon, all its vehicles marked with a circular red cross emblem, brings wounded men to a field hospital, southeastern campaign, 1941.

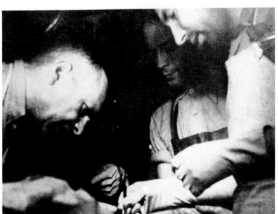

A doctor with a surgical team at a field hospital.

The Veterinary Services

A temporary veterinary hospital, a veterinary officer in white, well camouflaged in the woods.

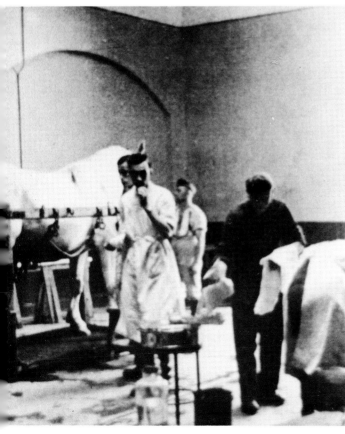

A veterinarian with his crew in a clean, bright operating room in a permanent building set up as a long-time horse hospital.

The War Horse

A team of horses in the mud at the eastern front, autumn 1941.

At 40 degrees below, mane, mouth and nostrils iced — the horse endures it quietly, without complaining.

280

Tough and spirited, used to the Russian climate, the little Panje horse from the eastern plains.

The Volunteers

He did his work loyally and willingly to the bitter end, the "Hiwi", here still wearing a Russian cap but with a German uniform jacket without insignia.

Volunteers in fur caps and German uniform coats drive an HF 2.

281

A "Hiwi" (wearing a white armband) is decorated by a regimental commander for his brave and dependable service in transporting many wounded men.

The Division Chaplains

A Catholic division chaplain with his fur cap, and rucksack on his way to the positions on the eastern front in the winter of 1942-43.

A Catholic chaplain in his full vestments giving the holy communion, at right the field altar with two soldier volunteers serving as acolytes, eastern front, 1944.

282

A Protestant division chaplain holds a burial service at the graves of fallen soldiers, southeastern campaign, 1941.

The Division Staff

An advanced division command post, the division commander (General) with peaked cap in the foreground, during the Polish campaign, 1939.

The division staff settles down in the forest during the French campaign, 1940.

283

The command unit of a division with its personnel, eastern campaign, 1942.

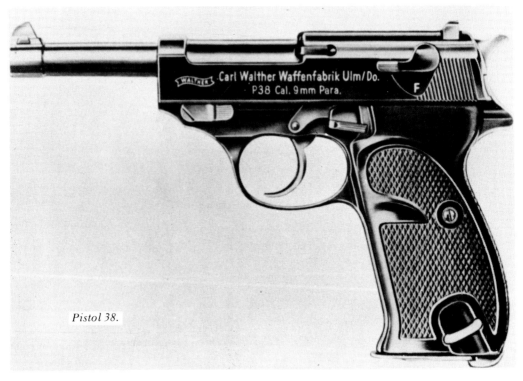

Pistol 38.

Machine carbine 42.

Assault rifle 44.

Only a few troops were completely armed with the new assault rifle. Here it is a Waffen-SS unit, easy to identity with multiple magazine pouches, western front, 1944.

A rifle grenade man in winter battle dress (camouflage side out) loading, beside him a case with explosive and antitank grenades.

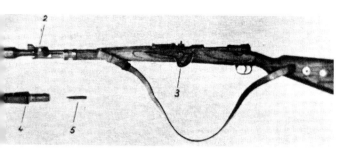

Rifle grenade device ("Schiessbecher") on a 98 k rifle: 1. rifled barrel, 2. bracket, 3. sight, 4. rifle antitank grenade, 5. propellant cartridge.

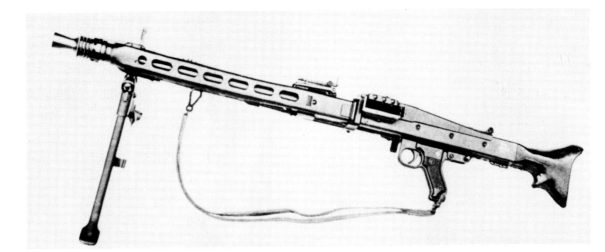

Light machine
gun 42.

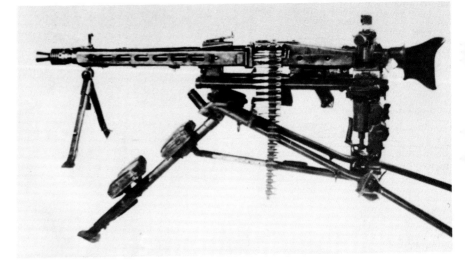

Heavy machine gun 42 with a half-used
cartridge belt.

Heavy 120mm grenade launcher 43 on a
chassis.

The Volunteers

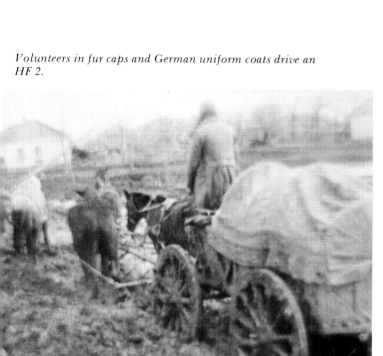

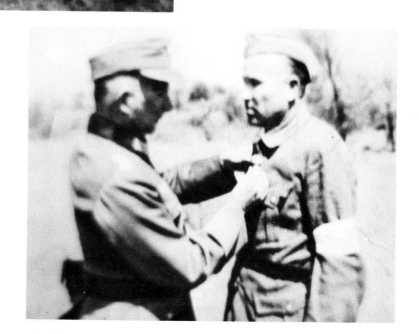

A grenadier with a tent cloth, 98 k rifle, stick hand grenades and small Panzerfaust, western front, 1944.

Small Panzerfaust 30.

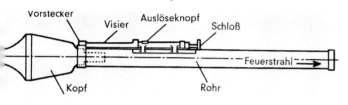

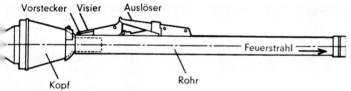

Panzerfaust 100.

A Gefreite *with a Panzerfaust 100 ready to fire, the sight up.*

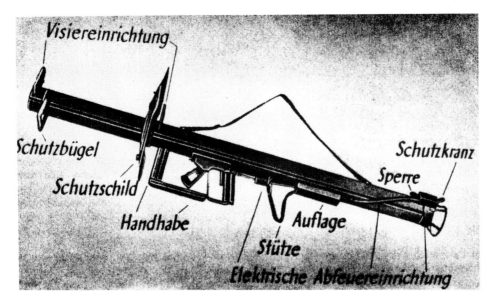

Panzerschreck ("Stovepipe").

Visiereinrichtung

Schutzbügel

Schutzschild

Handhabe

Stütze

Auflage

Elektrische Abfeuereinrichtung

Sperre

Schutzkranz

A Panzerschreck troop in position, Gunner 1 sighting, Gunner 2 loading a rocket shell.

288

Gunner 1 just before firing, Gunner 2 (lying at left) with the shell case.